ROME'S FIRST FRONTIER

THE FLAVIAN OCCUPATION
OF NORTHERN SCOTLAND

ROME'S FIRST FRONTIER

THE FLAVIAN OCCUPATION
OF NORTHERN SCOTLAND

D.J. WOOLLISCROFT AND B. HOFFMANN

TEMPUS

First published 2006

Tempus Publishing Limited
The Mill, Brimscombe Port,
Stroud, Gloucestershire, GL5 2QG
www.tempus-publishing.com

British Library Cataloguing in Publication Data.
A catalogue record for this book is available from the British Library.

ISBN 0 7524 3044 0

Typesetting and origination by Tempus Publishing Limited
Printed in Great Britain

CONTENTS

LIST OF ILLUSTRATIONS

TEXT FIGURES

COLOUR PLATES

ACKNOWLEDGEMENTS

This book could not have been produced without the help of a great many people, to all of whom the authors owe a great debt of gratitude. Almost 100 students and volunteers from 11 different countries have taken part in the Roman Gask Project's field programme to date, and space does not allow us to mention every participant by name. We would, though, like to give special thanks to our dedicated teams of trench supervisors: Dr N.J. Lockett, Mrs A.T. Lockett, Mr K.M. Miller, Dr M.H. Davies, Dr A.G. Keen, Mr M.T. Murphy, Ms S. Moore, Mr P. Murdoch and Ms A.T. Hamel, along with our survey team members, Mr D. Hodgson, Miss R. Hunt, Ms I. Hallyburton, Mr P. Smith and Miss R. Dundas. Others have provided analyses of artefacts and other material found on our sites and we would particularly like to thank Dr S. Ramsay and Dr J. Huntley for their environmental work, Ms A.C. Finnegan for her studies of our lithic finds, Prof D.C. Shotter for reporting on our coins and Dr A.T. Croom, Dr K. Hartley, Dr V.G. Swan and Mrs F.C. Wild for their pottery analyses. We also thank the Cumbernauld Historical Society for allowing us to work on finds from their fieldwalking programme. Dr D. Simpson has made his medical services available to our excavations and Mr P. Green has run our website since its inception. Mr W. Fuller has acted as pilot on all of the Project's air photographic flights and he, along with Mr T. Berthon, Mr A.S. Torrance, the RCAHMS and the Cambridge University Air Photographic Library have also made available air photographs of their own. Likewise, Prof S.S. Frere, Prof W.S. Hanson, Dr D. Emslie-Smith, Dr D. Gallagher, Mr T. Davis, Headland Archaeology Ltd and the Stirling Archaeological and Field Society have all allowed us to use illustrations.

A large number of colleagues have offered valuable ideas and suggestions and, on occasions, shot down our own more fanciful interpretations. Our thanks are especially due to Prof W.S. Hanson, Prof D.J. Breeze, Prof J.J. Robertson, Prof A.R. Birley, Prof F.W. Walbank, Dr B. Dobson, Dr A. Cheichoud, Dr J. Shepherd, Ms R. Jones, Mr G.S. Maxwell, Prof L.J.F. Keppie, Dr D. Strachan, Mr M.A. Hall, Dr T.M. Allan, Dr J.C.C. Romans, Dr F. Hunter, Dr R. McCullough, Dr P. Ashmore, the late Prof G.D.B. Jones, SUAT Ltd and the RCAHMS. We would also like to take the opportunity of thanking the various bodies who have funded our work. The Perth & Kinross Heritage Trust have financed most of our scientific and air photographic programme, as well as providing a great deal of other vital support. The Society of Antiquaries of Scotland, the Roman Society and the Roman Research Trust have all sponsored excavations and other field work, and our thanks are also due to Historic Scotland and The Derrick Riley Bursary for their support.

During the life of the Gask Project we have been made more welcome than we had dared hope by the farmers and landowners on whose sites we have operated. Without their support we could have achieved nothing and, to date, we have only once been refused permission to do anything we have asked for. We are especially grateful to Mr R.D. Baird, Mr R.M. Smith, Mr R.H.B. Smith, Ardoch Farming Co Ltd, Blackford Farms Ltd, Mr T.E. Ivory, The Dupplin Estate, Mr A. Simpson, Mr M. Bullough, Mr J. Christie, Mr J. Guthrie, Mr I.D. Brown, Mr W. Fotheringham, Mr W. Rob, Mr R. Hamilton, Mr D.W. Scougall, Mr A. Scougall and Mr D. Graham. We are also grateful to Mr and Mrs A.D. and E. Graham for providing accommodation for our often wet and muddy dig crews and to Mrs H. Fuller for spoiling us on our flying trips.

Finally we would like to thank Prof D.J. Breeze, Prof L.J.F. Keppie and Mrs V. F. Woolliscroft for reading the book in typescript, and offering many valuable corrections and suggestions. As always, any remaining errors are entirely our own.

INTRODUCTION

In the later first century AD much of what is now Scotland was invaded by the armed forces of what was then the world's leading superpower: the Roman Empire. For the first time in several hundred years, the exact date and circumstances under which this invasion took place are currently somewhat uncertain, but the results were remarkable. At the time, the Roman Empire was at the height of its power. It had been expanding for centuries, partly by diplomacy, but mostly by conquest, and now stretched (*1*) from the Atlantic to the Euphrates, and from the Rhine and Danube to the Nile. It took in most of Europe, North Africa and the Near East and there was no state left on earth strong enough to present it with a serious threat. Rome was so used to conquering that it had long seemed possible that expansion might continue indefinitely until the empire became a global state. As a result, Rome sometimes tended to see her borders as little more than jumping-off points for further conquests. Britain was only the latest addition, with the invasion beginning in AD 43 under the Emperor Claudius and, by the early 70s, what is now England and Wales were, for the most part, safely assimilated into an occupied province that was to last for over 300 years. Yet, in Scotland, things were to be very different. Initially, after supposedly crushing all resistance, the Romans seem to have had every intention of staying and of instigating a normal, permanent occupation: for a massive military building programme began, to hold down the newly won territory. Yet even here, we may see signs of a realisation that expansion might have to stop. Because, in the north, what was built does not appear to be just a standard garrison pattern, designed to monitor, police and control a conquered population. Instead they created what we shall argue was a massive and complex

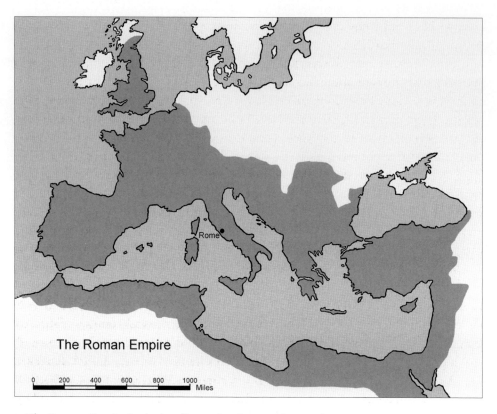

1 The Roman Empire in the late first and early second centuries AD

fortified frontier system. It revolved around a closely defended line, strung out along the Roman road between Dunblane and the Tay and, although it lacks a running barrier, such as a wall, ditch or palisade, it otherwise strongly resembles other, later, Roman frontier elements, such as Hadrian's Wall.

The first parts of this system to be discovered lay mostly on the Gask Ridge, which makes up much of the northern side of Strathearn, in Perthshire. It has thus become known as the Gask system, or even the 'Gask frontier' and some of its components have been known for centuries. Since the Second World War, however, many new sites have been found, mainly through air photography. These have more than doubled the known length of the line to at least 37km (23 miles) and there may well be more left to discover. Additional forts are known in the mouths of the main highland glens and, further north, in Strathmore, and the system as a whole shows signs of careful design, based on a remarkably thorough understanding of Scotland's wider strategic geography. It does, though, still seem to be a frontier. Much of the Highland massif remained outside it, as did some rich agricultural areas, particularly the area around the Moray Firth. Furthermore, although post-conquest military dispositions, in any time or place, are always likely to be fluid, the sheer building investment suggests that this was intended to be at least a semi-permanent situation. This in itself is curious behaviour, given Rome's previous track record. Britain was a (relatively small) island and at the time, faced few, if any, other overseas enemies. Yet, so long as any of its territory remained unconquered, the Roman occupied area still faced a potential external threat. The imperial logic might thus have suggested that the most efficient course would have been to seize every square inch to leave a province which needed little defending. To be sure, it would still have needed to be held down, at least in the short-term, but Rome had long experience of successfully integrating conquered peoples to the point where they could be run with minimal resort to force. Indeed, there were large areas of the empire where the population would rarely have seen a Roman soldier, and other island provinces, such as Sardinia, were held with a minimal military presence. The vast bulk of the Roman army was stationed to face external threats and it might have seemed realistic, in Britain, to expect total conquest, followed by a gradual run down of the occupation forces as internal stability increased, making the province more efficient and cost effective to run. In fact, however, the very opposite occurred and this is a second peculiar aspect of the Scottish invasion. The Romans had put themselves to considerable trouble in invading and conquering the country, and had invested massive resources in manpower and frontier installations. Yet, just as their occupation system was essentially up and running, they did something almost unprecedented in their entire imperial history to date: they left. It is true that they had also withdrawn from Germany beyond the Rhine some decades before, after ranging as far as the Elbe, but that was the result of a terrible military disaster. In Scotland, there was no such defeat. The pull-out appears to have been a unilateral and entirely voluntarily act. The Roman army simply gave up everything it had gained or built, and withdrew. It used to be thought that this was a phased process conducted in several gradual steps, but this no longer seems to be the case (Hobley 1989). Quite the reverse, they seem to have retreated by up to 80 miles, from Strathmore to what are now the southern border lands, in one fell swoop and, by the early years of the second century, they had fallen back on the Tyne–Solway isthmus where Hadrian's Wall would evolve in the 120s.

Aside from the more local strategic implications in Scotland, Rome's adoption of fortified borders was a huge historical turning point. They do, after all, show us what had been a supremely self-confident superpower, bent on unlimited expansion, slowly turning onto the defensive and covering itself with a kind of armoured shell. The British are understandably proud of Hadrian's Wall and the (sadly) lesser known Antonine Wall, but on the empire-wide scale, both are tiny. Their combined length is less than 120 miles. Yet there came to be literally thousands of miles of defences surrounding the empire as a whole, which have influenced subsequent history and military thought well into modern times; and vastly larger individual systems are known, for example, in North Africa (e.g. Baradez 1949). As a result, Roman frontier studies have long attracted a great deal of archaeological interest and one of the many questions needing answers is how these systems evolved over time. Were they refined and developed through the centuries? Or, was the initial design good enough to survive more or less intact, except for the later addition of running barriers such as walls? For this reason, it is particularly important to look at the first of these systems, because this was the prototype from which all else followed. The Gask belongs to a familiar class of early Roman defended lines, which also includes the Wetterau Limes in central Germany, but it seemed otherwise unexceptional. As a result, although good work had been done, few archaeologists had taken much notice of it. It seemed to be the earliest Roman frontier in Britain. For there was dating evidence to put its construction into the period of the Flavian dynasty of emperors and, perhaps, the reign of Domitian, in the AD 80s, 40 years before Hadrian's Wall. But it had always suffered because it was thought to be slightly later than the frontier in Germany. The German Limes (pronounced Leemase) was universally recognised as Rome's prototype fortified land frontier and, from the late nineteenth century onwards, received remarkable attention. At its peak this saw archaeology conducted on an almost industrial scale by the state funded *Reichs Limes Kommission*, whose eventual report filled 15 large volumes, published in the years before the Second World War (von Sarwey *et al.*). At the same time, the Gask languished all but neglected and, in particular, there was far less interest than one might wish in studying the line as a complete system, rather than as simply a collection of individual sites. As a result, it was lucky if it got a paragraph in books on Roman Britain and, in fact, most people, including many Romanists, had never heard of it.

In the early 1990s, however, a German postgraduate student conducted a thorough re-examination of the dating evidence for the birth of the German Limes (Körtüm 1998). The intention of this remarkable piece of work was simply to gain a little extra precision, but its results were utterly unexpected, because they showed that the accepted German start-date was so wrong that the line was not built before the Gask at all. Indeed, it was not even built in the first century. It now seems to be becoming generally accepted that it was not built until the reign of the Emperor Trajan (98-117) in the early second century. This means that

Britain's Cinderella system on the Gask becomes the prototype Roman frontier after all and it has consequently shot to international importance. It thus became vital that it should be studied in a more systematic manner and, in 1996, the Roman Gask Project was founded to contribute to this work. The Project, now in its tenth year, is based in the University of Liverpool, with the authors as Directors and has, since its inception, been engaged in an intensive campaign of surveys, excavation and archive work, which has included, where necessary, tracking down and publishing past research by other workers. To date, 27 excavations have been conducted, on 18 sites. Eleven more sites, including six entire Roman forts, have been subjected to geophysical surveys and we have been fortunate enough to be able to run our own air photographic flying programme which has generated thousands of pictures. In all, this represents a significant increase in data, but the Project has been far from alone, for other scholars have also been active in studying both the Roman remains and those of the contemporary native Iron Age population. The results have, again, been somewhat unexpected and, as in Germany, the shocks have often concerned dating. When the Project began we, like the Germans, believed that our chronology was reasonably secure. We had certainly hoped to refine it, but we never expected to rewrite Scottish history. Archaeology is full of surprises, however. That is one of its attractions, and although the Project's work remains far from complete, a new, more coherent picture is beginning to emerge and this book will try to present the current state of our knowledge (and, indeed, ignorance).

The Gask Project's remit was kept deliberately broad to cover all of Roman Scotland north of the Forth–Clyde isthmus and the line of the mid-second-century Antonine Wall. The present book will confine itself largely to the same area and to the first century AD, although later events and parallels from the wider empire will be relevant from time to time. The book is divided into two parts. The first will give a detailed outline of the archaeological remains of the first-century occupation and is best read in concert with large-scale (preferably 1:25,000) maps. Many of the sites mentioned are marked and six figure National Grid references will be given for every one. Alternatively, an electronic equivalent is available free of charge, on line, via the Royal Commission on the Ancient and Historical Monuments of Scotland's (RCAHMS) wonderful 'Canmap', map-based monuments database (www.rcahms.gov.uk). For some reason that we have never understood, such detailed archaeological treatments seem to have fallen out of fashion of late and, although there is a superb and frequently updated guide book available to the Roman remains of Scotland (Keppie 2004), this naturally concentrates on what can still be seen above ground. There has been no detailed overview covering the full state of knowledge in our study area since

O.G.S. Crawford's *Topography of Roman Scotland North of the Antonine Wall* was published in 1949. This beautifully written (if less than catchily titled) work is still much sought after on the second-hand market, but it is now hopelessly out of date and an attempt at a replacement seems long overdue.

Part two will try to put the archaeology into its historical context and explain something of what the military systems faced; what they were meant to achieve; how they were designed to operate and why they ultimately failed. It will also attempt to explain why the dating and the length of the occupation, which were once thought to be as secure as almost anything in the history of Roman Britain, have recently become controversial.

Until now, it has been more usual for books on Roman Scotland to provide a historical summary before giving an account of the physical remains, so our own reversal of this order might require explanation. In the past, we believed that we had such a good understanding of the basic historical narrative, that it could stand as a stable framework into which archaeological discoveries might be fitted. Yet, if archaeology is sometimes described (usually erroneously) as the 'handmaiden of history', there are times when it can also act as its midwife. As we shall see, there are now grounds for believing that our traditional history of Roman Scotland is flawed, and as the archaeology provides much of the evidence on which a new story can be built, it needs to be dealt with first.

PART I

THE ARCHAEOLOGY

1

ROMAN MILITARY SITES
IN SCOTLAND

The first part of this book contains detailed descriptions of Roman military installations such as forts, camps and watchtowers, but whilst the main text will make free use of technical terms (some in Latin), we are well aware that the general reader might find some of them unfamiliar. It thus seems sensible to begin with a brief guide to the first-century Roman army's organisation and fortifications, although this can be safely skipped if not needed.

The army was divided into two basic groupings. The first was the legions, which are what most people think of when they envisage the classic Roman soldier. They were elite, heavy infantry units, exclusively made up of Roman citizens (albeit drawn from many parts of the empire), and were highly trained for disciplined, close-formation fighting. They were also trained field engineers, who built their own fortifications, siege equipment and weaponry, and were accomplished road and bridge builders. Each legion had a strength of around 5,500 men on paper, including a small, *c.*120-strong, cavalry contingent, although as with all professional armies, their actual strength might vary with conditions. In the late first century there were four legions stationed in Britain, namely: *II Augusta, II Adiutrix, IX Hispana* and *XX Valeria Victrix*, a total of *c.*22,000 men. They were based in huge fortresses of up to 24ha (60 acres) in area, of which just one was built in Scotland: at Inchtuthil, near Caputh, on the Tay.

Each legion was split into 10 cohorts, each of *c.*500 men: except for the first cohort, which was almost double strength. The cohorts were subdivided into centuries, of which the majority were groupings of 80 men (not 100, as the name might suggest). Most of the cohorts contained six of these centuries, but the first cohort, held five of double strength. Each century was then further divided into 10, eight-man sections, called *contubernia* (literally, tent groups). The command structure was an interesting (and characteristically Roman) mix of long-serving professionals, and short-term, almost amateur, officers. Each legion was commanded by a Legate, who would be a relatively senior Roman Senator, who held his command for around three years as part of a mixed, political/public-service career, in which he might occupy a series of military and civilian posts. Under him was the *Tribunus Laticlavius*, which means Tribune with a broad stripe. The stripe refers to the fact that Senators were allowed to wear a broad purple stripe on their formal togas as a badge of status, and so we might expect this officer to be another Senator in uniform. In fact, however, he would usually be a teenaged boy or a young man in his early twenties. He would almost certainly be the son of a Senator, but not yet one himself. In theory, he was second-in-command, but in fact he was nothing of the sort. He was there to learn administration and to see something of military life, possibly including active campaigning: his period of military service (again probably around three years) was usually a prerequisite for beginning a political career. The real second-in-command, who would take over if the Legate was away or incapacitated, was the *Praefectus Castrorum*: the Prefect of the camp. Unlike his commander, he was a professional soldier with many years experience. He would usually be a senior ex-centurion and seems to have had no fixed term in this post. Below the *Praefectus Castrorum* were five *Tribuni Angusticlavii*, or Tribunes with a narrow stripe. Just as Senators were allowed to wear a broad purple stripe as a badge of social rank, Rome's second line aristocracy, the *Equites* (often mistakenly called the middle class), wore a narrower purple stripe and so these were equestrian officers. They too seem to have served for three years, but as part of a series of military commands which could themselves lead on to wider public service careers.

Surprisingly, the legionary cohorts do not seem to have had individual commanders, but the centuries were commanded by centurions. These were professional officers who might serve for decades. They seem to have had no fixed term of service or retirement age, and they have often been regarded as the backbone of the Roman army. Certainly, they were the principle repository of continuity and experience within the officer corps and the most senior centurion, the leader of the first century of the first cohort, who held the title of *Primus Pilus*, was a major figure in the unit. Many centurions came up from the ranks (although men from equestrian and even senatorial families could obtain direct commissions) and, in the past, this has caused scholars, led astray by the snobbery of their own day, to regard them as Sergeant Major figures. In fairness, it is virtually futile to try to equate ancient and modern military ranks, but it is far more realistic to regard them as fully commissioned officers, perhaps roughly equivalent to a modern Captain or, in some cases, Major and it was not unknown for different members of the same family to be found following senatorial, equestrian and centurial careers at the same time.

The second major grouping was the *Auxilia*, or auxiliaries. These were still highly trained men and certainly not the irregulars or mercenaries they are sometimes portrayed as, but they were provincials, not Roman citizens. They were organised into much smaller units, of which there was a variety of types. Firstly, the auxiliaries provided most of Rome's cavalry, an arm with which Rome herself had never been especially successful, and cavalry units were called *alae* (wings). The rest of the auxiliary troops were organised as cohorts. Most of these would be wholly made up of infantry, often of a lighter variety than the legions. But others were so-called '*cohors equitata*', which were part-mounted units in which about a third of the strength were cavalry. There were also a few special weapons units, such as archers, and some amphibious specialists, such as the Batavians from the area around the Rhine delta. Most *alae* and cohorts were described as *quingenaria*, in other words, 500 strong, but in later times there were also *milliaria* units, which were around 1,000 strong. In the late first century, the situation may have been somewhat in flux. We are not sure that the milliary units had yet formally come into being, but some units might have been held over the quingenary strength. Auxiliary units were usually commanded by Roman equestrian officers with the rank of Prefect or Tribune: these being the same men who at other stages of their career made up the legionary *Tribuni Angusticlavii*. Below them, the infantry were divided into centuries, which were commanded by centurions, just as in a legion. The cavalry were organised into troops of 32 men, called *turmae*, which were led by decurions. In most units, the commanding officer might be the only Roman citizen present, with even the centurions and decurions being non-citizens. That said, though, citizens were sometimes found serving in auxiliary units, and some units received citizenship *enbloc* for deeds of valour. Britain had a large auxiliary garrison which may have equalled, or more probably exceeded the number of legionaries. Exact figures are harder to provide than with the legions, as we still occasionally find evidence for more units, and it is harder to track transfers into and out of the province. Nevertheless, a total strength of 45-50,000 for the Roman armed forces in Britain might not be too far from the mark.

The auxiliaries certainly made up the majority of the first-century garrison of northern Scotland, with a minimum of 7,000 men present (as opposed to one 5,500-strong legion), and probably many more. They also manned the bulk of the known military installations. It seems likely that the small observation sites, such as watchtowers and fortlets, were manned by auxiliary detachments. The most distinctive auxiliary installations, however, and probably the most widely known Roman military site type, were the forts, which acted as their regimental barracks and administrative bases. It is sometimes said that Roman forts were completely standardised, so that if we excavate any fort anywhere in the empire, we can expect to find exactly the same design. Indeed, as we shall see, past excavators have been known to try to reconstruct an entire fort plan on the basis of a few small slit trenches. In fact, though, this is a gross exaggeration. As yet, no two identical Roman forts have ever been found and there can even be considerable differences between neighbouring forts which are obviously part of the same deployment. Nevertheless, they are usually variations on a relatively constant theme, so that it is still possible to discuss them as a single class. Fort design also tended to vary through time. The first author has already published a rough guide to the second-century forts on Hadrian's Wall (Jones & Woolliscroft 2001, 147ff), but the first-century forts of Scotland are sufficiently different for it to be worthwhile providing a new guide, with special reference to this period. Figure 2 represents a sample plan, but it is important to note that this is intended only as an illustrated key to the text. It is not the plan of any specific fort. Nor does it include every detail of the sorts of structures we might expect to find during a fort excavation. It is simply intended as an aid, to help the reader to put a shape to the technical terms, and what we know of the real forts in the area will be illustrated in the next few chapters.

One of the biggest differences between the first-century Scottish forts and those of Hadrian's Wall is the materials used in their construction. The Wall forts had their defences and internal structures built of stone, but this was rare in the first century (and indeed in the second century in Scotland). The legionary fortress of Inchtuthil had a stone facing to its defences, but otherwise, all of the first-century military installations had earth or turf built defences and timber internal buildings. Much of the layout remained broadly the same, however. Figure 2 shows a small fort of around 1.4-1.6ha (3.5-4 acres), such as might be occupied by a *cohors quingenaria*, and the first thing that will be apparent is the distinctive shape of its defences, which is almost always a quadrilateral with rounded corners. With some exceptions, the Scottish forts tend to be rather closer to squares than those of Hadrian's Wall, where the forts tend to show a more rectangular, playing-card shape, but there are always still easily recognisable short and long axes. The defences took the form of a rampart, outside which were a number of ditches. The rampart was usually constructed of turf, or turf-revetted clay or earth, and might rest directly on the ground or on a log corduroy, brushwood or, very occasionally, stone foundation. The ditches were usually V-shaped in profile and might be quite substantial. The rampart and ditch system was usually pierced by at least four gates:

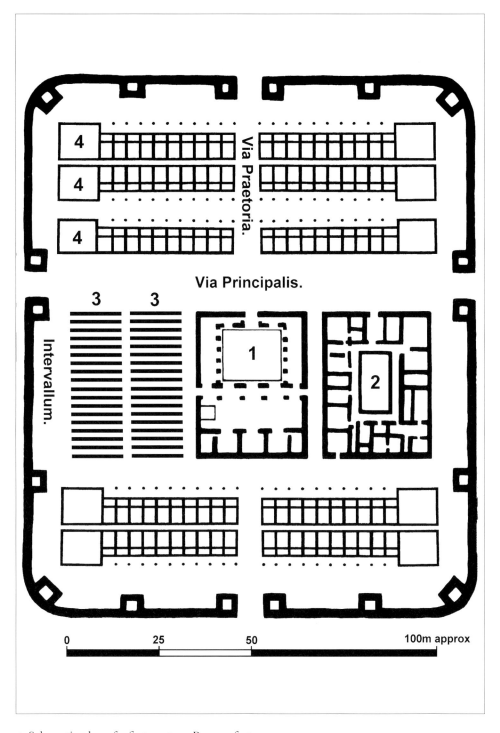

2 Schematic plan of a first-century Roman fort

one on each side. Those on one axis, usually but not always the short axis, were set centrally, whilst those on the other axis were set about a third of the way along, thus dividing the fort into two unequal parts. The smaller section was called the *praetentura* and was the front of the fort, which is usually though to have faced any likely enemy. The rearward section was called the *retentura*. The gates would normally be flanked by towers and there would sometimes be more towers set in the corners and at intervals around the rampart circuit, although these became more common in later times.

Inside the fort, the buildings were laid out around a regular street grid. Firstly, there was a road around the entire interior of the defences, called the *intervallum* road or *via sagularis*. Next was the fort's main street, or *via principalis*, which ran between the two off-centre gates. Lastly, apart from an assortment of alleys between buildings, was the *via praetoria*, which linked the centre of the *via principalis* with the front gate. Along the rearward side of the *via principalis*, and separating it from the *retentura*, we usually find a group of large buildings which are collectively known as the main range, or *latera praetorii*. These usually fall into at least three types. The first (2, 1) is called the *principia*. This was the fort's headquarters or administration block and it is generally divided into a number of distinct sections. At the front was an open courtyard, which often contained a well, and which was flanked by a colonnade, or by ranges of storerooms and offices. Behind this was a large, covered, transverse hall, which acted as an assembly area where courts martial, addresses by the commander and other formal events could be held. Finally, at the rear of the building was a further range of offices, in the centre of which was a room set aside as a shrine called the *aedes* (or *sacellum*). Here images of the gods and the emperor could be kept, under guard, along with the unit's standards (which were venerated as sacred) and its cash.

Next to the *principia* was another large rectangular building known as the *praetorium* (2, 2). This was the commanding officer's residence and was a large, Mediterranean-style, courtyard house in keeping with the aristocratic standing of the equestrian commanding officer. These houses could be very grand (although smaller than their legionary equivalents) and relatively luxurious. They may even have had second floors, although the evidence is stronger in later stone examples. They might contain stables as well as domestic areas and servants' quarters, for the commander could bring his entire household with him on his tour of duty, including slaves and horses. In keeping with Roman elite practice, his house might also have served in some degree as his office and as a place where diplomatic receptions and other public functions could be hosted. He thus needed to be able to reflect the power and status of Rome with a house that was able to both impress and contain a substantial staff.

The final standard element of the main range were the *horrea*, or granaries (*2, 3*), of which there were frequently two. As their name suggests, these were food stores, although they probably held more than just grain. Later stone granaries are instantly recognisable because they were supported by projecting buttresses to help their structure withstand extremely heavy loads, but the first-century timber equivalents also have a distinctive design. Their floors were supported well clear of the ground to provide some protection against damp and vermin, and they generally appear as either a series of sleeper beam slots (as in figure *2*) or as rectangular matrixes of postholes. Many forts also held a variety of other buildings, usually (but not always) in their central areas, including a workshop (*fabrica*), store houses and even perhaps a hospital (*valetudinarium*), but the three types described above were the basic minimum and are encountered virtually everywhere.

The remainder of the fort was filled with barrack blocks (*2, 4*), each of which was designed to hold one full century or, alternatively, a *turma* barracked along with its horses. Figure *2* shows an infantry fort and so the barracks are set up for centuries, but cavalry barracks were broadly similar in design. Each long block has a substantial area at the rampart end set aside for the officer, and these might be subdivided into rooms, although not to any standard plan. The remainder housed the men themselves and was thus divided into 10, two room sections called *contubernia*, after the eight-man squads who occupied them, and would also share a tent in the field. It is possible that equipment may have been kept in one room whilst the sleeping quarters were in the other, but this is not certain. The centurions' quarters were often broader than the *contubernia*, where the extra space might be used instead for a post-founded external verandah, presumably to provide some protection from the weather. One thing that was conspicuously lacking in Roman forts was a communal cooking and messing structure, so food would presumably have been eaten in the barracks. But there were usually ovens set into the rampart backs so that the men could bake bread without presenting too much of a fire or health risk to their accommodation.

Many of the Roman forts in Scotland also had extra fortified enclosures attached to, but outside their defences. The exact function of these so-called 'annexes' is still only dimly understood as few have been excavated in any detail. Parts of some appear to be empty and they may have provided secure accommodation for valuable, moveable goods such as wagons or even livestock. Others, though, may have acted as safety features, for they seem to contain structures, such as industrial facilities and bath blocks, that might have posed a significant fire hazard if sited amongst the timber fort buildings, which would have been all too flammable, especially in dry weather.

To date, 13 full-sized auxiliary forts have been discovered in our study area, along with two much smaller sites which could be categorised either as small forts or large fortlets, but are not large enough to have held a whole unit. This is quite a number, but it seems likely that there are more still awaiting discovery. The next few chapters will suggest possible locations for another four but, obviously, this is only an approximation.

Superficially, at least, legionary fortresses look like massively scaled up auxiliary forts (*23*). For example, they have the same round-cornered, rectangular shape; the same pattern of main streets and many of the same internal buildings, including granaries, barracks, headquarters and commander's house. Nevertheless, there are significant differences. Fortresses usually have huge amounts of extra workshop and storage space, which probably reflect a role as regional logistics centres. They are much more likely to have hospitals (albeit, these are rather hard to identify with certainty) and the main streets are often lined with a series of booths, whose exact use remains uncertain. Because the legions had an additional officer tier, in the six tribunes, the fortresses contain individual houses for these men (which resemble auxiliary *praetoria*), in addition to the legate's own, very much larger, *praetorium*. Lastly, the double centuries of the first cohort have special barracks. These are usually located to one side of the *principia*, with their much larger, centurions' quarters fronting onto the *via principalis*, rather than the *intervallum* road. Legionaries had higher status and may have been better paid than the auxiliaries (although the latter is now controversial) and so, not surprisingly, fortresses are also often qualitatively better than forts in terms of the size, elaboration, decoration and standard of construction of their buildings.

In addition to these large bases, the army also built numerous smaller posts in northern Scotland, of which the most common were towers. These are frequently referred to as 'signal towers', but this is probably something of a misnomer. Their primary role was almost certainly to provide observation cover but, as there is little point in having observers unless they can tell someone what they see, they probably were able to signal to speed up their communications in an emergency. We have ancient accounts of a number of Roman long-range signalling techniques, most of which operated visually (Woolliscroft 2001a), and there is evidence that the towers on the Gask were positioned so as to be intervisible with more major sites. The towers themselves were fairly simple timber structures, founded on four or more large posts and there is some evidence that at least some of the Scottish examples had wattle and daub side cladding to make them at least reasonably weather proof. Artistic representations (*3*) of such towers from other parts of the empire suggest that they were two to three times higher than their base width, which is all that we can now measure through

3 A Roman watchtower from Trajan's column

excavation. If so, this would have put the Gask examples somewhere in the region of 7-10m high and they may have had either roofed or open observation decks at their tops. The Scottish towers are unusual in that they were generally surrounded by small turf or earth ramparts but, like most Roman timber towers elsewhere, they also had one or more defensive ditches, with a single entrance break for access.

Next come a smaller number of tiny forts, which are generally known as fortlets. Like a fort they are rectangles with rounded corners, surrounded by one or two ditches. They are, though, very much smaller, at around 25m² over the ramparts, and they usually have only a single gate. Similar sites became very common in the second century, for example in the form of milecastles on the Hadrianic and Antonine Walls: but they were relatively rare in first-century Britain. On many Roman frontiers they probably acted as policing and customs posts and contained either one or two small *contubernia*-sized barrack blocks fronting onto the road to the entrance. The role of the Gask fortlets is currently open to question, however, because the three found to date have not produced internal structures.

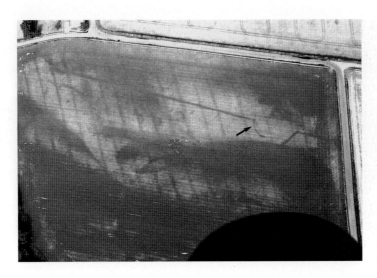

4 Stracathro temporary camp, showing claviculate gate

In addition to the permanent installations, it was standard practice for a Roman army to build itself a fortified camp every night whenever it was operating in hostile territory. The first-century historian Josephus (III, 84) tells us how quickly legions could construct such camps, and Scotland has produced one of the largest collections of these sites known anywhere. Some 70 are currently known to the north of the Forth and Clyde and more are still coming to light, mostly through aerial photography. They usually comprised an earth or turf rampart fronted by a V-shaped ditch and there are a number of telltale features that make them reasonably easy to identify from the air. They often have a fairly regular shape which, like a fort, is generally a rectangle with rounded corners (although far less regular examples are known). They also tend to show one of a number of distinctive entrance types. Camp builders did not have the time or materials to build proper gates, but the entrance gaps were often protected by short offset banks and ditches, just outside the camp, which were known as *tituli* (*colour plate 2*). Alternatively, the entrances might be marked by *claviculae*, or curved outward ditch projections. There is a particularly common variant on this theme in Scotland, which has become known as the Stracathro type, after an example discovered from the air in 1955, outside the Strathmore fort of Stracathro (4, arrowed). The fact that this name has stuck is something of an oddity, since the type was first identified some 200 years before, at another of the northern forts, Dalginross, but we will follow convention and use it. All of the known Stracathro gates are now ploughed out and so we can only see them as cropmarks caused by the ditches. Fortunately, however, the Dalginross camp was seen by Roy (1793, 64) in the 1750s when the rampart still survived and this allows us a far better idea of what the full design

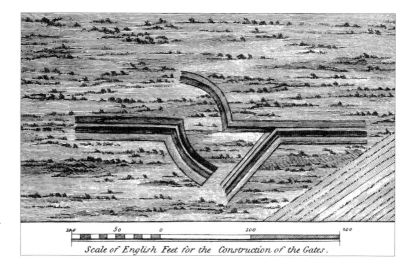

Scale of English Feet for the Construction of the Gates.

5 Roy's plan of a Stracathro-type gate at Dalginross

once looked like. His plan (5) shows the rampart following the ditch in its outward curve on the left-hand side (as planned) of the entrance. On the right side, the ditch also turns outwards, but this time on a straight course which overlaps the end of the left-hand *clavicula* to leave just a narrow break. The rampart on this side follows a separate course, however, continuing on straight until level with the outer entrance-break and then making an inward-turning curve. Both of these gate types were designed to force attackers to slow down and to approach the entrance at an angle, so that their shields would be turned away from at least parts of the rampart, making them more vulnerable to defensive fire from the camp. The more elaborate Stracathro type would have taken slightly more work to build, but should have been tactically more effective than a titulate gate, for it produced, in effect, a lengthy entrance passage, all of which was exposed to enfilading fire from the rampart on both sides. At the same time, it would also have been rather safer to operate because it achieved its effect without isolating friendly troops from the rest of the camp in the way that manning the detached rampart of a *titulus* would do.

At their largest, the Scottish camps can range up to nearly 59ha (145 acres) in area and there are numerous other examples of around 48 and 26ha (120 and 64 acres). There are also, however, quite a few very much smaller camps, some barely over an acre in area. Some of these might mark the passage of small detachments rather than whole armies. Others are sited outside forts and might have been built to provide security for personnel and stores during the construction of the permanent site, but some of the smallest might represent training exercises: for the Roman army conducted drills in camp building, as it did with virtually every other military skill.

In theory, Scotland's prodigious camp assemblage should be a great archaeological asset, not least because a number of distinct series have been identified in which camps of the same basic layout are found again and again across large stretches of territory. As has been pointed out for decades, these may well represent lines of march, with a particular campaigning army building essentially the same structure every night, whilst other Roman campaigns adopted slightly different designs. If this is correct, we should now have enough camps to follow the exact progress of individual operations. Camps also present problems, however, which have so far largely robbed us of this potential advantage. At one time, it was assumed that virtually all of them would have been extremely simple structures, occupied for no more than a single night and containing nothing except perhaps the occasional temporary field oven, since the occupants were assumed to have lived in tents. This has had a number of consequences, of which the most important has been a long-standing reluctance for archaeologists to excavate in camp interiors. The logic has been that their very function meant that there would be nothing to find there and that it would thus be a waste of time and resources to look. This might have been a valid viewpoint had the fundamental premise been confirmed first, but it was not and, as a result, we have very little dating evidence with which to put either individual examples or, indeed whole series into their historical context. Moreover, a number of often large-scale excavations in recent years, usually conducted ahead of road building or other destructive operations, have produced signs of a hitherto unsuspected level of complexity which may muddy the waters further. Some camps have shown signs of reasonably prolonged occupation. For example, Kintore camp in Aberdeen contains large numbers of ovens which show multiple uses. Others, such as Dunning, in Strathearn (Dunwell & Keppie 1995), and Dunblane, north of Stirling (Robertson 1970b), had more than one occupation. Still others might have had long-term occupations to perform some specialist function. For example, there are two small coastal camps on the Tay estuary and the Montrose basin, at St Madoes and Dun, which might represent fortified harbour facilities. Likewise, excavations in the 1990s on camps at Three Bridges, outside the fort of Camelon, near Falkirk (Bailey 2000), showed that they may have housed industrial activity. Camps might thus present a more complicated subject than we had thought and it is gratifying to know that there is now a major study of the Scottish examples underway (R. Jones, pers com). Given this ongoing work, however, it would probably be superfluous for us to attempt our own analysis and this book will, thus, confine itself to studying the more permanent installations, except where camps appear relevant, or occur in close association with more permanent sites.

FIRST–CENTURY SCOTLAND: THE MILITARY DISPOSITIONS

After the invasion, the Roman army settled down to consolidate its gains and created an occupation deployment which fell into two basic sections. To the south of our study area, in the southern uplands, the army set up a classic holding pattern along the main routes through the hills (6). The coastal areas were largely neglected, especially in the far west, and the principal object seems to have been to hold down the hill country and protect the main arteries of communication. There were two main roads to the north, which show signs of being linked

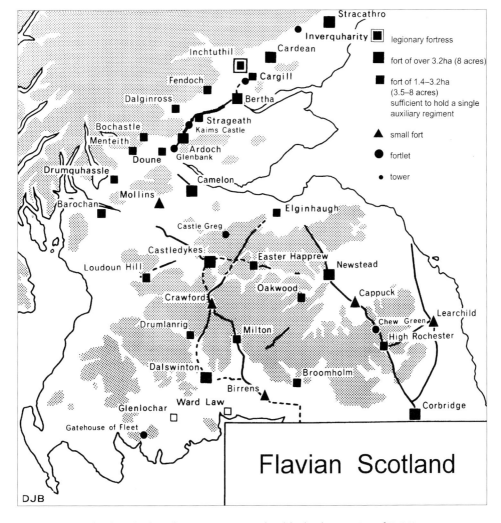

6 Roman Scotland in the late first century. *Reproduced by kind permission of D.J. Breeze*

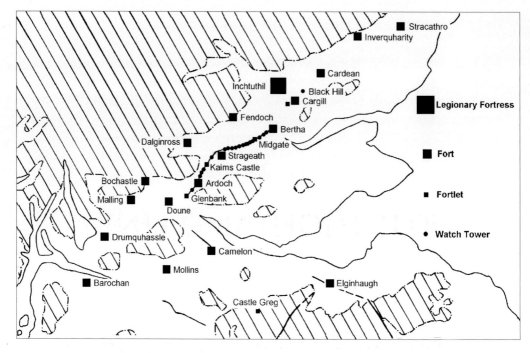

7 Northern Scotland in the late first century

together at several points to produce something of a ladder effect. The eastern route, now called Dere Street, ran from Corbridge in Northumberland, via Otterburn and Melrose to the fort of Elginhaugh, near the Forth. The western road ran from Carlisle, through Allendale and Clydesdale, with a branch through Nithsdale. In the central belt we lose track of these routes as most of the area is now built up or intensively cultivated, but at least one of the roads must have made for the fort of Camelon, near modern Falkirk. Here, to the north of the Forth–Clyde isthmus, the military dispositions seem to change from an occupation system to a denser, more defensive deployment, which looks more towards protecting the occupied zone from external attack (7). These arrangements consist of three main elements which will be dealt with in detail over the next four chapters. The first is a series of forts along the Highland fringe, between Loch Lomond and Strathtay, which culminate with the Inchtuthil legionary fortress. The second is the Gask system, which consists of a close-set chain of forts, fortlets and watchtowers along the Roman road from Camelon to Bertha (on the Tay) and which runs via the south side of Strathallan and the north side of Strathearn. The third is a series of additional forts which runs up Strathmore as far as Stracathro, near modern Brechin.

2

THE HIGHLAND LINE

DRUMQUHASSLE

If we work from south-west to north-east, the first known Highland line fort lies at Drumquhassle (NS 484872) to the south of the modern village of Drymen. The site occupies a strong position towards the southern end of a marked ridge summit, from which the ground slopes away steeply on every side except the north (*7* and *8*). It enjoys good views in all directions, extending as far as Loch Lomond, 3 miles to the west. Locally, it controls a number of natural corridors, notably the Endrick Water valley, Strathblane and the route north to Aberfoyle, now followed by the A811, 809 and 81. Its view over the whole of southern Loch Lomond, however, also confers more distant control over the routes into the Highlands which run on either side of the Loch: notably the line of the modern A82.

The fort is the latest of this line to have come to light, being discovered from the air by the RCAHMS in 1977 (Maxwell 1983, 168ff). In fact, though, the find was not entirely unexpected, for it was already clear that at least one more member of the line was missing in the south-west. Moreover, the place name means 'Castle hill', although no later fortification was known; gold coins of the Roman Emperors Nero (ruled 54-68) and Trajan (98-117) had been found in the vicinity in the eighteenth century: with the latter firmly datable to AD 100 (MacDonald 1918, 245). Nevertheless, the eventual discovery was an excellent piece of aerial spotting, since the site has never shown well from the air and many other observers would undoubtedly have flown on without noticing. Ironically, however, once one knows where it is, parts of the fort are plainly, if

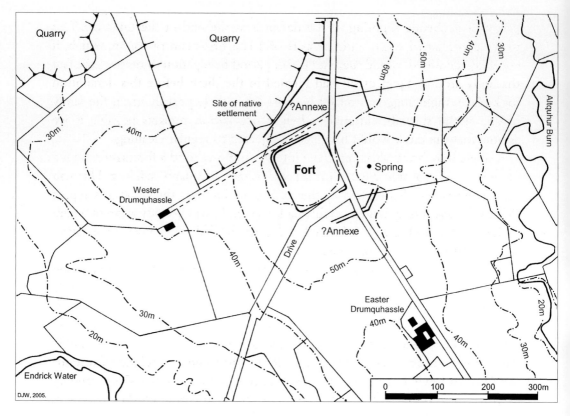

8 Drumquhassle fort, the aerial evidence. *Modified from original rectifications by Headland Archaeology Ltd and the RCAHMS*

faintly, visible on the ground. In particular, the south–east corner can be seen just inside the driveway entrance to Park of Drumquhassle House (*colour plate 3*), as a typically Roman, rounded fort corner. Whilst, in the field to the north, the north–east corner and parts of the western rampart can be made out as low earthworks. Taken together, the aerial and surface indications suggest a small fort of around 1.3ha (3.2 acres) over the ramparts, surrounded by a double ditch. Some parts, however, have been very badly destroyed by modern damage. For example, a minor road has removed parts of the east side, and the house drive has eaten into the ditches in the south.

Almost as soon as it was discovered a small excavation was conducted to confirm the fort's size and identity, and to look for dating evidence. Sections cut through the defences revealed a turf-revetted, earth and turf rampart, *c*.5m wide, fronted by a defensive ditch *c*.4.5m wide and a fraction over 1m deep. The ditch had been partly filled with rampart material, which may have been dumped as part of a deliberate slighting of the defences at the end of the fort's life. This material contained what could be part of a late first-century flagon, which, if correctly identified, would suggest Flavian period occupation. Moreover, the fact that only around 24cm of silt had formed in the ditch before this demolition took place might suggest a relatively short life-span (especially given the sandy nature of the subsoil), although a longer occupation remains possible if we assume that the ditch would have been subjected to regular cleaning.

A single trench was also dug in the interior and produced a foundation trench for what had probably been a timber and wattle and daub building. This had been deliberately demolished at the end of its life, but the published report (Maxwell 1983, 171) provides no further details and gives no indication of where in the interior the trench was located, so it is not possible offer any interpretation of what the structure might represent.

Although the fort itself shows poorly from the air, parts of a wider ranging series of ditches have shown far more clearly around it (8). In the north, a single ditch has been detected running roughly parallel to the fort ditches, which it is tempting to see as an additional outer ditch, facing what is tactically the fort's weakest side. Further out is an apparently heavier ditch (it becomes a double ditch in one section) which makes a series of turns before heading off towards the east. Meanwhile, to the south, two apparently lighter ditches run roughly parallel to the fort's southern side, before turning sharply towards the north-east. The southern ditches and the outermost of the northern features have often been interpreted as annexes, but this has never seemed very convincing. Roman defences of this period generally have smoothly rounded corners, whereas these ditches make a series of abrupt, angular turns. The features may well still be defensive in nature, but they would probably be more at home in a much later context, perhaps from some point between the Civil War and the Hanoverian campaigns. Likewise, the proposed third fort ditch shows no sign of an entrance break opposite the fort's north gate, and so might also be non-Roman.

In 1997 a second excavation took place in an attempt to rescue data after a quarry to the north of the fort encountered pits and ditches, one of which was misinterpreted as the so-called 'annexe' ditch. Fortunately the latter still lies beyond the lip of the now abandoned workings and would only come under threat in the (admittedly not improbable) event of a major collapse of the near vertical quarry face. Nevertheless, a pit was found, filled with what appeared to be midden debris from the fort. Amongst large quantities of burnt material, substantial amounts of Roman pottery were recovered, most of which falls into a date range between AD 75 and 95, which further supports a Flavian date. Meanwhile, fieldwalking and survey work in and around the fort has yielded a number of Flavian coins, some clay sling bullets, the handle of a bronze pan stamped with the mark of Publius Cipius Polybius (a Capuan bronze smith known to have been active in the mid-to-late first century) and a probable late first-century brooch, all of which provide further support for a Flavian date. On the other hand, nothing has been found to suggest reoccupation in the mid-second century, when some of the other forts in the north are known to have been brought back into use to serve as outposts for the Antonine Wall. Indeed, the only exception is the gold coin of Trajan already mentioned and, as its exact find spot is unknown, that may not derive from the fort. That said, however, we still have only a very sparse finds body from the site and only tiny areas have been excavated, so it is not impossible that this picture might change in the future.

The most recent work on the site has been a large-scale geophysical survey conducted by ourselves. Three pieces of work were completed: a resistivity survey of the fort and a large area around it, a magnetometer survey, just of the fort, and a magnetic susceptibility survey of its south-west quadrant. The resistivity survey (9) gave a far clearer image of the fort ditches than has ever been seen from the air. The whole of the north and west sides were revealed, including the gates, along with parts of the damaged east and south sides. The presence of a double defensive ditch, which had been suspected from the air, was fully confirmed, but the survey also showed beautifully clear indications of what have been nicknamed 'parrot beak' breaks at the gates. These involve the outer ditch swinging in at an angle of around 45° to join the inner on either side of each gate and are characteristic of first-century Roman forts in Scotland. The west gate lay about two-thirds of the way along the fort's long axis, as measured from the north, which means that the fort faced south-east towards Strathblane, whilst a very high resistance area in the expected position of the headquarters building might reflect the presence of stone floors.

The magnetometer data was badly scrambled by the presence of a pipeline, immediately north of the fort, which is kept magnetised to make it easy to find in an emergency. Nevertheless both it and, even more so, the magnetic susceptibility results (10) suggest that the rampart swung in to form a re-entrant at both the west and south gates.

Outside the fort, the survey confirmed the aerial evidence that there is no entrance break in the supposed third northern fort ditch, which is thus, again, unlikely to be Roman. It also cast unexpected light on the double ditches that had been thought to represent a southern annexe. From the air these ditches had appeared to be a parallel pair, albeit slightly further apart (c.11m lip to lip) than is usual in a Roman defence. This, however, proved to be a mere accident of the way that their cropmarks had shown. The survey shows the inner ditch

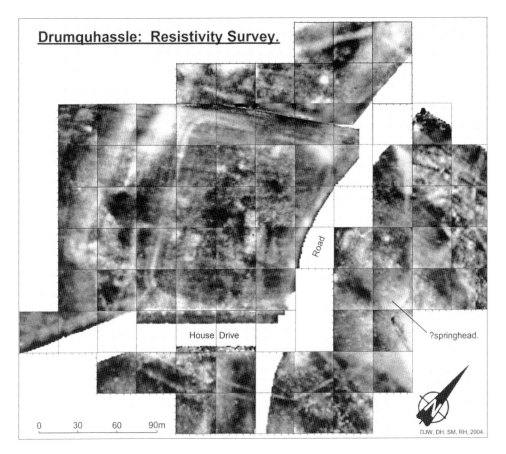

9 Drumquhassle, the resistivity survey

originating inside the fort and passing through the defences (something no annexe ditch would do), just to the west of the south gate. It then swings east, and only falls in with the outer ditch (which approaches from the west) just before entering the cropmark sector. The two then cross a modern minor road and turn to the north-north-east as expected. However, after leaving the cropmark sector, the inner ditch swings sharply to the east, crosses the outer ditch and runs off down a steep hill and out of the surveyed area. The outer ditch, meanwhile, continued straight on towards an area of very high resistance beside a spring, which represents the foundations of an old pump that supplied water to a number of local farms until well into living memory. The chances are that the supposed outer ditch is actually an old water pipe, perhaps heading for Park of Drumquhassle; another such feature, which can be seen running to the north from the pump, is probably a further pipe.

10 Drumquhassle, the magnetic susceptibility survey superimposed on the resistivity image

Yet a third possible ditch emerged from the fort's south-western quadrant. This started near the west gate and ran south across the house drive, before turning first east and then south and out of the survey area. This, too, seems unlikely to be Roman as it crosses the fort's defences. Instead, it appears to head for a rectangle of high readings inside the fort, which suggests a stone structure. As the fort buildings are likely to have been constructed entirely of timber, wattle and daub, this feature is probably post-Roman and it seems likely that it was also a pipe trench, perhaps for a drain or water supply. In short, the fort seems unlikely to have had an annexe and no temporary camps are known in the vicinity.

There is, though, one external feature that might be Roman. The spring to the east of the fort is famously reliable and never fails, even in the driest of summers (*11*). We have already seen that it was pumped to provide water in modern times and it is also the nearest water source to the fort, which means that it was probably used by the Roman garrison. It is thus interesting to find that the survey detected faint traces of a ditch around the spring, marking a rectangular enclosure, approximately 30m (north–south) x 35m (east–west) in extent. It is very far from proven, but it is possible that this represents a springhead feature of some sort: possibly a shrine, not unlike the famous Coventina's Well, outside the Hadrian's Wall fort of Carrawburgh.

11 The Drumquhassle springhead. The fort lies on the higher ground beyond the hedge

Finally, early air photographs of Drumquhassle (e.g. RCAHMS neg: ST2927) show a series of ring features to the north of the fort, which probably represent a native settlement (8). As we shall see, quite a number of Roman forts in northern Scotland had similar settlements around them, at least some of which might be contemporary with the occupation. This group would thus have been well worth investigating. Sadly, however, it has since been destroyed by quarrying, although it is possible that the 1997 midden pit with Roman pottery belonged with these features. Whatever the case, a possible opportunity to study interaction between the Roman army and the local indigenous population has been lost. Mercifully, however, the geophysical work detected similar ring features to the west of the fort, so that all may still not be lost. Indeed, there are even signs of such features inside the fort, which might be the homes of pre-Roman occupants of the site, or even a post-Roman settlement built inside what was left of the abandoned defences.

MALLING

Fifteen kilometres (9 miles) to the north-north-east of Drumquhassle, the second of the Highland forts, Malling (NN 564001), lies on the western shore of the Lake of Menteith (*colour plate 4*), to the east of both Aberfoyle and the two glens of Ard and the Duke's Pass. It sits close to the water, opposite a small island called Dog Isle, from where it has fairly wide views to the east and south. Nothing remains on the surface, but in 1968 it was discovered from the air as a cropmark by Prof J.K. St Joseph (1969, 109f), since when it has shown many times, with virtually the entire defensive circuit visible.

The fort's double ditches (*12* and *colour plate 4*) show a variation of the parrot-beak entrance in which even the inner ditches turn inward at their termini, to form a shape more akin to an eagle's beak. Three gates are visible, in the north, south and west, although the latter shows poorly from the air. In all, the fort measures approximately 185m (east–west) x 150m (north–south) over the inner ditch, an area of around 2.78ha (6.85 acres). To the east of the fort proper, further lengths of double ditch head down towards the water from the fort's north and south sides, but separated from them by two more entrance breaks, which some air photographs suggest are also of eagle beak form. At present, no eastern side is visible to link these ditches, but it may well lie in an uncultivated area along the lake shore, which does not produce cropmarks. Indeed it may even have been eroded. This extra area is generally assumed to be an annexe, but no ditches or other defences have been seen with certainty between this area and the rest of

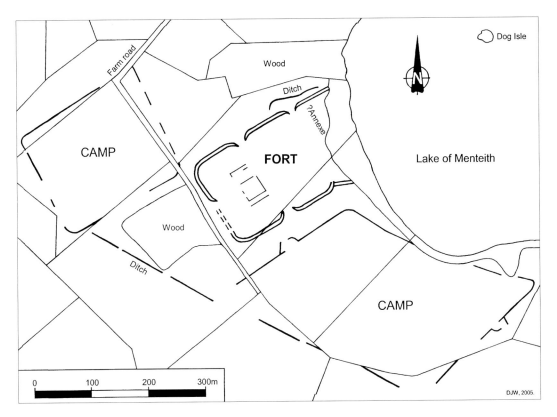

12 Malling Roman fort, the aerial evidence. *Modified from an original rectification by the RCAHMS*

the fort, as would be more usual for an annexe, so it is just about possible that the fort itself is larger than we had thought, with the eastern gates serving as posterns into a more elongated site of about 3.6ha (9 acres). This does, though, appear unlikely, thanks to an extraordinarily detailed air photograph taken by the RCAHMS in 1977 (neg: PT5515). This shows a faint trace of the fort's main road, the *via principalis*, running between the two western gates, to the west of which a number of postholes are visible as cropmarks, which define the outlines of a series of large square and rectangular buildings (*12*). These are too big to be barracks and so are almost certainly the fort's main range structures, including the *principia* and *praetorium*. If so, they would show the fort facing east towards the lake, rather than west, towards the glens. Assuming that the eastern ditch sections do represent an annexe, this would be a fairly conventional layout, but if they were part of a longer fort, the main buildings would be thrown unusually off centre in such a way as to make the *praetentura* massively larger than the *retentura*. Moreover, the same air photograph shows two extremely faint parallel linear features between the eastern gates (not shown on *12*), which just might represent ditches between the fort and the annexe. Finally, an additional stretch of single ditch has been seen just north of the site, which ends in a near right-angled corner. This may or may not be Roman but, if it is, it might be an additional defence for, or extension to, the annexe.

Surprisingly, almost no surface work has been undertaken on the site, although we are planning a geophysical survey. Otherwise, the only exception is a single section cut by St Joseph across the two northern ditches. This has never been properly published, but a brief note reports that they were V-shaped in profile. The outer was 3.66m wide and 1.52m deep. The inner, 3.05m wide and 1.22m deep, and there was a 1.5m gap between them.

Two temporary camps (*12*) are known in close association with the fort (St Joseph 1973, 223 and Maxwell & Wilson 1987, 29), at least one of which has the Stracathro-type gates that are thought to mark first-century activity. The larger of the two lies to the south, beside the lake and covers around 10.4ha (25.7 acres). It is somewhat irregular in shape, as it curves to follow the lake shore, and a small section of its defences is still visible close to a patch of woodland. The smaller camp, which sits a little to the north-west of the fort, is more regular in shape and occupies around 4.7ha (11.6 acres). The two are linked by a straight ditch, around 280m long, pierced by a single entrance break, which seems to lack either *clavicula* or *titulus* type defences and whose exact date and function remain uncertain. Air photography has also detected a number of circular features around the site, which probably represent native activity.

BOCHASTLE

The next Highland line fort, Bochastle (NN 615078), lies on low ground beside the River Leny, 9.3km (5.8 miles) to the north-east of Malling and just to the west of modern Callander (*colour plate 5*). It sits, with limited views, at the mouths of two glens: Strathyre and Strath Gartney, but despite being cut into by a disused railway in the south and the river in the north, significant lengths of its ramparts survive as surface features (*13*). Air photographs again show parrot- or eagle-beak ditch breaks at the surviving east and west gates, along with the parch mark of an internal road between the two (*14*). The fort is rather smaller and more square in plan than Malling, at around 137m (north–south) x 140m (east–west), an area of *c*.1.9ha (4.7 acres) over the ramparts and, like Drumquhassle, it does not appear to have an annexe. This omission is coming to seem unusual amongst the forts of Scotland, in both the Flavian and later periods, but it is noteworthy that both

13 Bochastle fort, the west rampart

Bochastle and Drumquhassle lie at the smaller end of the size range. It is thus possible that only larger forts showed these features, a possibility which might mean that annexes were related to the type of unit in garrison.

The site has been known since the eighteenth century, but often went unrecognised as Roman, despite the name 'Roman Camp' which became attached to it, and despite the discovery, before 1724, of a gold coin of Nero (Anderson 1956, 36f). Excavations were conducted between 1949 and 1953 by the Glasgow Archaeological Society (*15*), mostly by means of narrow slit trenches. The published report (Anderson 1956) is not a model of clarity, not helped by poor illustration and the discovery that the interior had been badly damaged by flooding. Nevertheless, it does provide useful information, not least the confirmation (through pottery and other finds) of a Flavian date and the suggestion of two structural phases in the defences. The ramparts were around 7m wide and consisted of turf work, mostly with an earth and rubble core. A number of turf and rubble features built against its rear were interpreted as

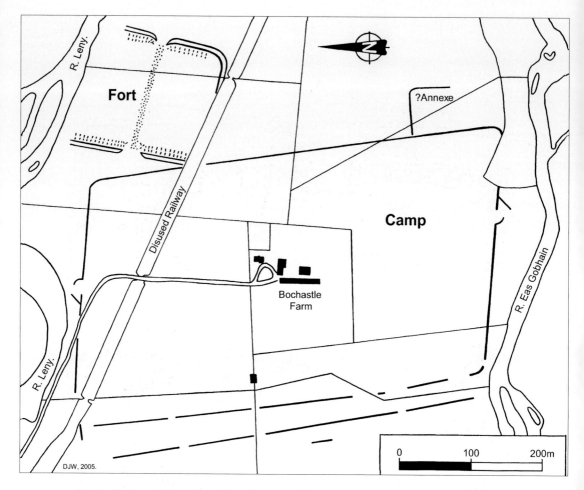

14 Bochastle Roman fort, the aerial evidence. *Modified from an original rectification by J.K. St Joseph*

ramps up to a walkway at the top, but could equally be secondary thickenings, and there were signs that the northern rampart angled towards the south, to the east of the north gate, to stay clear of flooding from the river. Roads were found emerging from the east and west gates, both of which turned to the south (probably in a secondary, perhaps post-Roman, phase), but these were not traced further.

The excavations claimed to be able to find only a single defensive ditch, whereas air photography reveals two. Interestingly, however, the southward running external road in the west seems to follow the aerial line of the outer ditch, in which case the excavator may have confused a ditch backfilled with stone (in effect an inverted field cairn), with a road. Whatever the case, the

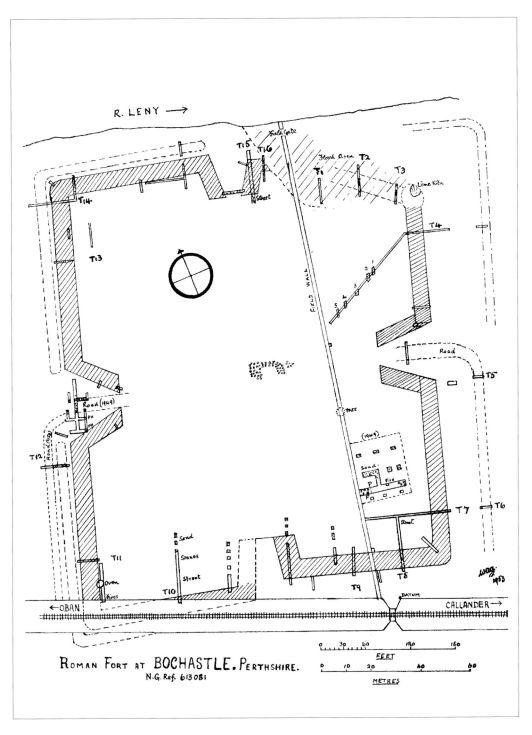

15 Bochastle, fort plan, from the Anderson excavations

ditch that was found was 3.66m wide and 1.53m deep and largely V-shaped in profile. The excavator also claimed that the fort is markedly off centre within its ditch system, with the west rampart only 1.8m from its ditch, compared with 22.6m in the east. The report becomes very confused at this point (and aerial views would suggest that this is an exaggeration), but Anderson does mention occupation levels under and around the road emerging from the east gate so it is perhaps possible that the fort was reduced in width here at some point, and that a primary rampart might be found further east, closer to the ditches.

The ramparts were found to turn inwards to provide deeply (up to 21m) recessed gates on all four sides, a fact that becomes more interesting now that Drumquhassle has produced a similar design. Indeed, gates of this type might prove to be more common than is currently suspected because, tactically, they fit well with the parrot/eagle-beak ditch breaks to create what amount to funnels that could be guaranteed to cause confusion amongst even an ordered rush on the gates. An attacking force would have been able to pass through the outer ditch on quite a broad front, c.25m wide. It would then find itself rapidly compressed as the outer ditch swung in towards an inner ditch break only c.15m wide. Some of its outermost members might even be pushed into this ditch, but the others would be forced inwards, causing confusion in the ranks at a time when they would already have been under fire from the fort. They would next pass down the rampart re-entrant, becoming still more crushed and disordered, to an entrance just c.6m wide and would there be faced with the barrier of the gate itself, whilst under enfilading fire from the rampart funnel, and with their escape route blocked by their own comrades forging on from behind. The result would be a killing ground and the funnel would have become a trap. No signs of towers or other gate structures were located by the excavation, except for two postholes outside the west gate, but this is hardly surprising since they were looked for in what, on this defence model, is almost certainly the wrong place, in the mouths of the rampart re-entrants, rather than their throats. The published plan does, though, show the re-entrants and, to a lesser extent, the fort corners, to be more angular than is usual on first century Roman forts, something that provoked comment in the report (Anderson 1956, 46f). In truth, however, it is difficult to believe that the real shapes could have been accurately determined by the limited trenching undertaken, and air photography certainly shows more rounded curves.

Few internal features were revealed and fewer still were properly understood, although ovens were found built into the rampart back. One of these was overlain by a later phase of the 12.2m-wide *intervallum* road, but only after a 22cm-thick layer of earth had had time to form over it. A second seems to belong with the later road level. Otherwise little was found in the interior except patches of metalling. This might mean nothing, however, since the few, very narrow, slit trenches dug would have stood little chance of finding timber building remains on ground that had suffered flood erosion. Indeed, the one reasonable piece of area excavation that was conducted, recorded a floor and a line of posts, which might have been part of a barrack. The report appears to give the find little significance, however, and (sadly) did not even trouble to provide a plan. Likewise other remains towards the north-east corner were brushed over with hardly a word and it is to be regretted that an important site could still be treated in such a cavalier manner at a time when archaeological technique was otherwise fairly advanced. Nevertheless the excavation's finds, coupled to the known Neronian coin, are enough to suggest occupation in the Flavian period only.

To the west of the fort is a temporary camp with Stracathro-style gates (*14*). It is unusually large for the type, for although its exact dimensions still need some clarification, it seems to measure around 530m (north–south) x 365m (east–west), an area of *c*.19.4ha (47.8 acres). Curiously, the only excavation yet undertaken on the camp, a series of tests for the north ditch (DES 1998, 93), failed to locate it, despite the strength of the cropmark, but geophysical work is currently in preparation. There is a small rectangular enclosure attached to the southern end of the east rampart which might be an annexe. This too requires confirmation, however, for although there is a series of temporary camps in Scotland which are known to have annexes (e.g. Keithock in Strathmore), these are even larger sites of *c*.26ha (64 acres). They also have titulate, rather than claviculate, Stracathro-type gates and, at present, no other Stracathro camp has produced the least evidence for such a structure.

DALGINROSS

Twenty kilometres (12.7 miles) to the north-east of Bochastle, the fort of Dalginross (NN 772210) sits just to the south of Comrie, watching Glen Artney and Strathearn (*colour plate 6*). The site occupies a raised bluff which provides reasonable views in all directions. Indeed parts of its west and north sides have been eroded by the River Ruchill, although this has since meandered away again and now runs, at closest, about 100m to the west. The fort has been known for many years and two plans published as early as the eighteenth century (Anon plan of 1786 in Perth museum and Roy 1793, PI XI) have been little improved upon today, whilst a third, less detailed example (by McFarlane, now also in Perth Museum) was drawn in 1802. Moreover, coins of Titus (or perhaps Vespasian), Domitian and, more surprisingly, Severus Alexander (emperor 222-35) have long been known from the site (Macdonald 1924, 326), although the latter could be a native, or antiquarian loss.

The site presents a double enclosure, with one set inside the other. The probability is that both represent different fort phases, although the outermost fort is less certainly identifiable as such from the almost exclusively aerial evidence available (*16*). The inner fort was originally around 2.43ha (6 acres) over the inner ditch. The outer was obviously larger, at least 3.6ha (9 acres), but no more accurate size can be determined because, as only the two eastern corners survive, we are unable to extrapolate its entire circuit. In the eighteenth century the ramparts and ditches were well-preserved earthworks and they are still faintly visible as slight undulations on the ground, but the site now shows far more clearly from above. Fortunately, it is a superb air photographic target (e.g. *colour plate 6* and Frere & St Joseph 1983, 130), which shows well as crop, soil and/or germination marks in most years, and occasionally shows detail like few other sites. The inner fort shows as a double-ditched enclosure with parrot-beak entrance breaks at the surviving gates. Some air photographs show the rampart and *intervallum* road within and it is possible that the south gate, at least, might have been recessed, like (although perhaps not quite as markedly so) those at Bochastle. A much lighter ditch, which might be an annexe, can be seen defining a smaller rectangular area projecting from the southern half of its south-eastern front.

The outer fort is bounded by a wider single ditch with simple entrance breaks. There is some possibility that it too had an annexe. For in 2005, an archaeological evaluation by SUAT Ltd, ahead of proposed building work to the south-east, revealed what seemed to be another ditch and rampart (SUAT Report CM047). Re-analysis of one of our own air photographs (GPAP04 BW01#12) might seem to refute this identification by showing the ditch running on a heading which would not intersect with the fort (*16*), and thus suggesting that it represents a separate enclosure, but more work will be needed before the situation becomes clear.

In 1996 the RCAHMS took a series of remarkable colour air photographs of the site which show clear traces of timber buildings inside the inner fort (e.g. neg: C67788). Amongst other things, these show what seems to be a vast beam-founded granary in the fort's south-eastern quadrant, close to the south-east gate (although it may actually be two such buildings sitting side by side). This fronts onto a road which, as the granaries are usually part of the main range, is presumably the *via principalis*. If so, the fort faces south-west, towards Glen Artney, and the *via principalis* (unusually, but not uniquely) runs along the

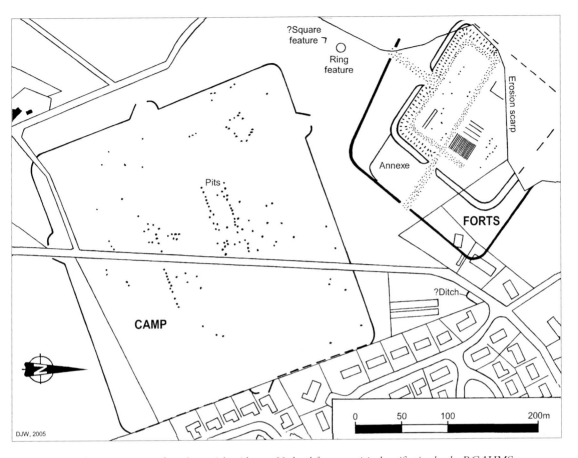

16 Dalginross Roman fort, the aerial evidence. *Updated from an original rectification by the RCAHMS*

fort's long axis. Other structures are visible, if harder to identify. To the north-west, there appear to be two long, narrow buildings beside the granaries and, beyond these, close to the north-west gate, are faint indications of a square structure which could be the *praetorium*. To the west, in the presumed *praetentura*, more rectangular buildings can be seen whose long axes run parallel to the road (north-west to south-east). These should be barrack blocks, but the aerial indications are too faint to be certain and only a few scattered pits can be seen in the *retentura*.

Interestingly, although the inner fort is shown as a cram of buildings, the same air photographs show almost no signs of structures within the outer site, except for ring features from earlier (or later) native houses. Indeed not even an internal road system is visible. This may be an accident of cropmark formation, but it is possible that the larger enclosure is actually an annexe, or even a fort that was never completed. Roads have been recorded, both from the air and by antiquarian writers, projecting from the south-west and south-east gates. Neither have been traced far from the site, however, and these may be little more than spurs produced as part of the fort's construction in the expectation of being connected to a wider inter-fort network that was never actually built.

Some fieldwork has taken place on the site. Prof A.S. Robertson (1964, 196ff) excavated a trench in 1961, but her report is a little hard to follow. Indeed, as no location plan was provided, it is not even clear exactly where in the fort the dig took place. It appears, however, to have examined the outer enclosure, not far from its eastern corner, and sectioned a V-shaped ditch. This was crossed at a slight angle and so would have appeared slightly wider than it actually was, but the figures within the trench were 4.88m wide and 1.22m deep. It had silted to a depth of over 30cm and then been filled with earth and turf, some of which, at least, may have derived from a rampart. No rampart material survived *in situ*, however, having been presumably ploughed away. Instead, the first internal feature uncovered was a *c.*3m-wide stretch of gravel, starting 11m inside the ditch, which was interpreted as an *intervallum* road. No other internal features were found (except some presumably modern furrows) and no Roman finds were made. This deficiency was made up in the 1970s when the Cumbernauld Historical Society conducted fieldwalking on the site. The finds were only analysed much later (Woolliscroft 2002b, 40ff) but were sufficient to prove that the site was occupied in both the Flavian and Antonine periods. Given the site's morphology, this might suggest that the inner fort, with its parrot-beak ditch breaks, was the Flavian fort, whilst the larger, single-ditched, outer fort was Antonine. This is far from proven, however, especially given the uncertainty as to whether the outer site is a fort at all. Sadly, the exact find spots of the fieldwalking finds were not recorded, which means that no clues can be gleaned from their distribution and it is to be hoped that similar work can be undertaken in the future now that GPS logging would allow this type of spatial information to be recovered quickly and cheaply, without excavation.

To the south of the fort lies a 9.5ha (23.5 acre) temporary camp with Stracathro-type gates. In 1990, excavations conducted on the east gate in advance of housing development (Rogers 1993, 277ff) showed that the ditches had been recut after being apparently deliberately backfilled with turfy material, perhaps from the rampart. This would suggest two distinct occupation phases, possibly separated by a significant period of abandonment. No dating evidence was recovered for either phase, but air photographs show a series of what might be rubbish pits in the interior, which might well repay future study.

FENDOCH

The final auxiliary fort on the Highland line sits 17.2km (10.7 miles) to the north-east of Dalginross on a steep-sided, but flat-topped, plateau between the River Almond and the Fendoch Burn (NN 919283). The site lies partly under the now ruined farm of East Fendoch (*colour plate 7*) and stands on very strong ground which slopes away steeply in all directions except the immediate north-east. It dominates the mouth of the Sma' Glen and also controls the natural route from Crieff into Glen Almond. The fort was known in the eighteenth century, when it was mentioned (i.a.) in the *Old Statistical Account* (vol 15, 256), but memory of it faded until the 1930s when it was rediscovered and partly excavated by Richmond and McIntyre (1936 & 1939). The plan produced by this excavation has become famous. It purports to show the site's full internal layout and is often taken as the archetypal late first-century Roman fort in northern Scotland, despite being markedly more elongated than any of the others, thanks to its need to fit onto the plateau's rather narrow summit.

Figure *17*, shows the published plan, and a number of features are marked. The rampart, which encloses a 1.8ha (4.5 acres) area, is *c*.5.2m thick and has a number of ovens built into its back. The long axis runs south-west to north-east, and the *via principalis* cuts across it, about one-third of the way along, so that the fort faces south-west. The short axis is shown as narrowing slightly towards the south-west (from 92m to 86m internally) and four gates are depicted: all with single portal entrances flanked by towers, with the exception of the south-east gate which was thought to be topped by a single tower. There was no indication that the gates lay in rampart re-entrants, as at Bochastle, but a post, interpreted as holding a door jamb for the north-west gate, was recessed behind the line of the rampart and tower fronts, so that something of the same defensive approach might have been in use by another means. No angle or interval towers were located (or looked for). Outside the rampart, the excavators believed that there was a double ditch towards the north-eastern end (inner 3.9m wide and 1.8m deep, outer slightly smaller), but only a single ditch elsewhere. They also found signs of an annexe ditch running south-east from a point just over halfway along the south-east rampart. A few small test pits dug inside this feature revealed no structures, but burning was found, along with a few shapeless pieces of iron which might suggest metal working activity. This has since been borne out by fieldwalking by the authors, which produced fragments of raw lead.

Inside the defences, the plan shows the usual *intervallum* area running right round the fort and averaging *c*.11m wide. Behind this lies a complex series of internal buildings and, interestingly, although almost all of these seem to run

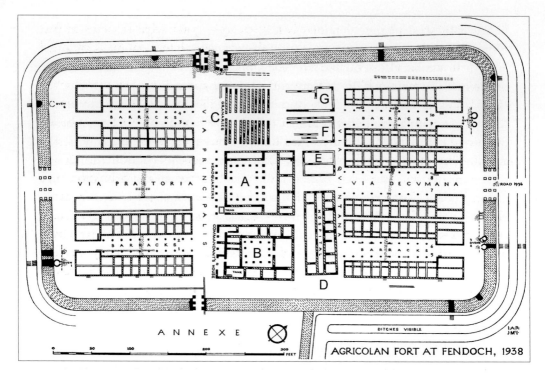

17 Richmond and McIntyre's plan of Fendoch

parallel to each other, the plan shows them at a noticeable angle to the defences. To a degree, this is the result of the narrowing of the fort's short axis and so, not surprisingly, the plan shows the north-west *intervallum* area narrowing by 6.7m towards the south-west as the rampart closes in. Ironically, however, the *intervallum* actually widens very slightly towards the same end of the south-east side, albeit by only 1m.

With a few exceptions, the internal buildings are much as we would expect. The main range buildings lie on the rear (north-east) side of the *via principalis*, with the *principia* (17, A) in the middle, flanked on the south-east by the *praetorium* (B) and on the west by two beam founded granaries (C). The *praetentura* and *retentura* are both filled with barracks and only the buildings immediately behind the main range stand out as unusual. The published plan shows four. The first (D), a long corridor building, was interpreted as a hospital, albeit on no excavated evidence. It lies at a slight angle to the rest of the interior with its long axis (unlike all the other internal structures) running north-west to south-east. Further to the north-west were three more, less clearly defined structures (E–G) that were interpreted as workshops and/or store buildings.

The published plan of Fendoch is not, though, quite what it seems at first glance. In fact most of it is invention or, at the very least, interpolation. Richmond and McIntyre would have taken decades to excavate the whole fort with the resources they had available, so instead they dug a series of narrow slit trenches; recorded what foundations they encountered and then simply joined the dots to extrapolate plausible building plans. Indeed the site has sometimes been labelled the best planned, unexcavated Roman fort in Britain. Figure *18* shows what was actually dug and the difference is manifest. In fairness, much of the published plan probably does represent at least a reasonably accurate approximation. The granary beam slots are unmistakable and the *principia* and *praetorium* are fairly clear. Nevertheless, the barracks were hardly touched and, although these are a universal fort feature, their design and layout can differ. The structural interpretation of the supposed hospital and the other features to the rear of the main range is still more debatable. Indeed, even the number of buildings present here is open to question (with as many as six being possible), and the south-west and north-east gates were not dug at all, so their reconstruction is entirely conjectural.

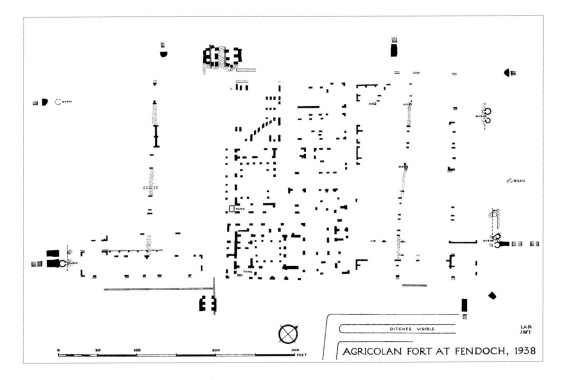

18 Fendoch as actually excavated

19 Fendoch, ovens. *Photograph by kind permission of Dr D. Emslie-Smith*

Richmond and McIntyre (1939, 151) claimed that the building dimensions were so standardised that they might have been prefabricated off site and then assembled from kits. Moreover, a pollen analysis suggested that, as elsewhere in the area, there seem to have been few if any major timber trees in the surrounding (largely grassland) landscape in ancient times, so the building timber may well have been shipped in from elsewhere. Even so, nothing like enough was excavated to give a reliable picture of how standardised the structures really were and so the idea must remain conjecture. Worse still, the published plan was drawn on the assumption that all of the foundations would belong to the same structural phase and thus form a single, contemporary whole. In other words, the excavators seem to have assumed such a short occupation for the fort that none of the buildings had complicated their plans by needing repair or rebuilding work. If so, they may have been mistaken. For example, some of the rampart ovens were replaced at least once, after intensive use and we were recently given a set of photographs taken by a former schoolboy volunteer on the dig (*19*) which seems to show an oven complex with three phases. Three postholes were found amongst, but not in line with, those of the north-west gate towers (Richmond & McIntyre 1939, 117f) which might also suggest more than one phase. Likewise a drain or conduit had been buried beneath the rampart at the south-east gate, but not covered to prevent its being blocked by rampart material, and this, again, might suggest that it had gone out of use when some, otherwise undetected, rampart modification took place. Most importantly, however, one of the first trenches dug in the interior revealed a slot dug for a 1ft (30cm) sectioned sleeper beam (Richmond & McIntyre 1936, 404). The timber had later been dug out in an act of demolition and the void filled in with occupation debris. The backfilled slot was then cut by a series of postholes for a subsequent structure. The excavators later tried to retract this analysis (Richmond & McIntyre 1939, 122), claiming that the postholes had merely cut an eaves drip, but the structure described in the earlier report sounds too big for such an interpretation (the eaves drips elsewhere on the site were only 7-10cm deep) and even if the later analysis is correct and it really was an eaves drip that was cut, this must still have existed before the posts or there would have been nothing for them to cut. In other words, there must still have been an earlier building a little to one side, whose roof drained onto this channel. The chances are, therefore, that this part of the site had a rather longer and more complex history than the single phase plan might imply. If so, a similar degree of complexity could be expected elsewhere in the fort and the multiple foundations slots in building F (*17*) could certainly be interpreted as a two-period structure.

The finds from the excavation were mostly Flavian in date, with no Antonine material present. Some of the pottery was surprisingly early, however, with some Samian from the beginning of the reign of Vespasian (69-79) or even late Neronian (54-68) times. The fort's exact occupation period thus remains uncertain but at the end of its life it was systematically demolished.

The most recent work on the fort, a large-scale geophysical survey by the authors (*20*), has refined the structural picture. Demolished timber structures rarely respond well to geophysics, so little more can be said about the internal buildings, but the defences show well and here we can add a good deal. For example, the excavators thought that the fort had only a single ditch over most of its circuit and did not study the ditch entrance arrangements. The survey showed that there is, in fact, a double ditch around almost the entire fort, with the now familiar parrot-beak breaks at the gates. Perhaps the biggest gain, however, is in our understanding of the annexe. The excavations found its eastern defences and traced them far enough to the south-east to suggest that the southern end had

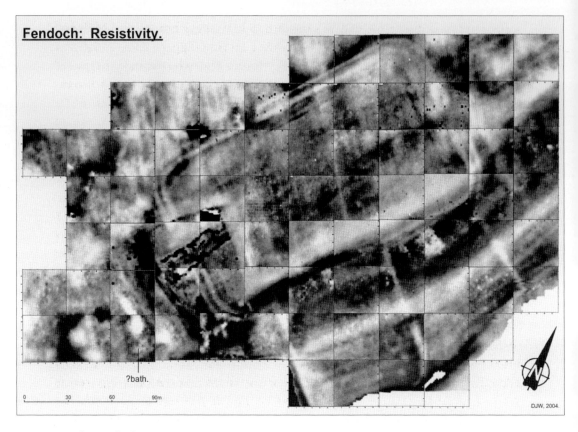

Fendoch: Resistivity.

?bath.

0   30   60   90m

DJW, 2004.

20 The Fendoch resistivity survey

been eroded by the Fendoch Burn. They were not, though, able to locate its western limit and so could not estimate its size. Moreover, air photography has since suggested that there might be a second annexe to the east of the known enclosure (RCAHMS neg: c55038) but, again, knowledge of its size and form remained sketchy.

Fortunately the survey was able to trace the full surviving extent of both annexes. As expected, the east side of the Richmond/McIntyre annexe is attached to the fort defences a little to the north-east of the south-east gate. It has a single ditch which was traced for 74m (including a single entrance break) before it began a typically Roman, rounded-corner curve towards the south. It was then cut off by erosion from the burn, but the survival of the corner allows us to say that the enclosure measured 96m (north-west to south-east). The west ditch was located 77m to the south-west of the eastern ditch (with no entrance break) and, once one knows where it is, it can still be dimly made out on the surface, running just to the east of a modern field wall. Richmond and McIntyre believed that the fort ditch had been destroyed by land slippage towards the west end of the south-east side. But the survey found that what actually happened is that the fort's outer ditch fell in with the annexe ditch at each end, leaving only the inner to run across the annexe interior. This was partly obscured by high resistance areas caused by rabbit warrens, but does still seem to survive, to leave the annexe with an internal area of 0.5ha (1.2 acres). This ditch pattern would suggest that the annexe was part of the original design, and this might explain why the fort's southern gate was less heavily defended. For it would not have given access to the outside, but could only have been attacked if the annexe itself had fallen. No Roman buildings were traced in the annexe, but a 10m diameter ring feature was detected, which presumably represents a pre- or post-Roman roundhouse, and this is the only sign of native activity found within the survey area.

The eastern enclosure proved to be rather different in form. Firstly, both fort ditches continued across its northern end, which might suggest that it was a later addition. Indeed, there are even hints that it may not be Roman at all. In particular, its south-east corner is marked by a sharp, angular turn rather than a normal Roman curve and, although this may not be a sufficient disproof by itself, it will be interesting to see what any future excavation might reveal. Whatever its date, however, the north-eastern ditch began 54m to the north-east of the west annexe and was traced for 57m to the south-east. It then made a turn of rather less than 90° and ran south for a further 90m before being lost to erosion just before falling in with the west annexe's south-east ditch (at a point 83m from the outer fort ditch). The internal area was thus c.0.35ha (0.86 acres) inside the ditch lips, and no entrance breaks were detected in its ditches. The north-western thirds of both annexes occupy the steep slope down from the fort plateau, and it is doubtful whether much use could have been made of these sections without artificial terracing. The rest of their area lies on even ground beside the burn, however, and it was here, in the western site, that signs of metal working have been found.

Finally, Richmond and McIntyre (1939, 138ff) suggested that the gully entering the south-east gate may have marked the line of an aqueduct bringing piped water to the fort. The site does, of course, stand markedly higher than its surroundings and so this would involve water flowing (very sharply) uphill. The excavators attempted to get round this by suggesting that the gully would have contained a wooden pipeline held together by iron collars and set up as an inverted syphon, to bring water from a source on still higher ground. Pipelines of this type are known on Roman sites, as are inverted syphons, but they do not generally occur together: for timber pipes cannot withstand much pressure. Known Roman pressurised water systems usually have heavy concrete jackets which would have left archaeological traces, yet none were found at Fendoch. More importantly, there are no higher water sources in the vicinity, so there was nothing to feed such a system, and the gully seems far more likely to have been a drain.

The geophysical survey did, though, produce one unexpected feature which might be water related. Some 50m to the south-west of the fort's southern corner (and almost 20m below it) is a patch of ground overgrown with swamp grass, which probably hides a spring. It was assumed that the area would yield uniformly low resistance readings and this was largely the case. Nevertheless, there was also what looked to be an ordered pattern of very high readings, of a type normally caused by stone (20). This took the form of a square structure, almost 15m across, at the south-east end of which was a more rectangular (18m north–south x 9m east–west) area with an almost apse-like curve at its southern end. Where the square and rectangular features meet, two much smaller square features (only c.4m across) were detected in what looks to be a symmetrical pattern: one on either side of the junction. Nothing can yet be said with any confidence about the meaning of these readings. They could represent a modern building, or just a geological anomaly. They would, however, be perfectly in keeping with a Roman bath building and, if so, this would be the first to be discovered for 100 years on a Flavian military site north of the Forth and Clyde. Alternative possibilities include a stone-built temple or other shrine, and, again, it will be interesting to see what future exploration might reveal.

No temporary camps are known with certainty around Fendoch. One was claimed, to the north of the fort, on a map (now in Perth Museum) drawn in 1778 by J. McOmie, but the plan does not resemble that of any other Roman camp, and the identification is highly questionable. More recently, however, another associated installation has been claimed in the form of a possible watchtower. This can be seen as a well-preserved earthwork on higher ground on the southern side of the mouth of the Sma' Glen (NN 908284) and takes the form of a ring ditch surrounding a circular ridge or rampart with a hollow centre (*colour plate 8*). The remains have been interpreted as a timber tower surrounded, like those on the Gask line, by a ditch and rampart. Certainly, it has the fort in full view, which would have allowed Roman-style visual signalling (Woolliscroft 2001a), and an early warning post against attacks down the glen would seem eminently sensible. Nevertheless, although no certainty will be possible until the site has been excavated, there are reasons to cast doubt on the traditional identification. For example, there seem to be no entrance breaks in the rampart and ditch, which are a universal feature of such towers. Moreover, although great play has been made in the past of the site's supposedly crucial view up the glen, this is actually very limited. *Colour plate 8* shows the site photographed from the top of a tall telescopic pole designed to mimic the likely height of a Roman tower, and thus gives a fair approximation of such a site's field of view. It should be noted that the picture was taken with a wide angle (24mm) lens which makes everything seem about twice as far away as it actually is, and it is immediately apparent that a tower on this spot could only have seen a few hundred metres along the glen bottom. As a result, it could have given little more than a few minutes warning and it is doubtful whether this would have justified leaving men in such an exposed position. In fact, the site sits amongst a series of ruined barrows and it is highly possible that it is actually an old burial mound that has been burrowed into, perhaps during treasure hunting activities, or even early, unrecorded archaeological work. Had the Romans really wanted to install a warning tower it would probably have been on the northern side of the glen mouth, where it would have been closer to the fort and from where it really would have enjoyed a good view up the glen. Yet nothing can be seen in this area, despite an intensive search by the authors, and no similar towers have been claimed for other Highland line forts, such as Bochastle, where the need would seem to have been at least as great.

One thing that seems conspicuous by its absence on the Highland line is much sign that the forts were linked, either to each other, or to the Gask, by road. There are a number of vague (mostly eighteenth-century) antiquarian references to old roads in the area, but almost no firm evidence to back these up. Air photographs and old plans show roads leading out of the fort of Dalginross, but these cannot be traced for more than a 100m or so, and even less can be seen at the other sites. Indeed, perhaps the only indication of cross-country road building comes from a recent aerial find by A.S. Torrance (neg: Torro3CN8#11, now in the Gask Project archive) of a *c.*200m-long section to the north of the River Earn, opposite the Gask fort of Strageath. We will see in chapter 3 that the Roman Gask road is now known to turn east at the fort, to cross the Earn at Innerpeffray, but there was once a competitor line. For Roy (1793, PL XIX) showed the road passing to the west of the site (running approximately north–south) and crossing the Earn *c.*400m upstream (west) of its confluence with the Pow Water (*c.*NN 894186). He then shows it turning to the east crossing the Pow, and running to the north of Innerpeffray towards Parkneuk. There had, however, been no modern evidence for such a course and modern scholars have tended to discount it (e.g. Crawford 1949, 51). Torrance's photograph, however, shows a road crossing the Earn almost exactly where Roy said it should but, once across, there are still no signs that it then turned east. Quite the contrary, the aerial indications are that it headed north-west. Of course aerial evidence alone is not enough to show this road as Roman. It may well be a later track associated with an old ford at this point, and the fact that it heads in the direction of modern Crieff might suggest an early modern date, perhaps close to Roy's own time. Nevertheless this would also be a reasonable heading for a link from Strageath to Dalginross and/or Fendoch and there is an antiquarian record of a possible Roman road being discovered in Crieff when the current Burrell Street was first built (NSA vol x, 502). It thus remains possible that a Highland line road network was begun, even if it was never completed, and future work might yet augment our meagre evidence.

INCHTUTHIL

As the base of the only legion permanently based in Scotland, Inchtuthil (*colour plate 9*, arrowed) was the key site of the whole military occupation, and single-handedly accounted for up to a third of its entire garrison. It lies just north of the Tay at NO 125397, 23.3km (14.5 miles) from Fendoch, 12.9km (8 miles) from the end of the Gask line at Bertha, and 4.4km (2.75 miles) from Cargill at the foot of Strathmore. It is also about 10km (6 miles) downstream of Dunkeld, where the Tay valley becomes a near gorge. The legionary fortress occupies the northern part of a large, steep-sided plateau (*21,1*), which stands well above the surrounding flood plain and represents a strong defensive position with a good all round field of view.

The fortress dwarfs all of the auxiliary forts we have seen: measuring 472.4m (north–south) x 460.2m (east–west), over the ramparts, to give an area of 21.74ha (53.73 acres). It had just a single (albeit large) V-shaped defensive ditch (6.1m wide and 2m deep), behind which stood a turf rampart. The latter was modified after construction by the insertion of a 1.52m-thick stone wall into its front, which is the only stone defensive structure known from the entire occupation. There were four gates, of which only three now survive. These had no rampart reentrants, but seem to have had dual-carriageway entrances flanked by massive timber towers, which stood on nine posts each. In the interior, the *via principalis* runs across the short axis, about two-thirds of the way towards the south, so that the fortress faced south-west. Long stretches of the defences are still visible on the ground and it is even possible to see individual demolition dumps in the ditch, although these are clearer in pictures taken before the site was partially landscaped for a short-lived golf course in the mid-twentieth century (e.g. *22*).

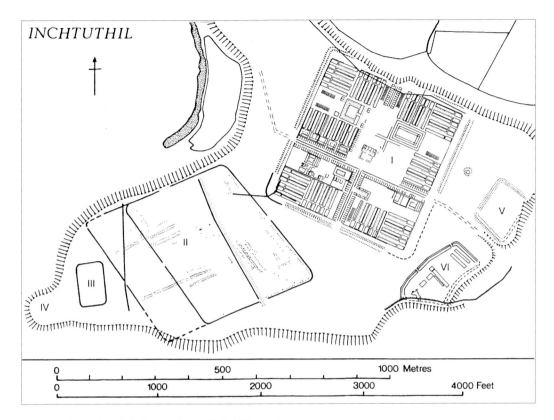

21 The Inchtuthil plateau. *Drawn I.A. Richmond*

The site has been known for centuries and three excavation programmes have been conducted. The first, by Abercromby (1902) in 1901, looked largely outside the fortress proper, amongst a series of other Roman structures to the south-east. The second, and by far the most extensive, was by I.A. Richmond and J.K. St Joseph, who conducted large-scale trenching between 1952 and 1965 (Pitts & St Joseph 1985). Finally, Barclay and Maxwell (1998) excavated a pre-Roman mortuary feature inside the fortress in 1989 and, in the process, acquired further information on two barracks. Thanks largely to Richmond and St Joseph's work we now have what appears to be a complete plan of the fortress (*23*), but the techniques used were much the same as those used by Richmond at Fendoch. In other words, the site was sampled by (mostly narrow) slit trenches and the features found extrapolated in what amounts to a gigantic dot to dot puzzle, to form a plausible, but not necessarily accurate plan. The only difference being that some of the Inchtuthil internal features have also appeared on air photographs (e.g. RCAHMS neg: B18501), which should allow a degree of control.

22 Inchtuthil, the eastern fortress ditch. *Photograph by kind permission of D. Emslie-Smith*

One of the most noteworthy aspects of the fortress is that it was never fully completed. It probably did become operational as a legionary base, but there were still structures missing, which left open areas in the interior. Moreover, these are genuine blanks and not just a reflection of an absence of excavation in certain sectors. For example, the *principia* is clearly recognisable in the centre (*23*, A), but there is a large open area next to it (B) where we would normally expect the *praetorium*. The building was apparently never started. Indeed, even the *principia* has a provisional look to it, because it is far smaller than we would expect for a legionary fortress (albeit still larger that an auxiliary *principia*) and takes up only a small part of the plot provided for it. It is also set much further back from the *via principalis* than would be normal, and it is possible that we are looking at a quickly built temporary structure designed to occupy the courtyard area of a planned much grander building. In other words an interim measure to get things up and running, which could be used whilst the final *principia* was built round it and then dismantled without causing a break in operations. Likewise, six beam-founded granaries can be seen (C), each with post-founded loading bays at each end, but space has been left for at least two, and possibly four more. We also see a number of large courtyard houses (D) reminiscent of auxiliary *praetoria*. These are the tribunes' houses, but only four were built, whereas the legion had six tribunes, and we might also expect a house for the camp prefect. Indeed some legionary fortresses have still more and plenty of space has been left for these structures. Many of the missing buildings were, at least in part, luxuries: in particular, the grand houses for senior officers. By contrast, the finished granaries would be enough for day to day provision, if not for an emergency reserve, and it is immediately apparent that a full complement of barracks was provided. For the most part, the latter were built in neat groups of six, each of which represents a cohort. Most can be found in the *praetentura* or *retentura*, as we might expect, but one normal cohort group lies at the east end of the *via principalis*, next to the plot left for the *praetorium*. The first cohort barracks can be seen at the other end of the main street, where they are clearly recognisable as a group of five larger blocks. Here the centurions' quarters are essentially miniature versions of the tribunes' houses and the largest (E), which lay in the place of honour on the *principia's* right hand, was that of the *Primus Pilus*.

Behind the main range lay the two largest completed buildings. The first (F) is a courtyard structure with an aisled hall running around three sides and a range of rooms, fronted by a timber colonnade, on the fourth. In all, the structure measures 59.74m (north–south) x 58.52m (east–west), an area of close to an acre (0.35ha). Furnaces and other finds suggest that this was a *fabrica* and, when the fortress was abandoned, large numbers of iron objects were buried here, mostly in an unused state. These included iron wheel-tyres and almost 10 tons of nails (close to 900,000 in all), presumably to deny them to potential enemies. In short, this was more than just a workshop. It was a veritable factory for manufacturing military matériel.

Further to the east is a truly colossal building (G), measuring 58.52m (north–south) x 91.44m (east–west), an area of over 1.3 acres (0.54ha). It consists of two concentric rings of small rooms, separated by a corridor, arranged around a central courtyard. This is usually described as a hospital (*valetudinarium*) and might well be so: for, although there was little evidence to confirm it at Inchtuthil, similar buildings at other legionary fortresses are better attested and there is literary and epigraphic evidence to show that such buildings did exist (Pitts and St Joseph 1989, 91ff). Whatever it was, however, the very fact that it was built before the *praetorium* must suggest that it had a reasonably high priority.

To the south, in the eastern part of the *praetentura*, an elongated courtyard building (H) was found, fronting onto the *via praetoria*. Richmond thought that

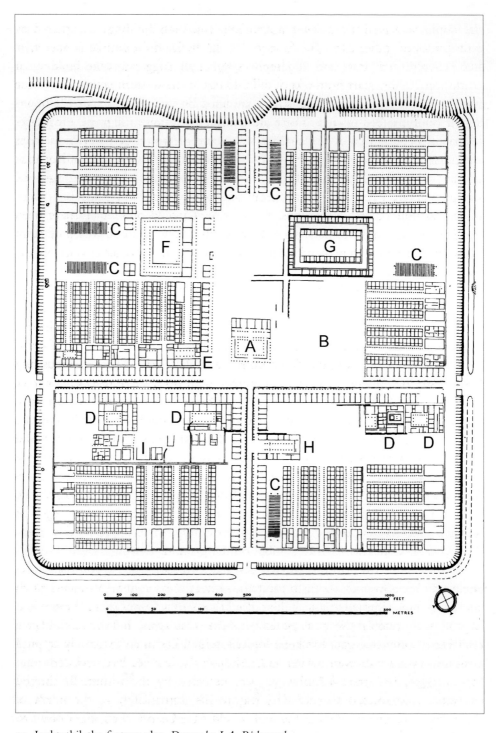

23 Inchtuthil, the fortress plan. *Drawn by I.A. Richmond*

this could be a *basilica exercitoria* (a drill hall) and such buildings are attested by inscriptions on other sites. The function of the Inchtuthil example is uncertain, however, although Pitts and St Joseph (1989, 127f) suggest a store building or workshop. Finally, apart from a knot of buildings in the western *praetentura*, whose function is unclear (I), the main streets are lined by numerous, apparently open-ended, booths called *tabernae*. These are common features in legionary fortresses (although almost unknown in auxiliary forts) and are also found serving as shops on civilian sites. Their military function is not altogether clear and they may, in fact, have filled a variety of roles such as offices and filing rooms, general storage, stabling or garaging for wagons and other machinery (such as artillery pieces), armouries and workshops. Some at least would presumably have been equipped with shutter or barn-type doors, so that they could be closed off from the elements and potential pilfering, but these would leave little trace in the archaeological record.

Much of the rest of the plateau is also filled with Roman installations. To the south-west of the fortress, a large temporary camp has been detected from the air (*21, II*). It is shaped like a parallelogram, to fit into the space available, and originally covered 19.91ha (49.2 acres). It was thus almost as large as the fortress itself, although it was later cut down from the west to 14ha (35 acres). Unusually, both phases have simple gap ditch entrances, with no signs of *claviculae* or *tituli*, and some aerial shots show large numbers of pits in the interior, which were probably rubbish dumps or latrines. It is possible, although not certain, that the site acted as a labour camp from which the fortress could be built and it would certainly be large enough to hold an entire legion in tents, with room to spare for work areas and construction materials. Further west, a much smaller camp (III) of 0.94ha (2.33 acres) has been seen from the air and, beyond that, on the western tip, is an Iron Age promontory fort (IV). The latter contains stone which seems to have been robbed from the fortress wall, so it is presumably post-Roman and its defences remain visible on the ground.

To the east of the fortress (*21, IV*) lies a well-preserved, if slightly irregular, enclosure. It consists of an earth rampart, protected by a single V-shaped ditch and has been variously named as 'the redoubt' or 'stores compound'. The site is as large as many auxiliary forts, at (at least) 1.65ha (4.08 acres), but the resemblance ends there. Only one gate has been located, which lies in an extremely atypical position in the south-west corner and, although the interior has produced some Flavian finds, no internal buildings were detected by the admittedly limited excavations conducted to date. The feature sits immediately to the north of the easiest route up to the plateau and would have been a convenient point to which to bring heavy supplies. Alternatively, it may have served as a demolition base at the end of the occupation. None of these possibilities can be more than suggestions, however, and without additional archaeological data, its true function must remain unknown.

The final major site on the plateau is often referred to as the 'officers' compound' (*21, VI* and *24*) and may be a double structure. The 1901 excavator reported a rampart and a (4.88m wide x 2.1m deep) ditch running south-east from the fortress, along the south side of the modern path up to the site (*24,* A). He did not determine the stratigraphic relationship between the fortress and these features, so we do not know which came first: but two parallel, rectangular stone buildings (B) were located with their short axes parallel to the rampart (A) and which might, thus, be associated with it. No dating evidence was reported and the buildings were badly preserved, but they were 8.2m wide and 76.25m long. This gives them a similar size and shape to the fortress barracks and seems far too large (and regular) for them to fit well with a group of relatively modern cottages to their east. To the south-east of these structures was another defensive enclosure, of somewhat irregular shape. This had two entrances: one a little south of centre on its south-west side and the other in the north-west corner, where it provides a symmetrical reflection of the south-west corner gate of the redoubt. The enclosure was defended by a 2.9m-wide x 1.37m-deep V-shaped ditch, backed by a 6.1m-wide rampart, and enclosed an area of 1.5ha (3.75 acres).

Several internal buildings were found, some of which show more than one structural period. In the north-east were timber barracks (C), which are unusual in having 15 *contubernia*, but no centurions' quarters. Initially, there was only a single block, but this was later demolished, along with the enclosure defences, and replaced by a pair: one of which encroached onto the line of the former rampart. To the south of these was a large, apparently open area and then another long rectangular structure (D) which shows the basic shape of a normal barrack with centurions' quarters, but was heavily modified to a more luxurious standard, that included some rooms with hypocaust under-floor heating. This has been interpreted as an interim *praetorium*, to serve whilst that in the fortress remained unbuilt (Pitts & St Joseph, 1989, 210f) and this is not impossible, especially as the layout is reminiscent of the north wing of the palatial, Flavian villa at Fishbourne in southern England (Cunliffe 1971, 75). Indeed, a not dissimilar building existed outside the milliary *ala* fort of Heidenheim (Rabold 1988), in Germany, which has even been discussed as a possible residence for the provincial governor. The Heidenheim building lasted for at least 150 years, during which it underwent several rebuilds (some in stone), although we do not know if the *ala* fort had its own *praetorium* at the time. Whatever the case, the Inchtuthil structure ran parallel to what seems to have been a rectangular shed (E), to the south-west of

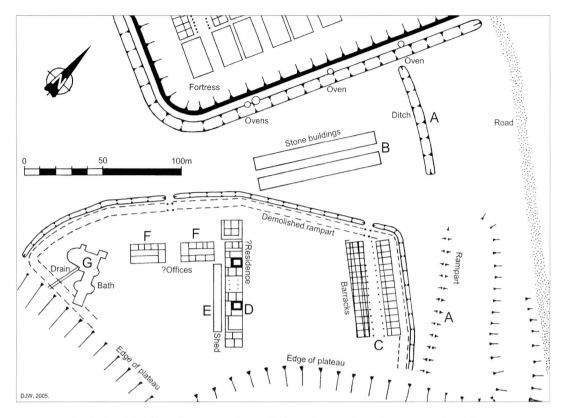

24 The Inchtuthil 'officers' compound', combining evidence from the Abercromby and Richmond excavations

which two more rectangular buildings (F) ran off at right-angles. The latter are often referred to as offices, but, although slightly smaller, they closely resemble the houses of the first cohort centurions in the fortress and so may have been meant to accommodate centurions for the barracks further north. Alternatively, they look similar to two structures at the villa of North Leigh in Oxfordshire, which initially formed a detached wing, but were later incorporated into the main structure when it was extended to form a quadrangle (Wilson 2004, 81ff & fig 4). Indeed, the supposed commander's house appears almost to beg to be finished as such a four sided complex, and there is enough room, both to its north and south, for the work to be done. All of the buildings inside this compound are roughly parallel inter-se, but all lie on a distinctly different orientation to the stone structures (B) outside it. As a result, none seem likely to be fully contemporary with those structures, or part of the same design, which means that we might have up to three structural phases on display.

Finally, at the south-western end of the enclosure, lies a stone-built Roman bath block (25), one of only two known with certainty on a Flavian site north of the Forth and Clyde. This too overlay the demolished enclosure defences, making it late in the sequence, and it is set on a different alignment to all of the other buildings. Opinions differ as to how much use it received. Richmond claimed that its stoke holes had never been fired (Pitts & St Joseph 1989, 216), but Macdonald (1919, 116) pointed out that it had stood long enough for settling cracks to both develop and be repaired. One thing is certain, however: this structure is far too small to have served as the main baths for a legionary fortress. At just 33m long, the building is much the same size as many auxiliary fort baths, whereas legionary baths were vast structures, many times this size. In the eighteenth century a possible second bath was reported (albeit at second-hand) by Maitland (1757, 199) and Pennant (1774, pt 2, 70), lying to the west of the fortress, but even this would be unusual: for legionary baths, unlike their auxiliary equivalents, were usually built inside the defences. Indeed, the so-called 'drill hall' (23, H) in the fortress *praetentura* has a large space behind it that had not yet been built on when the site was abandoned, and it is possible that it was built as a timber exercise hall for a planned stone bath that was never built. If so, a similar hall and bath pairing is known in exactly the same part of the fortress of Caerleon in south Wales, and another has been recorded not far from the same part of Chester (Mason 2001, 164). As a result, this might be a hint that the Romans had planned to build many of Inchtuthil's remaining major buildings in stone.

At present the Inchtuthil plateau lies on the north side of the Tay, but it is obvious that this has not always been the case. There is a line of oxbow lakes around its western and northern sides, and the eastern sides of the 'redoubt' and 'officers' compound', as well as parts of the fortress' northern defences have been eroded away in post-Roman times. It seems certain, therefore, that the river has flowed to the north of the site at some point. Whether it lay to the north or south in Roman times remains unknown, however. Indeed, the plateau might even have been an island, as it can still become today during floods, and it is to be hoped that the issue will eventually be studied by a geomorphologist.

The stone for the Inchtuthil rampart came from a quarry on the Hill of Gourdie (NO 109423), some 2.8 km to the north-north-west, and a road seems to have been built to allow efficient transportation. This can be seen from the air, to the north of Spittalfield (NO 115411-107415), as a series of cropmarks caused by its quarry pits (Gask Project neg: 05CN09#35), and excavations in 1983 found a gravel road bed c.5.95m wide, laid on a low turf *agger* (Pitts & St Joseph 1989, 256). Towards the east end of the Hill of Gourdie (NO 115427) lies

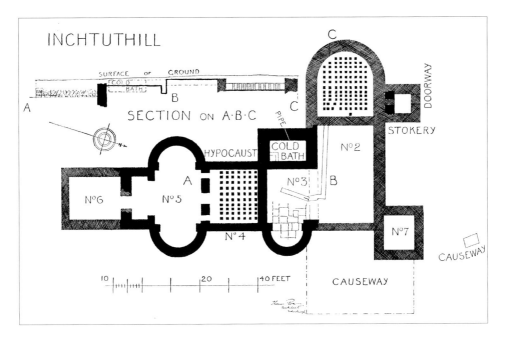

25 The Inchtuthil bath block

a small temporary camp of 1.6ha (4 acres), which may have formed a base for the quarrying (*colour plate 10*). The site is curious in being divided in two by an internal ditch, which has its own gate break to allow movement between the two halves (*26*). There are clear aerial indications of an entrance break in the SE ditch and much fainter signs of south-west and north-east gates just to the north of the transverse ditch. There are also faint signs of what is probably the north-west gate, although this is not directly opposite the south-east entrance or the gate through the transverse ditch.

The camp is best known for a series of seven prominent, roughly tadpole-shaped, artificial hollows which local legend ascribed to stabling: thus giving the site its modern name of Steed Stalls. The visible examples (*colour plate 10*) form a line running parallel to the camp's north-west defences, but air photography has revealed a further seven, which turn through a neat right-angle to run south-east. Quite what these features represent is uncertain. No excavation has yet taken place, so there can be no guarantee that they are even Roman. They might be quarries, although a wider working face would have been more efficient. They might be lime kilns, although none face into the prevailing west wind. It is even possible that they might form a base for stone vaulting, perhaps for a victory monument of some kind to celebrate the occupation. The Roman geographer

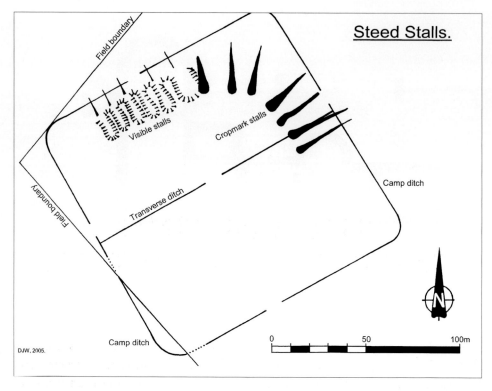

26 Plan of Steed Stalls camp

Ptolemy (II, 3, 7) mentions a site called *Victoria* somewhere in this area, which has sometimes been linked to Inchtuthil (Rivet & Smith 1981, 499). Indeed, for this reason, the fortress plateau is one of the many places to have been claimed as the battlefield of Mons Graupius. In fact, however, Roman victory monuments were by no means always set up on, or even near, the battle site and Steed Stalls would have been an excellent position, since it would have been visible for many miles across Roman occupied territory. Whatever the case, the aerial data provide signs that the stalls might not be contemporary with the camp. One overlaps part of the internal division ditch. Two more cross the camp's north-east defences and five narrow cropmarks, which run from the visible stalls across the north-west defences, probably show the same sequence. Likewise, the visible features seem to block the camp's north-west gate and, as they come to within 6m of the camp ditch, they would not have left room for a rampart. As usual, one cannot be certain of stratigraphic relationships from aerial data alone but, in this case, it does seem probable that the camp predates the stalls since it seems unlikely that a north-west gate would have been created that was blocked from the start.

3

THE GASK LINE: CAMELON TO STRAGEATH

The backbone of the first-century defence of northern Scotland was a line of fortifications along the road between Camelon, on the outskirts of Falkirk, and Bertha, just upstream of Perth on the Tay (7). This was not the most powerful component in terms of manpower. That accolade undoubtedly lies with the Highland line, whose garrison included the Inchtuthil legion. It was, though, the most closely watched and co-ordinated sector. In particular, it is the only defensive element known to have been linked by a road. That said, although the line of this road is known over much of its length and long sections still survive, it is surprisingly poorly dated. There have been relatively few excavations, of which fewer still have been properly published and, so far as we are aware, no closely datable finds have been recovered from its structure and no associated milestones have come to light. This is quite common with Roman roads, but it is particularly galling here, for we know that many of the forts on the route, although Flavian foundations, were brought back into use in the mid-second century, as outposts to the Antonine Wall. It is thus possible that the beautifully engineered, all-weather road that we know today is of second-, rather than first-century date: especially as it has never been traced to the south of the Antonine Wall. There is, though, one strong hint that the road did exist in Flavian times, albeit it remains possible that the early version was of lighter construction. For all of the military installations along it have their entrances oriented onto its line, even those that were not reoccupied later.

At least parts of the Camelon to Bertha road were exceptionally closely monitored and have become known collectively as the Gask line or Gask frontier. This consists of a series of watchtowers and small fortlets strung out along the road between the main garrison forts, and it has already been traced over roughly two-thirds of the road's length: from Bertha to Glenbank (just north of Dunblane). This may be all there ever was, but that does seem rather unlikely and it is probably just a reflection of the fact that the modern agricultural regime to the south of Glenbank is more pastoral in nature than that further north. This is crucial because many of the small installations have been found from the air. There are exceptions, and there are sites along the Gask Ridge, on the north side of Strathearn, which have been known for centuries (hence the system's name). Nevertheless, the Ridge provides exceptional preservation conditions, and almost all of the remaining sites are air photographic finds discovered since the Second World War. Aerial archaeology, however, depends on buried sites causing visible cropmarks and, unlike cereals, or crops such as oil seed rape, pasture land only shows marks under severe drought conditions. This makes it far less revealing, although not completely beyond hope, and we can only wait to see what future flying might bring.

CAMELON

The Roman road emerges from the Antonine Wall at the milefortlet of Watling Lodge (NS 863809), and just 1,070m to the north lies the fort of Camelon. Accounts from the sixteenth century (Buchanan, in Aikman 1827, 1, 89) reported it to be still in good condition and, in the mid-eighteenth century, Roy (1793, PI 29) was still able to produce a reasonably accurate plan from the surface features alone. Sadly, it has since been badly damaged, having been ploughed, partly built over and cut by a railway line. Nevertheless, its northern part survives on a golf course and fragments of the defensive circuit remain faintly visible on the ground, whilst internal features still show from the air during droughts (e.g. CUCAP neg: CNB 14). It occupies strong ground on a steep-sided (if quarry damaged) promontory, south of the River Carron and has good views in all directions, which take in large swathes of the Wall and the Carron valley, and stretch for miles to the north, across Larbert and Stenhousemuir. The site is best known as a second-century outpost (or, perhaps more correctly, outlier) to the Antonine Wall, but as early as 1726 at least one coin of Vespasian (69-79) had been found (Gordon 1726, 23) and excavations have shown that it had at least one first-century predecessor.

The first excavation programme took place in 1900 (Christison et al. 1901) and was, in effect, a rescue dig in response to imminent industrial construction

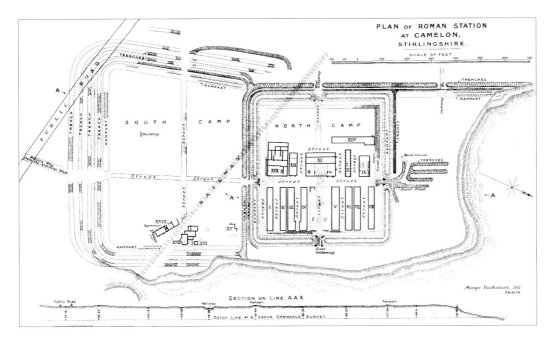

27 The Christison plan of Camelon

over the southern part of the site. Somewhat illogically, given this motivation, the dig's efforts concentrated on the northern area. It did, however, succeed in tracing a turf and timber fort, containing barracks and the normal main range buildings (*principia, praetorium,* granary etc.), flanked by large defended annexes to the north and south (*27*). The south annexe (the excavators called it the 'south camp') contained a number of stone buildings, including a bath house, but little sense was made of its northern counterpart and the bath house may be Antonine. The enclosures all seem to be Antonine in date, but Flavian finds were recovered, including pottery, a surprisingly early (AD 70) coin of Vespasian and an equally surprisingly late (AD 88) coin of Domitian (81-96). Other inconsistencies were also apparent. For example, one of the buildings (*27*, building XVIII) in the 'south camp' lay at a distinct angle to the rest of the layout, but parallel to a set of ditches found crossing the site's south-west corner (not shown on the 1901 plan). The bath block (building XVI) proved to be secondary, for it had needed buttresses to be added after it began to subside into some earlier feature and, as early as 1919, Sir George Macdonald (1919, 130f) felt able to suggest that there was at least one, and probably two, Flavian forts underlying the Antonine levels. This view has since gained more archaeological support. For example, work in advance of quarry damage to the north annexe in 1962, found structures that might predate the Antonine defences, although they could be native in origin (McCord & Tait 1978 and DES 1962, 44f). Flavian material has been found amongst soldier burials to the north-north-west of the site (Breeze *et al.* 1976) and building work for a factory storage tank has revealed a pit containing Flavian pottery (DES 1959, 40f).

Better information has come from excavations conducted by V.A. Maxfield in the 1970s, again ahead of development in the south camp. The full report still awaits publication, but enough has reached print (e.g. Maxfield 1979, 1981 & 1984) to allow us to say a little more about the first-century occupation. In essence, the south camp seems to have been a Flavian foundation and was only later reused as an annexe for the Antonine fort: albeit with its defences on a somewhat different alignment. It contained timber buildings which, although badly disturbed by later activity, seem to show at least two construction phases, with another change of alignment between them. Signs of at least one Flavian U-shaped (rather than the normal V) fort ditch were found (up to 5.4m wide and 1.5m deep), which itself cut a pit containing Flavian material which, again, suggests more than one building period. There are also signs that the Flavian fort may have been large, perhaps over 300m long, although its width (and thus its area) is less certain. In addition, possible temporary camp ditches and what may be a Flavian fort ditch have been found outside the northern annexe (DES 1974, 63) and what might be an annexe to the east of the Flavian fort was found in 1998 (DES 1999, 45). In short, the situation is very confused and we are still not in a position to draw an accurate outline (let alone a plan) of the Flavian fort. We are, though, now able to say with confidence that there was such a fort, and that it was probably a major installation with more than one construction period. Furthermore, both Maxfield (1984) and Caruana (1997, 46) have pointed out that the fort has yielded a suspiciously large amount of very early Flavian material, which might point to an earlier than expected start-date. At the same time, the presence of a coin of AD 88 might suggest that it also stayed in use rather later than current wisdom might lead us to expect, although the piece could easily derive from the Antonine occupation.

The fort stands on a major natural route-way and in ancient times it might also have been the lowest bridging point of the Carron. It is no coincidence that the railway and several roads to the north (including the M9 motorway) pass close by and it is clear that Camelon was also a major staging point for Roman forces heading north. For the area around the site holds one of the densest concentrations of temporary camps found anywhere in the Roman world. At present, at least 10 are known with certainty (for a plan see RCAHMS 1997, 21), some of which may have had more than one period of use; the discovery of possible camp ditches on the fort plateau might suggest that there are yet more for us still to find. They range in size from relatively small enclosures of around 2ha (5 acres), to the vast 52.6ha (130-acre) camp of Dunipace, but their dating is poorly understood. There is also a long-standing tradition that there were Roman harbour works on the Carron, including antiquarian reports of the discovery of an anchor beside an old channel, close to the fort. Sadly, however, although there may well have been such a harbour and the possibility of a link between sea transport and the Roman road network would make perfect logistical sense, its existence remains far from proven.

Finally, quite a number of native Iron Age sites have been found in the fort's vicinity, mostly from the air. Few have been excavated, so little can be said about their dating, but one site, which lies just north of the fort, has produced Roman material from the second and late first centuries and so may have been in use at the same time as one (or even both) of the fort occupations (Proudfoot 1978). There are also aerial indications of prehistoric field systems around the fort (e.g. CUCAP neg: DH29) but, once again, their date is unknown.

Moving north, the exact point at which the Roman road crossed the Carron is uncertain: for the channel has moved significantly over the last two millennia, eroding away archaeological remains in the process. It may, though, have crossed a little upstream (c.NS 856820) of Larbert Bridge, where a ford was later recorded. The eighteenth-century antiquarian Nimmo (1777, 21) then reports it passing just west of Larbert church (c.NS 856822). After this, it again fades from the realm of certainty until Tor Wood, 2km to the north-north-west, where a 1.6km length is (or, in places, was until recently) preserved amongst the trees. This ran from NS 838843-828854, passing just west of the famous Iron Age broch of Torwood (sometimes Tappoch, NS 83338498), which may or may not have been in occupation when it was built (Dundas 1866). There is though a linear parch-mark on two RCAHMS air photographs (negs: ST2961 & B62132) that might represent the line from Larbert. If so, it runs from a cottage called Inverwoods (NS 845839) and heads west-north-west for c.500m to NS 840841, before swinging north-west to line up with the Tor Wood stretch.

Beyond the wood, the road continues on the same alignment to West Plean Cottages (NS 822863) where it makes a slight turn to the west and falls in with a modern road; 1,200m further on (NS 815872), this road veers off to the north, but the Roman line carries straight on (RCAHMS neg: A64010) through the grounds of West Plean House (where it forms part of the drive), before making another slight turn to the west and rejoining the modern road at NS 811878. Just north of West Plean House a marked ring feature (28) is clearly visible on a hilltop close to, but well above, the level of the road (NS 81078762). This sits on strong ground with a quite beautiful field of view, which stretches northwards over Stirling to the Highland fringe. The surface feature is strongly reminiscent of a Roman watchtower and for years that is exactly was it was believed to be (Crawford 1949, 18). Excavations in the 1950s (Steer 1958), showed it to be an Iron Age homestead, however, and thus, as so often in archaeology, an attractive story died a death.

From West Plean the route follows the modern road for a further c.500m until the latter veers off at Croftsidepark (NS 808881), after which the exact line again becomes uncertain. It probably continued on to the north-west, passing just to the west of the service station and motorway interchange at Pirnhall, for a road answering its general description was found during excavations (NS 803 889 & 804888) ahead of their development, and again in 2004 (DES 1972, 39 & 2004, 129). It must then have turned slightly more to the north to run towards the built-up area of Stirling, probably a little to the west of the modern A872. In 1962 a coin of Hadrian was found in St Ninians (NN 798915), suggesting that the route might not have been far away, and a series of excavations in the 1970s by the Stirling Archaeological and Field Society (DES 1971, 42, 1972, 39 & 1974, 65) managed to trace it at several points in house gardens (29), where it was usually c.6.7m wide, with a structure of packed gravel on a foundation of larger stones. Earlier records would support this line (Crawford 1949, 23f) and the general course ran through Boreston (from c.NS 713919) and passed west of St Ninians church to Drummond Place (NS 792927). Hereabouts it turned slightly to the west and has been traced through the gate of what is now the King's Park as far as NS 791929.

Stirling has long been the strategic key to the Highlands of Scotland. Much of the Forth valley was wetland until early modern times, but Stirling itself was dry land and provided a route around the eastern end of the mosses where the valley is fairly narrow. It also lay at the lowest convenient bridging point on the Forth, and at a point just below its confluence with the Teith, where there is only one river to cross. It is thus no coincidence that so many battles were fought in this area in medieval times (e.g. Bannock Burn and Stirling Bridge), nor that it became the setting for a major royal castle. At the same time, a garrison point here is relatively easy to supply by sea and there has long been an assumption that there would have been a Roman fort in the vicinity. It might be natural to look to the Castle Rock, which dominates the countryside for miles around but, in fact, Roman fortifications tend not to occupy obvious strong points of this kind. Roman forts were essentially armoured barracks, not defensive strongholds like medieval castles: and the Romans preferred to take on enemies in the field, rather than hiding behind defences. They thus tended to pick easily supplied and

28 The West Plean ring feature

29 The Roman road under excavation at 6 Drummond Place, Stirling. *Photograph by kind permission of the Stirling Archaeological and Field Society*

watered strategic points, often near places where a Roman road crossed a river. This means that, although the Romans might well have placed an observation post on the Rock, the fort, if there was one, is more likely to have been on lower ground and, for centuries, archaeologists' eyes (e.g. Crawford 1949, 22) have fallen on the site of a much later set of formal gardens called the 'King's Knot' (NS 789937). These still survive as earthworks to the west of Stirling Castle (*colour plate 11*) and the projected line of the Roman road as it enters the King's Park, 750m to the south-south-east, would pass right through them. It must be said, however, that at present there is no hard evidence for a fort at this point. Nor is there any significant concentration of Roman finds known anywhere else in Stirling to point us to a different site: so, although it still seems likely, we simply do not know whether a Stirling fort ever existed. The same applies to a possible alternative: a fort in, or around, Dunblane. This would fill a similar strategic niche and, unlike Stirling, there are known temporary camps in the vicinity. We have already seen that camps sometimes cluster at forts, and so these might serve as an indicator. There is still no evidence for such a fort, however, and a site at Dunblane would tend to unbalance the spacing pattern: being that much further from Camelon, and closer to Doune and Ardoch.

The line of the road from King's Park to the river has so far defied investigation, but there are a number of options. Indeed it is not beyond the realm of possibility that there were actually two routes: one directly to the north and the other to the north-west to link up the fort at Doune. The line from the south seems to be heading as if to pass to the west of the Castle Rock, but its last known position still leaves room for it to veer off to the north-north-east towards the medieval bridging point, around NS 797946. It is even possible that a branch road might already have left the known line by this point and been missed by the few archaeological views we have had of it through this very old built-up area. Alternatively, it could have continued more or less straight on and, although an attempt to test this possibility failed to find it (DES 1975, 53), this was only able to study such a very small area that even a slight deviation of the road's course would have by-passed it. If this was the route taken, the road would have passed below the western side of the Castle Rock on or close to the line of the modern B8051 and would have reached the river somewhere around Kildean Hospital (NS 785950). The river here flows in a broad, flat flood plain and may have followed a very different course in ancient times. As a result, the fact that recent work by a group of able amateur archaeologists failed to find signs of a crossing need not be very significant, and there are earlier reports of a possible paved ford here (Crawford 1949, 25). The third, rather circuitous possibility is that the road turned west along the approximate line of the modern A811 and then used the ancient 'Fords of Frew' along the so-called 'Kippen road' (now the B8031) which, until surprisingly recently, was the only firm path through the Forth mosses. This route crosses the river at Bridge of Frew (NS 668960) and then returns to the north-east past the Iron Age broch at Coldoch (NS 696981), from where there are a number of possible routes to Doune.

Which of these potential courses was chosen remains unknown and perhaps the only clue is that there are no Roman temporary camps known along the Fords of Frew route, whereas there are three within easy reach of the direct northern line. These lie at Dunblane (NN 775006), Craigarnhall (NS 756985) and Ochtertyre (NS 745982), although the latter lies south of the Teith and its Roman identity is less certain. Whatever the case, however, the road cannot yet be followed for almost 11km (7 miles) beyond its last known point in Stirling and, when it does reappear, to the north of Dunblane, it has passed to the north of Doune. As a result, we do not know how, or even if, that fort was linked to it.

DOUNE

The fort of Doune (NN 727012) was discovered from the air by the RCAHMS in 1983 (DES 1984, 4), but there had been earlier hints of Roman activity. For a start, the fort sits on what had long been known as Castle Hill, despite the fact that Doune's famous medieval castle is built on lower ground to the south-east. More tellingly, however, a coin of Vespasian had been found near the site (Robertson 1950, 147). The fort lies 22.5km (14 miles) from Camelon (9.6km (6 miles) from the King's Knot in Stirling) and sits atop a steep-sided, but flat-topped, promontory on the southern side of the modern town. From here it overlooks the River Teith and medieval castle to the south and two burn valleys to the east and west, and has reasonable long-distance views. The site itself is partly overlain by a school and modern housing (30) and, as even the remaining area lies in permanent pasture, it rarely shows well from the air. Nevertheless, enough can be seen to show that at least the south-east and north-east sides have a non-standard, triple-ditch system, with parrot-beak entrance breaks, a configuration we shall see again at the Strathmore fort of Cargill. The full defensive circuit has never been traced, but the fort is probably around 2.25ha (5.6 acres) over the ramparts.

A small excavation was conducted almost as soon as the fort was discovered, but the full results have never appeared and it is difficult even to tell what was done from the short published notes (e.g. DES 1984, 264), let alone exactly what was found. The work does, though, seem to have confirmed the identification of

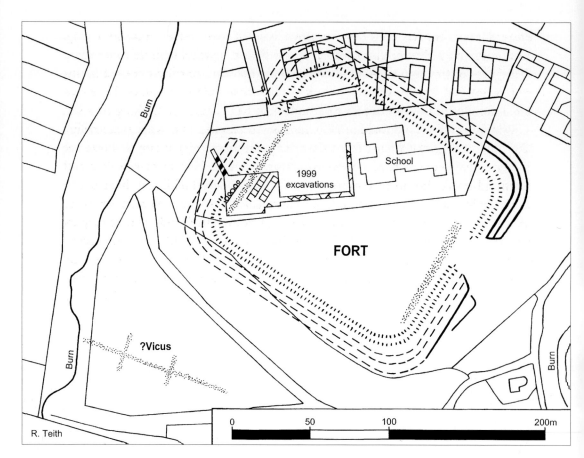

30 Doune Roman fort

the site and suggests that it had just a single period of occupation, after which at least some parts were deliberately demolished. The site was assumed to be Flavian because of its entrance design, but little in the way of datable material seems to have been recovered to prove it.

In 1999, more extensive excavations were conducted by Headland Archaeology in advance of the construction of a new nursery building at the school. This work also remains unpublished, but short notes and a plan (*31*) have reached the public domain (Maloney, in Keppie 2000, 381f and www.headlandarchaeology.com). The excavation found the rampart at the fort's north-west side and confirmed that this area too had a triple ditch. Inside the defences, five ovens were revealed, which were built into the rampart back and surrounded by copious burnt material, as if they had been used for a considerable time (*colour plate 12*). Behind these ran the *intervallum* road, beyond which a number of timber buildings were encountered, founded on sleeper beams. Some of these were found in a long, narrow trench and were thus so fragmentary that it is probably futile to do more than guess at their nature, although none show the characteristic close-set beams or postholes of a granary. Near complete plans were, however, found of the two buildings closest to the rampart (*31*), and these have caused something of a stir. They take the form of parallel, long, narrow rectangles, *c*.5m wide (externally). The one nearest the rampart is 22.5m long, whilst its neighbour is shorter at *c*.18.2m. They seem to have a common building line at their north-east ends and it is possible that they fronted onto a road. The north-west building is divided into six roughly equal sized rooms, *c*.3.3m² (internally). The more easterly structure has only four such rooms (of which one is of double size) and, interestingly, its rear wall coincides exactly with the partition between the fifth and sixth rooms of its neighbour, as if the two were originally designed to be the same length. Somewhat oddly, there seems to be a considerable open area to the south-west of these structures, whilst the next building to the east seems to be offset to the south-west, thus leaving another open space.

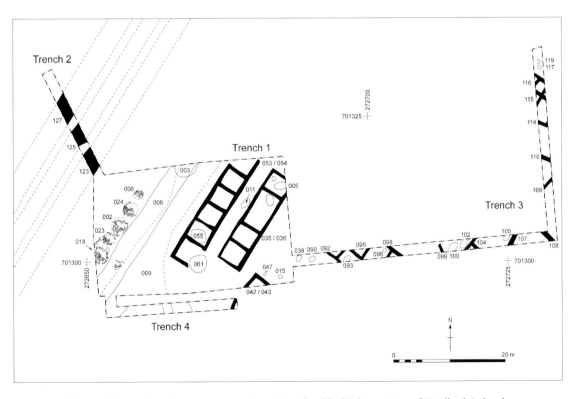

31 Doune Roman fort, the 1999 excavations. *Reproduced by kind permission of Headland Archaeology*

The excitement over these structures was caused by their supposed similarity to the so-called hospital at Fendoch, and they have been reconstructed in this role as being, in fact, a single building in which two ranges of rooms were separated by a roofed corridor. Whether or not there is any more evidence for this identification than there was at Fendoch will not be known until a full report is published. The structures do, however, look remarkably like the buildings marked B on figure 75 at Cardean, whose own (almost certainly false) claim to being identified as a hospital will be discussed in chapter 5. On present evidence, therefore, it might be safest to regard the Doune structures as exactly what they appear to be: two separate sheds, which may have served as stores buildings or the like. Nevertheless, this excavation did throw a great deal more light on an otherwise poorly studied site. Unlike the 1980s work, it provided firm dating to the Flavian period, the details of which should prove interesting and, unlike many of the other sites in the area, no signs of rebuilding, or any other phasing, are recorded, apart from some pits which may be demolition features.

One would normally expect buildings such as this to be located in or around the main range and, if they do front onto a road, it might well be the *via principalis*. This would certainly come as no surprise, despite the fact that it would then run down the fort's long axis. For the air photographic indications are that the south-east gate lies north of centre on the fort's short axis, which would put the *praetentura* to its north and leave the fort facing north-east, away from the river. On this analysis, the north-west gate should lie around 10m north of the excavated area and it will be interesting to see if our own planned geophysical work at the site will confirm this. There is, however, one major objection: for the narrow exploratory trench cut into the fort's central area makes it clear that any such road would be blocked by buildings, whereas a normal *via principalis* would pass through the site without interruption. This being the case, the main street is more likely to have run south-west to north-east, beyond the eastern limit of the 1999 excavations. The south-west and north-west gates have not yet been identified but, on this scenario, they probably lie to the east of the fort's long axis centre line and, if so, the supposed hospital will lie in the *retentura*, with the fort now facing south-east.

No temporary camps are known in the site's vicinity, although both Ochtertyre and Craigarnhall are only *c*.3.75km (2.3 miles) away. There are, though, a number of air photographic features which might indicate other activity around the fort. In particular, there is a series of parch-marks to the south (*30*), on the much lower ground beside the river (RCAHMS neg: A64136). These show at least one length of road, with what look to be lighter tracks running off it at right-angles. There is also the faintest suggestion of a feature linking that area with the fort, and one could think of a number of Roman scenarios to explain these. Firstly, they might show internal roads for an annexe, something the site so far lacks. The very steep bank separating them from the fort might seem to argue against this, but the slope to the Fendoch annexes is almost as sheer, and so provides a plausible precedent. Secondly, they might be part of an external civilian settlement, associated with the fort. Such *vici* are common, indeed almost universal, around Roman forts in other parts of the empire, but they have so far proved very elusive in northern first-century Scotland. Consequently, the opportunity to study one would be extremely valuable, but only Doune and (as we shall see below) Strageath have so far shown even the slightest indications. Finally, the features might represent military activity on the river bank: possibly some form of bridgehead to control a crossing, or even a quayside of some sort. For although the Teith cannot really be described as navigable at this point, very light craft can still move here and might have been useful logistically. It must be stressed, however, that for the moment, none of this can be anything more than speculation. No excavation has been done on these features and, as always, they cannot be dated from aerial data alone. It is thus perfectly possible that they are not Roman at all and it will be interesting to see what any future work might reveal.

As already stated, we do not know how (or even if) Doune was linked to the Roman road north, but the line finally reappears close to the Allan Water, running to the north of the modern A9, on an old quarry lip near Glassingall (NN 792045). The first detectable sector is a long straight, running to the east-north-east and, if one projects that alignment backwards, it would have run onto lower ground to cross the river at Ashfield (NN 787042), after which it would take only a slight turn to the north (albeit through rough country) to put it on a heading for Doune. Nevertheless, it might just as easily have kept to the higher ground and turned south-west onto the approximate line of the modern B8033 towards Dunblane. It is, thus, probably futile to speculate on its true course, and we can only wait to see if firmer data will emerge. To the north-east, however, things become a lot more certain. From the Glassingall quarry the road follows a straight fence-line for 1,030m onto Kinbuck Muir and in 2004 the Gask Project (neg: 04CN17-35) discovered a ring feature immediately to its north at Lower Whiteston (NN 800051). This was initially suspected of being a Roman tower ditch, but closer examination suggests that it is probably a native feature. At NN 801050 the line falls in with a field track, which continues the same heading for another 720m, after which it continues straight on for further 200m beside another fence. At NN 809056 it swings briefly to the north to cross the Todhill Burn. It then resumes its course to the east-north-east, falling in with an old farm road for about 250m, past the ruined farm of Glenbank, where the Gask system, as we currently know it, begins (*32*).

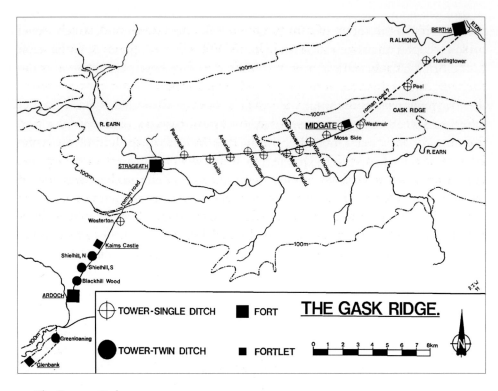

32 The Roman Gask system

To the south of the road, just opposite the farm house, we meet the first of the Gask installations: the fortlet of Glenbank (NN 812057). The site was discovered from the air by the RCAHMS in 1983 and nothing is now visible on the surface. Nevertheless, the aerial results, when combined with a geophysical survey, are enough to show that the site had a double ditch with a single entrance break, which faced towards the road. It is slightly rectangular and has curved corners, with the outer ditch measuring 51m (north–south) x 49m (east–west) and the inner 41 x 39m, so that the entrance lies on the short axis.

A small excavation was conducted by G.S. Maxwell shortly after the site was discovered (DES 1984, 4) and the authors have recently carried out larger-scale work (*33*), the report for which will include both sets of data. The combined results show that the ditches varied unusually in size and their entrance breaks showed simple butt-ends, rather than the parrot-beaks seen at the forts. The ditches also showed several recuts, suggesting that the site had been in use for some time. The rampart had been all but ploughed away and only one significant turf patch survived to show its position. As a result, the internal area is difficult to estimate, although it was probably in the region of 27m (north–south) x 24m (east–west), which would make it roughly the same size as a Hadrian's Wall milecastle (Jones & Woolliscroft 2001, 78). The single entrance gate was marked by four huge posts, up to 40cm in diameter and set 1m deep into the ground, which suggests that it carried a tower. The biggest surprise, however, came from the interior. We would normally expect a fortlet to hold one, or more probably two, small barracks, separated by a road from the entrance, again much like a Hadrian's Wall milecastle. Instead, the entire internal area was covered by patches of badly plough-damaged metalling, and even when this was lifted, there was no sign whatever of internal buildings. Indeed only one posthole was found in the interior and even that need not necessarily be Roman. No dating evidence was found during our own work, and amphora sherds found by the 1980s dig cannot now be located, but the site seems to fit into the spacing pattern of the Flavian system and is probably first century in date.

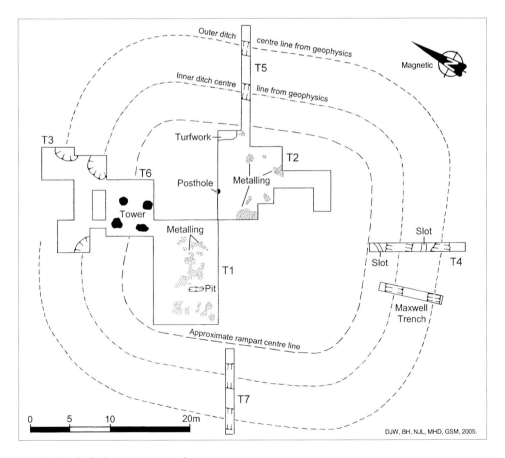

33 Glenbank fortlet, excavation plan

At NN 810058 the Glenbank farm road swings to the south, but the Roman road holds its course, as a field track, for a further 75m. It then turns north-east to run on lower ground closer to the Allan Water and so avoids a series of deep burn valleys. In 2002 the Gask Project found a c.250m-long section from the air, running east-north-east past the farm of Woodside of Balhaldie (NN 815061–818063), and a long series of RCAHMS air photographs (confirmed by occasional test trenching) have traced it on much the same course, from NN 824067 to 070829 at Woodlea. These air photographs show an interesting characteristic of the Gask road, which differs in one important respect from many other Roman roads. Often such routes can be traced from the air, even where the actual structure has been completely ploughed away, because they have side ditches, which can show in air photographs as a pair of parallel running cropmarks. The Gask road seems largely to lack these features, however. Instead, the line is often marked by a series of small pits from which the rock and gravel for its structure was quarried. These quarry pits are occasionally visible on the surface but, for the most part, they show from the air as lines of dot-like cropmarks (*41*) along one, or both, sides of its course.

At Upper Quoigs (NN 821063), a RCAHMS air photograph (neg: A64658) detected a ring feature, c.200m to the south of the road line, which looked like a Roman tower ditch. But excavations by the Gask Project in the 1990s (DES 1995, 97 & 1996, 82) make it seem more likely to have been caused by relatively modern sand working.

At Woodlea the road makes a turn to the north and becomes visible at the surface again for around 150m. Here, it forms the boundary between two fields and is conspicuously marked by an electricity pylon. Test trenches dug by the former estate factor, R. Baird (2005), found it to be more badly damaged than had been expected, but it still showed a clear construction pattern, with a rammed gravel surface set on a foundation of larger boulders. Beyond the surface feature, the line has been traced from the air continuing on the same course, past the hamlet of Greenloaning towards the Allan Water, which it probably crossed just upstream of the bridge for the modern A822 (NN 835079).

The first firmly attested watchtower (NN 829071) lies just to the south of the road as it passes Greenloaning. Nothing is visible on the surface, but the tower was discovered from the air by the RCAHMS in 1986 and excavated by the authors in 1995 (Woolliscroft & Hoffmann 1997). Like Glenbank, the site has a double V-shaped ditch with a single entrance, 3.6m wide, facing towards the road (*34*). The ditch circuits were approximately circular and had separate butt-ends at the entrance, rather than fort-style parrot-beaks. The outer ditch was 24.7m in diameter, 1.91m wide, but just 0.4m deep, whilst the inner was 15.5m in

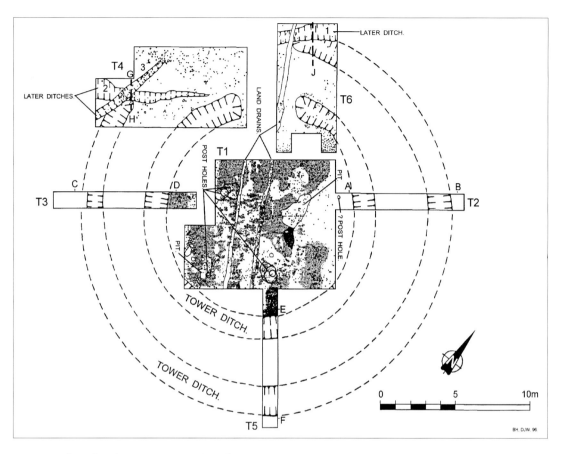

34 Greenloaning tower, excavation plan

diameter, 1.45m wide and 0.54m deep. Inside the ditches, the interior was heavily metalled and contained a timber tower, which measured 5.25m (north–south) x 4.25m (east–west) and was founded on four large posts (only three had survived). This may have been surrounded by a turf rampart, like many (if not all) of the Gask towers: for although no remains were found *in situ*, the ditch fills contained a great deal of turf, which may have been displaced from such a rampart by ploughing or deliberate demolition. Certainly there were signs that the site had been systematically demolished at the end of its occupation, with the structural timbers being dug out and burned on site. Close examination of the tower posts showed them to have been completely replaced at least once and possibly twice, suggesting that the structure had remained in use long enough for the timbers to need replacing. The only dating evidence recovered was a small quantity of coarse pottery which, although probably Roman, could not be dated more closely.

Once across the Allan Water, the road turns sharply to the north and is intermittently visible (as far as NN 836086) in woodland, and then from the air as a parch-mark. It crosses the little River Knaik at NN 838093, just upstream of a small sewage works, and is then again intermittently visible on the surface past the next major fort: Ardoch.

ARDOCH

The fort of Ardoch (NN 839099) sits on a rise, immediately north-east of the modern village of Braco and 14km (8.75 miles), as the crow flies, from Doune. To its west, the ground falls sharply into the deep, near gorge-like valley of the Knaik and, to the south, it drops into a smaller valley, now largely filled by an artificial lake belonging to Ardoch House. The ground is more level towards the other sides, but the site has a good view in all directions, especially along the Gask line itself, where the fortlets of Glenbank and Kaims Castle (see below) would both have been in view from its gate tower tops, at a range of 5km and 3.6km (3.1 and 2.25 miles) respectively. The site is probably the best-preserved Roman fort in Scotland (*colour plate 13*). It has consequently been known for centuries and boasts a superb and complex ditch and rampart system, which suggests multiple periods of occupation. This has been partly ploughed out in the south and is cut by the modern road to Crieff in the west, but elsewhere it remains untouched and, despite on-going rabbit damage, the site today looks much as it is shown in a plan drawn by Roy (1793, PI 30) in the 1750s. The eastern side is the most impressive, with no fewer than five ditches (35). There are five again in the north, but here the outer three are separated from the inner two by a rampart, showing that the obvious fort visible today (35, A), was preceded by a somewhat longer one (B), which was cut down in such a way that part of its northern end remained visible when the later fort ditches were cut across it. At present, only a single ditch survives in the west, but accounts written before the construction of the Crieff road in the mid-eighteenth century suggest that there were originally at least two, and possibly as many as four (Gordon 1726, PL 6), with at least three more in the south.

In the last years of the nineteenth century, Ardoch was subjected to a year-long excavation by the Society of Antiquaries of Scotland, which examined around half of the interior (Christison & Cunningham 1898). The team concerned developed methods well ahead of the norm for their time and, in particular, they discovered (on site) how to trace timber features, such as beam slots and postholes, when most archaeologists before them had simply chased walls and

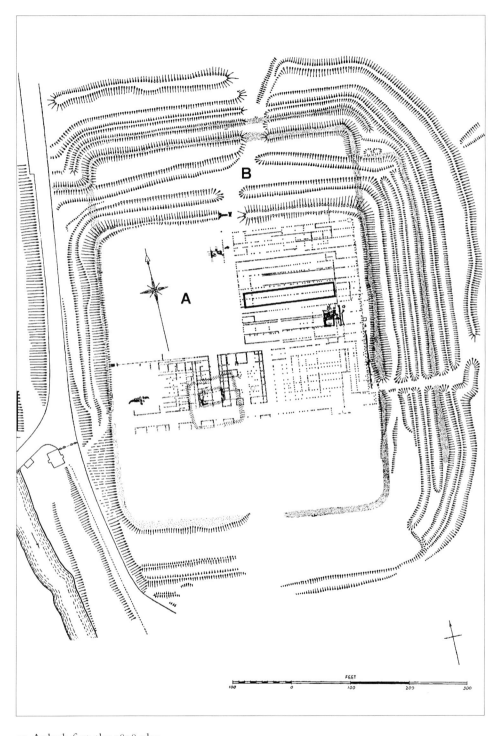

35 Ardoch fort, the 1898 plan

other stonework. The report gives a detailed description of their methodology and, a century later, their excitement at this discovery still shines through the formal, Victorian academic prose. The improved techniques were vital on the site, where all but a few of the buildings were of timber, and enabled them to draw up a convincing plan (35). Their detailed findings include a clear *principia*, a *praetorium* and a number of long narrow buildings (at least one of stone construction) that are clearly barracks. The *via principalis* runs across the fort's short axis from the east to west gates, with the main range structures to its north: so the fort faces to the south, rather contrary to what might have been expected. No clear granaries were uncovered, nor are there visible indications of one of the double, supposed hospital, structures encountered at Fendoch and Doune. Otherwise, however, all of the main elements of a Roman fort were found and at least three buildings showed evidence for hypocaust heating.

What seems, at least partly, to have escaped the original excavators, but was pointed out later by Macdonald (1919, 122ff), is that it is extremely clear that the timber elements found belonged to several different periods. In the northern part of the fort there are clearly at least three sets of barracks, on top of one another. The *principia* and *praetorium* also show signs of at least two periods whilst, to their east, a jumble of postholes and beam slots was found that is difficult to make any sense of, but which again must contain several periods. To a degree, this much was to be expected, since the excavation also produced finds evidence for both Flavian and Antonine occupation, including coins from Nero (AD 54-68) to Hadrian (117-38). But that is not enough by itself to account for this degree of complexity. As a result, there have been a number of attempts to disentangle the site's detailed construction history. Macdonald (1919, 122ff) himself pointed out that some of the timber buildings extend right up to the fort's eastern rampart. Indeed some postholes were found beyond it, outside the east gate. Yet early Roman forts always have a fairly wide *intervallum* area between the defences and the internal buildings, to accommodate a road and, perhaps, to give the buildings some protection from missiles. As a result, this particular set of buildings cannot belong with the rampart of fort A. Nor, though, can they belong with fort B because, although this projects further north than fort A, the two forts' east and west sides coincide. On the other hand, some of the other buildings do leave room for an *intervallum*, as do the few stone buildings found, which themselves appear to post-date the timberwork. Macdonald thus suggested that the stone structures belong with fort A, the timber buildings that lie clear of the *intervallum* with fort B and the other structures with at least one more fort that was earlier still, and rather wider. Moreover, there seems to be a somewhat random mix of posthole and beam slot construction in the buildings that impinge on the rampart, suggesting that there were actually two building periods within this early fort, which used different building techniques. Later, Crawford (1949, 34ff) pointed out that the early buildings had been burnt at the end of their lives, to produce a thick layer of charcoal, and that the nineteenth-century excavation had found a similar demolition layer, underlying the northern rampart of fort B, but beneath a thick abandonment layer. This suggested that the early fort had extended still further to the north, and thus that it was also longer than the two visible sites. He suggested that forts A and B were both Antonine, whilst the abandonment layer separating the early fort burning from the later remains might suggest a long enough gap for the former to be Flavian.

Crawford also attempted to use this model to separate out different periods in the ditch system, but a clearer and more thorough account has since been provided by Breeze (1983). His analysis shows three successive forts, all facing south, but with each progressively smaller so that, as each was built, more ditches were needed so ensure that at least some were close enough to the ramparts to be within effective missile range. In other words, the great multiplicity of ditches for which the site is so famous are not the result of a garrison which felt more than usually under threat, but are simply a by-product of the site's complex history. He suggested that the large Flavian fort (36, a) would have measured something in the region of 3.5ha (8.6 acres) over the ramparts, with the two Antonine forts (b-d) measuring 2.5ha (6.3 acres) and 2.25ha (5.8 acres) respectively. This analysis seems eminently plausible, but it is interesting that none of the gates show the parrot-beak ditch breaks so common in other Flavian forts in Scotland. That said, these do appear to be less universal on the Gask system, which may or may not prove to have implications for their contemporaneity, with the rest of the Flavian deployment. The Flavian rampart does not survive in good enough condition for us to tell if the fort had re-entrant gates, but the outer ditch on the east side shows another unusual trait, for it seems to have an outward turn, or *clavicula*, at its southern terminus. This is a common feature amongst the temporary camps of Scotland, as we have seen: but it is unique amongst the forts. It is thus possible that Ardoch also has a camp in its developmental ancestry, although it is equally likely that a local commander or military surveyor was simply experimenting with the design.

To the north of the fort is a large, somewhat irregular, defensive enclosure (with a camp inside it) which has generally been assumed to be an annexe (*38, G*), but analysis of a thermal line-scan image in 1994 has now suggested that it is actually an independent monument and nothing to do with the fort (Maxwell, in Keppie 1995,332). Likewise, there is a conspicuous rampart passing around the north-east quadrant of the fort's outermost ditch, but the nineteenth-century

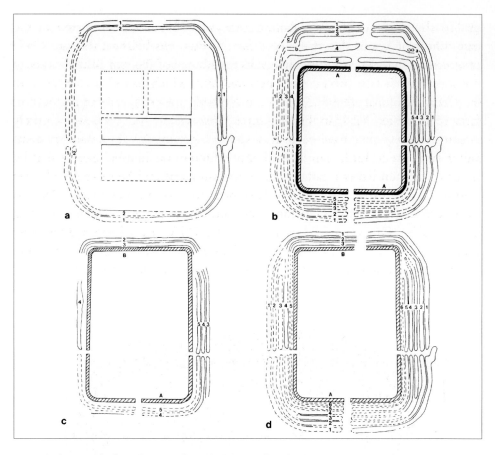

36 Ardoch, possible fort phases with a) the Flavian fort, b) the late Antonine fort and c & d possible early Antonine layouts. *Reproduced by kind permission of Prof D.J.Breeze*

excavations showed that this was a post-Roman feature. Finally, we have a small human touch, a tombstone (RIB 2213) which, uniquely amongst the Roman forts of northern Scotland, tells us what the Roman (and probably Flavian) garrison of Ardoch was (*37*). The stone reads:

Dis Manibus

Ammonius Da-

-mionis (filius) C(enturio) coh(ortis)

I Hispanorum Stipendiorum

XXVII Heredes

F(aciendum) C(uraverunt).

94

or: 'To the shade of the late Ammonius, son of Damio, a centurion of the first cohort of Spaniards, who served for 27 years. His heirs set this up.' *Coh I Hispanorum* is known at other periods in the history of Roman Britain, when it was a milliary (1,000-strong) part-mounted unit, which served at Maryport on the Cumbrian Coast (RIB 826) and then Netherby (RIB 977), one of the outpost forts of Hadrian's Wall. In Flavian times, however, it was probably a purely infantry unit and may have been only 500 strong, although if so, the fort seems rather large for it. Little can be said about Ammonius himself, except that he seems to have an eastern, rather than a Spanish name and he served for longer than the 25 years that is thought to have been the norm for auxiliaries. He was an officer, however, and centurions were sometimes known to have very long service careers. His age at death is not given, but if, like many, he joined the army at around 18, he would have been somewhere in the region of 45, which would not have been a particularly untimely age to die in the ancient world.

37 The Ardoch tombstone. *Drawn R. Stuart, 1852*

As at Camelon, there is a significant concentration of temporary camps in the vicinity of the fort, mostly just to the north (*38*). At least five overlapping camps are known, extending up to 52ha (130 acres) in area and some seem to have been modified in, or between, uses. Several sections of the defences remain visible on the surface, including long sections of the east and west sides of the 130-acre camp, which include *titulus*-style gateways (*38*, Camp C,2), along with smaller sections of camps A and D. The series seems to span most of the known Roman campaigning periods in Scotland (Hanson 1978).

The Roman road passes to the east of Ardoch fort, where the nineteenth-century excavators found it to be 7.61m wide, cambered and 'as smooth as a cyclist could wish' (Christison & Cunningham 1898, 432). It remains visible at the surface for most of the next 1.1km (*38*) – at first running north–north-east. It crosses a modern minor road at NN 843103, where it turns to run north-east alongside the defences of the 130-acre temporary camp and, at NN 845108, passes the next tower: Blackhill Wood. This was the first of the Gask towers to be recorded, with the earliest published plan dating to the mid-eighteenth century (Roy 1793, PL 31), and it remained faintly visible as late as the 1980s (Keppie 1986, 149). Since then, however, the burrows of a resurgent rabbit population have reduced the densely wooded site to a virtual lunar landscape and, of the two excavations conducted here, the most recent (Glendinning & Dunwell 2000) was a rescue dig designed to retrieve information before it was too late. Like Greenloaning, the tower had a double ditch (*39*) with a single entrance which, like all of the Gask installations, faced the road. Inside was a turf rampart, with a timber tower in the centre, which was rather smaller than Greenloaning at 3.6m². The site has a number of interesting features. Firstly, it was cut by the defences of the 130-acre camp (which was thus later), and an oven – probably also belonging to the camp – had been built into its outer ditch. Secondly, although only three of the four tower posts had survived rabbit and tree root damage, at least one had been removed and replaced, so that, again, we have evidence for a rebuild or major repair to the structure whilst in service. At the end of its life, the tower posts were dug out and the postholes filled in with burnt material containing nails, which suggests that the demolition materials were burnt on site.

From the north-east corner of the 130-acre camp (NN 847110) the road disappears from view, but can be traced on aerial photographs continuing on essentially the same heading for a further 1.7km. It first passes what appears to be a Bronze Age barrow-field (CUCAP neg: BQN93), then begins a long, gentle climb up to the hill of Drum Coillie. At NN 848113 – as it crosses a farm road – it turns a few degrees to the east and, at NN 850115, it becomes briefly visible

1 The Gask fortlet of Kaims Castle

2 The Roman temporary camp of Grassy Walls, showing titulate gate. *Photograph by kind permission of W. Fuller*

3 Drumquhassle fort, the south-east corner

4 Malling fort from the air

5 Bochastle fort from the air. The tractor lies just inside the west rampart

6 Dalginross fort from the air

7 Fendoch fort from the air

8 The supposed Roman tower in the Sma' Glen

9 Inchtuthil fortress from the air

10 Steed Stalls from the air

11 Stirling, the King's Knot. *Photograph by kind permission of A.S. Torrance*

12 Doune fort, the ovens and timber buildings under excavation

13 Ardoch fort from the air

14 Strageath fort from the air

15 The Innerpeffray cutting

16 Parkneuk tower

17 Ardunie tower faintly visible on the surface, with the Roman road behind

18 The Roman line intersecting a modern minor road near Roundlaw

19 Kirkhill tower from the air. *Photograph: W. Fuller*

20 Muir O' Fauld tower in the foreground, with a long stretch of the Roman road heading west, towards the top left

21 Witch Knowe tower

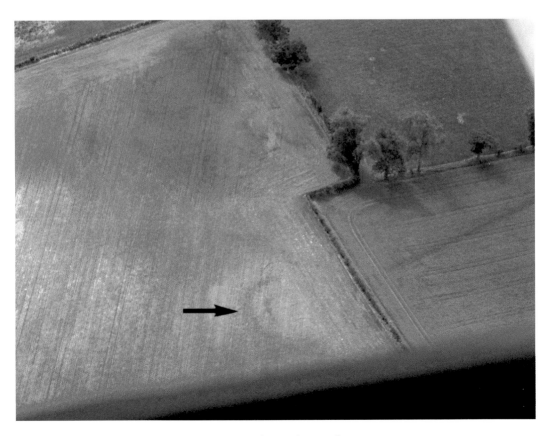

22 The double ditched enclosure at Woodhead. *Photograph: W. Fuller*

25 The Cleaven Dyke from the air, seen as a cropmark in the foreground and in a forest clearing behind.
Photograph: W. Fuller

Above: 26 Cardean
fort from the air

Left: 27 Inverquharity
from the air

28 Carpow fortress from the air

29 Barryhill hillfort from the air

30 An isolated roundhouse showing as a cropmark at Innerdunning

31 Dun camp, from the air

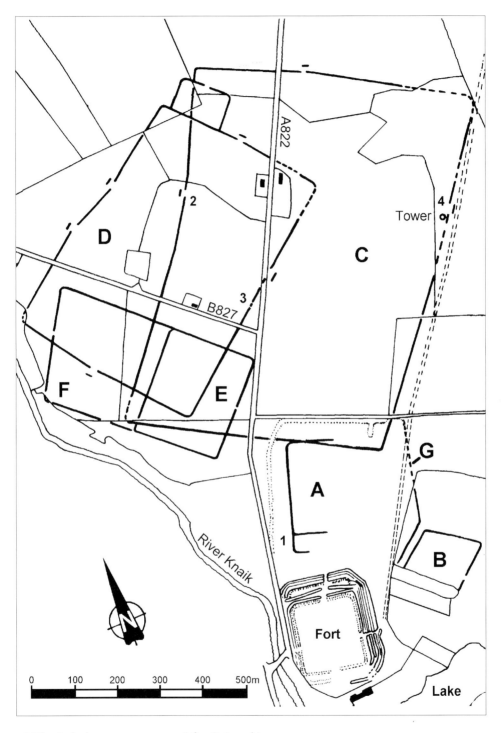

38 The Ardoch temporary camps (after St Joseph)

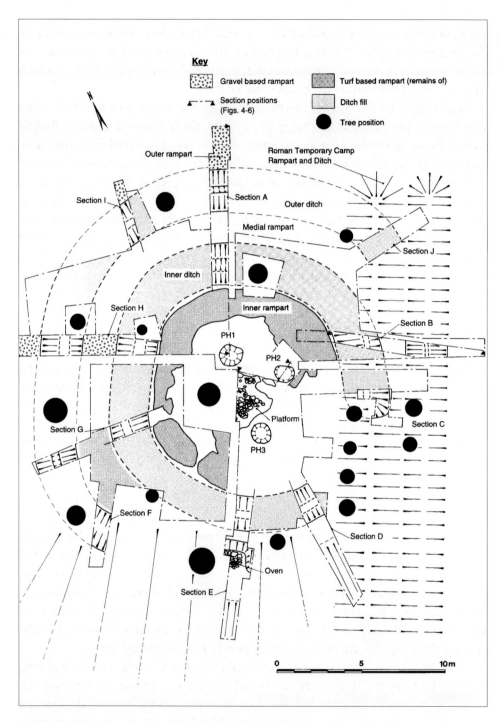

39 Blackhill Wood tower: the Dunwell and Glendinning excavation plan. *Crown Copyright, Historic Scotland*

again, crossing the steep-sided valley of a small burn. Here, we see something of the engineering detail that was lavished on this strategic road: for on both sides of the stream, the gradients are lessened by cuttings through the valley lips, which give way to an embankment towards the bottom.

Immediately to the west of the burn crossing, the next tower, Shielhill South (NN 850115), sits right on the valley lip, with its ditch system extending slightly over it. Nothing can be seen on the surface and it was discovered from the air by St Joseph (1976, 22), in what was a magnificent piece of spotting, as it has never presented more than the faintest of cropmarks (e.g. CUCAP neg: BOQ38). St Joseph himself led a brief excavation, shortly after finding the site, and larger-scale work was conducted by ourselves in 1996 (Woolliscroft & Hoffmann 1998). The tower was, again, protected by double ditches (40), of which the inner is rather more rectangular in shape than those of the towers further south. There may also have been an internal rampart, although this could not be proved beyond doubt. The tower itself was somewhat irregular in shape, with no two sides quite the same length (they ranged from 3.1-3.7m) but, as always, it was founded on four large posts. The interior had been surfaced with gravel metalling, which also extended through the ditch entrance breaks, and may have extended, as a light path, as far as the main road. Datable finds have been vanishingly rare on the Gask towers, but the site did yield a single, blue-green body sherd from a late first- (or early second-) century Roman, cylindrical glass bottle (Isings form 51), which appears to support the assumed Flavian date.

Once again, there are signs that the tower stayed in service for some time. For the ditches had been completely recut – after a considerable depth of silt had formed in them – and at least two of the four posts had been dug out and replaced during the occupation. The others were too badly damaged to tell but, in practice, it is virtually impossible to replace just one, let alone two, posts in a four-post tower without demolishing the whole structure, and so the chances are that the entire building had been rebuilt. Whatever the case, the tower had been thoroughly demolished at the end of its life. The posts were rocked or dug out and the postholes capped off with clay. The timbers were then burnt on site, along with large quantities of wattle and daub – which presumably came from side cladding. Indeed, so intense was this demolition fire that it had baked the clay posthole caps to the consistency of poorly fired earthenware.

Once across the burn, the road continues on its old north-easterly heading, visible only from the air or, very occasionally, as a barely discernible bump in the fields. On a slight knoll at NN 853119 it makes another minute turn to the east and then continues on to the next tower: Shielhill North (NN 856122). Here, however, a series of superb air photographs taken by St Joseph (e.g. CUCAP neg: BKE51) show

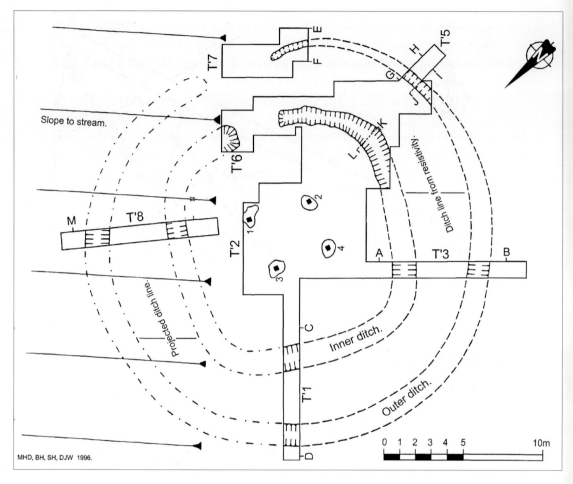

40 Shielhill South tower

it to do something which is, so far, unique on the line (Woolliscroft 2002b, 68ff). The photographs show the road approaching the tower, c.7m wide and on a heading to pass just to its east (41). Unusually for the Gask, clear traces of side ditches are visible as cropmarks, albeit intermittently, as well as the ubiquitous quarry pits. But, at NN 85591215, c.40m south-west of the tower, it appears to fork. One line then continues on much the same heading as before, to pass within 9.7m of the tower's outer ditch. Immediately to the east of the tower, however, it narrows abruptly (with an inturn of its southern side) to leave it c.4m wide within the side ditches. It then descends into a deep, narrow valley to cross another small burn, immediately to the south of the modern A822. There are surface and air photographic indications that it may have done so on a small embankment, but

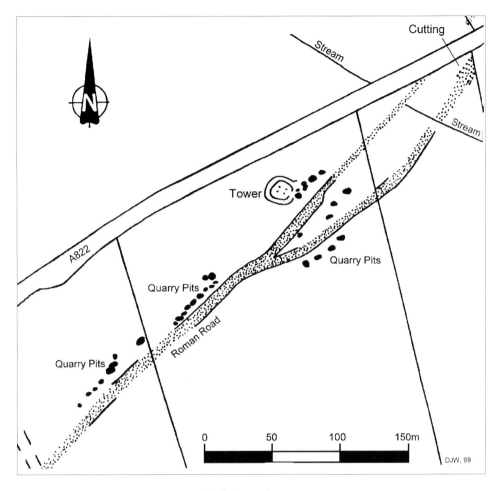

41 The Roman road by-pass loop at Shielhill North

without excavation it is difficult to separate the ancient works from the modern road crossing – which involved the construction of an arched, stone-built tunnel to canalise the burn. Whatever the case, however, the Roman line then crosses the modern road and continues on the same course.

The second arm retains its original width throughout and follows a more southerly track, to reach a maximum separation from the northern branch of *c.*28m. Until August 2000, the air photographic evidence only allowed it to be traced as far as the burn's southern bank, but a Gask Project air photograph (neg: 00CN7#16), taken that month, showed clear indications of a linear feature continuing up the far side of the valley, until it disappeared at a dry stone wall at the northern edge of the modern field. A surface examination revealed signs

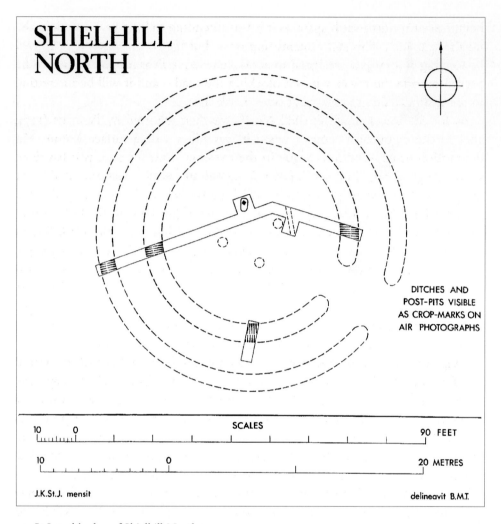

SHIELHILL NORTH

DITCHES AND
POST-PITS VISIBLE
AS CROP-MARKS ON
AIR PHOTOGRAPHS

SCALES

10   0   90 FEET

10   0   20 METRES

J.K.St.J. mensit   delineavit B.M.T.

42 St Joseph's plan of Shielhill North

of a slight embankment running north-east from the stream, which confirmed
the air photographic line, although, sadly, the feature was damaged, soon after,
by cable laying. More interestingly, however, the road meets a low, but almost
vertically sided knoll *c.*20m south of the field wall, and from here to the edge
of the field it runs in a slight, but still clearly defined, cutting which does not
appear to have been noticed before. The arrangement is, thus, similar to that seen
at Shielhill South. In the next field to the north, all surface trace of the road has
been ploughed out, but this short extra segment was enough to provide another
surprise. For its course, if extrapolated, would suggest that the road fork had

begun to turn northwards again, as if it was intending to loop back to rejoin the northern branch. This still remains unproven, but if it is the case, we may well be looking at a by-pass, designed to allow vehicles, such as supply wagons, to be parked outside the tower without blocking the road – and it will be interesting to see if similar sidings emerge at other Gask sites.

As for the tower itself: Shielhill North was first reported by Pennant (1774, 100) in the eighteenth century, when it was still a visible surface feature. His description of its position is vague in the extreme, however, and, as it has since been ploughed out, little was known about the site until it was relocated by St Joseph, on the same air photographs which picked up the by-pass loop. The site sits on a small knoll beside the A822 and enjoys a quite superb field of view to the south, which stretches well into Strathearn and has the entire Gask line in view, as far as Kinbuck Muir. A small excavation was conducted by St Joseph, soon after its discovery, and we have added geophysical work (Woolliscroft 2002b, 68ff): but much of our knowledge still comes from the aerial indications. The site, again, has a double ditch with non-parrot-beak breaks for the single entrance. St Joseph's excavation plan (42) shows the circuits as circular, but the aerial (41) and geophysical indications make it clear that they are actually sub-rectangular. No sign of a rampart was traced in the interior, but turf was found in what was clearly a demolition deposit in the inner ditch, which may have come from the slighting of such a structure. Only one of the tower posts was excavated, but the discovery air photographs are so clear that all four postholes can be detected and show a regular, rectangular building, whose short axis faces the entrance. No signs of ditch recutting or posthole replacement were recorded, but this does not necessarily mean that the tower was shorter lived than the others we have seen. This is partly because the excavation was so small, and may easily have missed such evidence, but it also has to be said that St Joseph failed to recognise signs of rebuilding during work at Shielhill South and Blackhill Wood and might easily have done so here.

The site was demolished at the end of its life and, again, the demolition materials, including wattle and daub, had been burned on site. No datable material was found, but there is one interesting aspect of the aerial and geophysical evidence that might be a pointer to the chronological relationship between the tower and the road: because one of the latter's quarry pits is set right in the tower entrance and would have blocked it almost completely. If this had been open during any part of the tower's occupation, it would have been inconvenient to say the least, which might suggest that the two are not fully contemporary. Two scenarios might be envisaged. Firstly, the road may have been built before the towers were installed, and at a time when their exact positions had not yet been fixed: in which case the pit may have been backfilled later to allow access to the tower, perhaps using spoil dug from its ditches. Alternatively, despite the evidence provided by the apparent by-pass loop, the road may have been built, or repaired, after the tower had gone out of use, when the blocking of its gate no longer mattered. If so, the pit might be Antonine. Unfortunately, the excavation did not take in this feature to determine its relationship with the tower and so it is not possible to speculate further.

After crossing the A822, the reunited road turns very slightly to the west and can be seen as a clear ridge in a field corner, restored to its original width. One hundred metres later (NN 857124), the modern road swerves sharply to the west and re-crosses the Roman line, which has been seen from the air (CUCAP neg: BKE44) continuing straight on, through a small field to the south of Drum Coillie Lodge (NN 858125). It is then intermittently visible in woodland for c.70m, before being rejoined by the modern road for a further 100m, where it is flanked by some of the few, still visible quarry pits. Beyond this, it reappears to the north of the A822 as a faint mound and, although a section was recently damaged by the construction of a driveway, it can otherwise still be seen for around 150m, running behind a cottage garden, past the fortlet of Kaims Castle (NN 861129).

Kaims (*colour plate 1*) is the best-preserved fortlet on the line and has been known for centuries. It stands on a slight knoll at the summit of Drum Coillie, with its entire rampart and ditch circuit plainly visible at the surface. Its hilltop location gives it what would have been a breathtaking field of view, although it is now obscured in the north by a dense conifer plantation. To its south, the view appears to be quite limited at ground level – because the hill top is relatively flat and the summit stands close to its northern end – but, from the top of a Roman tower, it would have taken in Ardoch fort, at a range of 3.5km (2.2 miles), along with Glenbank, Greenloaning and much of Strathallan. This would have made it a potentially vital signalling link, because it is also, from tower height, intervisible with the next major fort, which lies 6.3km (3.9 miles) to the north-east, at Strageath. The site also marks a distinct change in the design of the minor installations because, although Glenbank fortlet and all of the towers we have seen so far, had double ditches, Kaims, and the sites beyond, have only one. Moreover, the sites to the south seem to show a fairly regular spacing pattern: for Kaims Castle is exactly 6 Roman miles from Glenbank and the towers are set at 0.6 Roman mile (887m) intervals, but those to the north have more random spacings.

The site was excavated at the end of the nineteenth century by Christison (1901, 18ff), whose results were similar to our own at Glenbank. He found that the single entrance (*43*) – which had been deliberately blocked – faced south-south-east towards the road, with a paved trackway linking the two. The fortlet

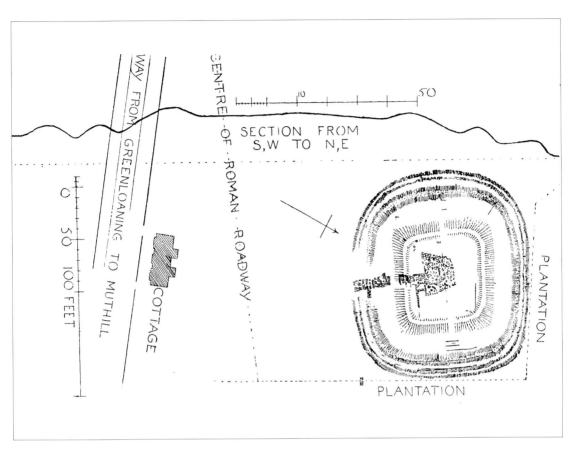

43 Christison's plan of Kaims Castle

measured 20m (south-west to north-east) x 22m (north-west to south-east) internally, and so the entrance lies on the long axis. The gate arrangements were not studied, which means that we do not know if there was a tower: but this would be a normal provision on a Roman fortlet and its existence can probably be assumed. Like Glenbank, no internal structures were detected. Instead, the interior was surfaced, this time with flat flags, rather than cobbling. Unlike the authors, however, Christison's team did not look under this surface so, although (as at Ardoch) their methodology was sufficiently advanced that we can be confident that they would not have missed postholes or beam slots cut into the flagging, it is still not impossible that there may be features from some earlier period beneath it. No signs of ditch recutting were looked for, however, and no datable material was recovered so, at present, the best that can be said about the site's date and life-span is that it seems likely to be Flavian.

Once clear of Kaims Castle, the road continues to be visible (as a firebreak) in woodland for a further 200m and, from here, it begins a long downhill run towards its crossing of the Machany Water. At NN 863131 it falls back in with the A822 for *c*.100m, then emerges onto moorland to the east – again accompanied by a few visible quarry pits – and remains traceable on the ground for a further 150m to NN 864133. Its course over the next 700m is somewhat obscure. Ordnance Survey maps show it veering by 11° to the north but, in fact, it almost certainly carried straight on. For air photography has shown quarry pits running immediately east of a large lay-by beside the modern road, at NN 869140 (RCAHMS neg: A29669), and then continuing on the same heading, to the first of the single-ditched towers: Westerton (NN 873146).

The tower was discovered from the air by St Joseph (1951, 62) and nothing is visible on the ground. It stands on a high point with a good field of view, especially to the north. The site stands 2.3km (1.4 miles) from Kaims Castle, which is an abnormally long spacing, and so it is probable that we have at least one intervening tower still to find. Unfortunately, although Westerton itself is in arable land, much of the intervening area is moorland pasture, which does not show cropmarks. That is why the road is so poorly defined in this sector, and we can only hope that some chance discovery, or extremely severe drought, will eventually provide more data.

Westerton was excavated by Hanson and Friell (1995) in 1980 (*44*) and, with its single ditch, it is not surprisingly smaller in overall diameter than its southern neighbours: at 18.4m (as opposed to 25.75m for Blackhill Wood). The ditch profile was of the Punic-type – rather than the normal, symmetrical, V-shape – which means that it had a steep outer face, but the inner side sloped more gently. It was also more substantial than the very light, double ditches of the southern towers: at up to 2.5m wide and 1m deep. The circuit was roughly circular in plan and no signs of recutting were encountered, but the fill did yield a single sherd of what is probably a Flavian *mortarium*. Turf was found in the ditch, which may or may not have come from a rampart, but no trace was found *in situ* in the interior. The tower itself was small – but markedly rectangular – at 2.5m x 3.8m, and its short axis faced the single (south-east-facing) entrance break. Not all of the four tower postholes were fully excavated, but those that were showed posts, *c*.30cm in diameter, set *c*.75cm into the ground, which is a little deeper than those of the towers further south. They appeared to have been dug out at the end of their lives, as part of the usual systematic demolition.

Interestingly, one of the front tower postholes showed two separate posts in the same post pit. It was not possible to determine their chronological relationship, but the excavators suggest that one might represent the main structural timber,

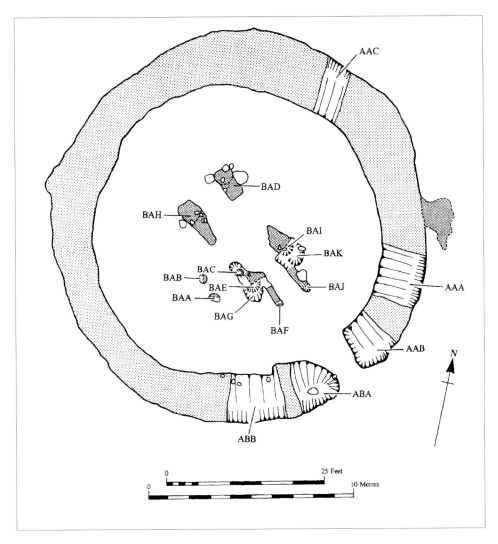

44 Westerton tower, excavation plan. *Reproduced by kind permission of Prof W.S. Hanson*

whilst the other formed a support for a balcony close to tower top level. This has never seemed a very satisfactory interpretation, however, for although there are, near contemporary, artistic portrayals of Roman towers with balconies (*3*), these always show them as carried – via cantilevers – by the tower itself, rather than by independently founded supports from the ground. This is certainly a more elegant engineering solution and it seems just as likely that the two posts were not contemporary and that they, thus, represent yet more evidence for rebuilding, similar to that seen on the towers further south. Finally, the structure showed one oddity that has not, to our knowledge, been seen on any other Roman timber tower: either on the Gask or elsewhere. Two short slots were uncovered – approximately 2m long and set *c*.1.4m apart – running from the front of the tower towards the ditch entrance. They seem likely to have contained sleeper beams and certainly predated the end of the site's service life, but their function and relationship with the tower, are uncertain. The excavators interpreted them as an entrance structure, or as the base for a ladder, or flight of steps, up to the observation platform. This seems eminently plausible, and it is possible that similar features will be found on other towers in the series.

As it passes Westerton, the Roman road makes a 12° turn to the north to run north–north-east, and cropmarks caused by its quarry pits show regularly from the air, as far as NN 874150, where it crosses the A823. There are then faint signs that it ran through the next field to the north, which has long been in permanent pasture, before crossing the Machany Water at, or very close to, the modern bridge at Bridgehill (NN 875154). Once across the river, it crosses the A822 and then swings through 25° to run north-east, up Crosshill. At present, no towers are known between Westerton and the fort of Strageath, but this is a distance of 4.2km (2.6 miles) and there are almost certainly two, or more, still to find on the stretch. If so, Crosshill would be a perfect location for the first. The ideal spot would be at, or around, NN 878157. The site is 1,150m from Westerton, with which it is intervisible and, from tower height, enjoys widespread views, especially to the north and east. It stands well above the river, whilst still being close to it, and has the Bridgehill crossing point in full sight. That said, careful observation of the neighbourhood from the air, over many seasons, has failed to find any trace: but there is a small knot of cottages within metres of the ideal position and it is possible that the site has been built over.

At NN 879157, the Roman road crosses the A822 for the last time, after which its cropmarks can be seen from the air through two fields until, at NN 881160, it enters the parklands of Culdees House. For the next 900m little trace can be seen, even though the clearance of woodland, that used to cover much of this stretch, has provided a much better aerial view. Nevertheless, the line continues its north-easterly heading, before crossing the modern Muthill to Auchterarder road, at NN 887165, and entering Pirnhall Plantation. As it enters the woodland, the road makes a 23° turn to the north, and returns to a north–north-easterly heading, almost exactly parallel to its course to the south of Bridgehill. Its state of preservation also changes dramatically, as we enter the first really well-preserved length. Parts of the plantation itself have recently been felled, but the road survives for *c*.500m, as a plainly defined forest track (*45*) and then, for a further 150m, as a less clearly marked line. At NN 890172, it is crossed by a (now disused) railway

45 The Gask road in Pirnhall Plantation

cutting, but then emerges into open country to run, slightly more strongly, for another 200m, as far as NN 891174. By this point, we are probably missing at least one more tower and there are two knolls within Pirnhall Plantation which would make good positions. One of these lies at NN 888168 and the other at NN 891171, but careful searches by ourselves have failed to reveal any surface trace of a ditch. Geophysical work might one day be more revealing, however, for the site may still exist underground but, as we currently have no evidence either way, nothing more can be said.

Once clear of the Pirnhall sector, the road vanishes for 250m, but then re-emerges (from the air), on the same heading, at Cuiltburn (NN 892177). Here it passes immediately west of a curious structure for which we have been unable to

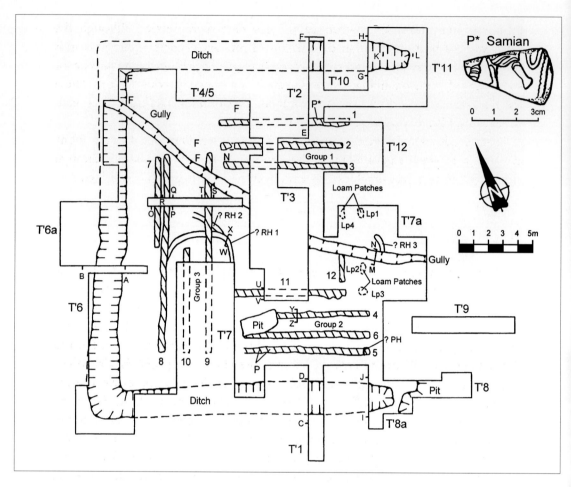

46 Cuiltburn, excavation plan

find a parallel. The site appeared from the air as a rectangular, ditched enclosure (e.g. RCAHMS neg: PT4692). At first, it resembled a fortlet, but a closer analysis showed it to be too small – at 18m (north–south) x c.23m (east–west) over the ditch – and excavations by ourselves showed a radically different structure (Woolliscroft & Hoffmann 2001). The ditch proved to go round only three of the four sides, with the open side facing away from the Roman road, and with no entrance break towards it (*46*). Inside were three sleeper-beam founded buildings (overlying native roundhouses) running around the three ditched sides, whilst a series of postholes suggested a timber colonnaded facade on the open side. The finds included Roman coarseware and a piece of Flavian, Samian ware decorated with a gladiatorial scene. When combined with the Roman style of the internal buildings, this makes a first-century Roman date seem certain, although the ditch was flat bottomed, rather than the usual military V-shape. Quite what this site represents remains a mystery, however. It might be a Roman civilian site, or some official, but non-military, structure such as a *mansio* (posting station). These are just guesses and, whether or not it formed part of the Gask line, it does seem to leave us with a wholly new site type.

From Cuiltburn, the road maintains its previous heading for a further 300m, crossing a modern minor road in the process. It then turns sharply through almost 90° to run, just north of due east, into the next major garrison fort.

STRAGEATH

Like Ardoch, Strageath fort is a complex stratigraphic layer-cake and, until the eighteenth century, it was almost as well preserved (Roy 1793, PL 32). Sadly, ploughing has now left little more than a vague rectangular platform visible in the field, but it still shows well from the air (*colour plate 14*). The fort sits on a promontory, at NN 901183, with steep-sided drops overlooking the River Earn to the east and a small burn valley to the south. Elsewhere, the ground is fairly open, but whilst its views, although reasonable, are not particularly impressive, the site is ideally suited for controlling the Gask road's crossing of the Earn. From the air, the site can present a bewildering palimpsest of ditches, roads and annexes: but an extensive program of trenching by Frere and Wilkes (1989), along with a geophysical survey by Lockett (2002) have radically improved our understanding of its history. This has allowed full plans to be produced and, although these still contain extrapolation and conjecture, they are fully able to differentiate several periods of Flavian and Antonine defences and internal buildings.

The Flavian fort (*47*) seems to have had a double ditch, but, although some air photographs give the appearance that the gates had parrot-beak breaks, this is not yet quite certain. On the southern half of the fort's west side, was a rectangular annexe, which sat parallel to the incoming road. No excavation has taken place in this structure, which means that any analysis is bound to be largely conjectural, but it seems likely that it was an integral part of the site's design, since the fort's outer ditch deviates to enclose it: leaving the inner ditch to continue across its east side. There was no ditch on the northern side, alongside the road, but a rampart is assumed, which would give the feature internal dimensions of *c.*100m (east–west) x 57m (north–south): an area of *c.*0.58ha (1.42 acres). The annexe had a single entrance at the eastern end of its north side, right beside the fort's own west gate, but nothing is known of its internal arrangements.

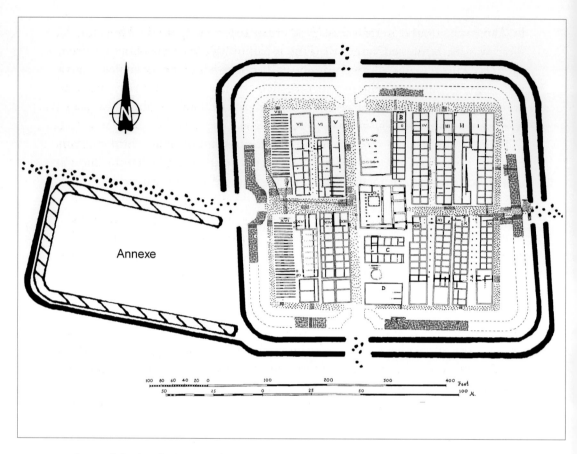

47 Strageath in the Flavian period. *Reproduced by kind permission of Prof S.S. Frere*

The fort itself was 1.77ha (4.36 acres) over the ramparts. The gates seem to have been single carriageway structures and at least one (the east gate) was topped by a tower. The west gate was recessed, with Bochastle-style rampart re-entrants but, although the north and south gates have been reconstructed in the same way, the east gate seems to have been flush with the rampart line. The defences are not quite a regular rectangle: for the east rampart lies at a distinct angle to the others, so as to leave the northern rampart *c*.15m shorter than the southern. The rampart itself was turf built, on a foundation of laid branches, and around 5m thick.

In the interior, the rampart was backed by the usual *intervallum* road. The *via praetoria* ran north to south across the short axis, about two-thirds of the way from the fort's east end and, as the main range buildings lie its east, the fort as a whole faced west. The excavation plan shows a clear *principia* in the centre, flanked by a poorly preserved (slightly irregular), rectangular building (47, A), which is presumably the *praetorium*, along with a double structure (C), reminiscent of the so-called 'hospitals' seen elsewhere. To the south of the latter was a large water cistern – around which were ill-defined traces of another timber structure – followed by a further rectangular building (D), which might be a *fabrica*. A range of 10 rooms (B) behind the *praetorium*, which looks like a miniature barrack block, was interpreted as an administrative building, or as quarters for staff personnel, but its exact function remains uncertain. Unusually, the granaries were not on the main range, but stood in the *praetentura*, facing each other across the *via praetoria*, immediately inside the west gate: both were unusually large, with a combined floor area of 652m² (as opposed to a more normal 312m² at Fendoch). The rest of the interior was filled with a total of 12 barracks, along with a possible second *fabrica* (II) and one large shed (V), which may have been a storage building. The barracks are a less than homogenous collection; no two are quite identical and some differ markedly. The finds from the Flavian barracks included horse equipment, and the excavators suggest that the number of barracks, combined with their design differences, might suggest the presence of a mixed cavalry and infantry *cohors equitata*, or possibly parts of two. A water pipe ran through the fort, from the west gate towards the *principia*, and there are aerial indications that this might have followed the north side of the Gask road for some distance, to bring in water from a spring, *c*.570m to the west.

As with so many of the Flavian sites in northern Scotland, there were signs that the fort had been remodelled in service to some degree. In particular, building V was preceded by a small granary, which was demolished to make room for it, but there are also signs of reworking in building II. These are fairly subtle adjustments, however, when compared with other sites in the area and, still more so, when compared to Strageath's own later history: for the Antonine fort was almost completely rebuilt during its operational life.

Outside the fort a number of additional features are known, mostly from the air. Four hundred metres to the west is a large temporary camp – of 13.1ha (32.3 acres) – and there are another two examples, across the Earn to the east. The nearest, Innerpeffray West, is 600m away and measures *c*.26ha (64 acres), whilst the second, Innerpeffray East, is almost 1.3km away and still larger, at *c*.52.6ha (130 acres). Yet another large camp – of *c*.9.1ha (23.5 acres) – has been found at Dornock, some 2km to the west-north-west (NN 877188) and, although this too lies on the far side of the river, it can be reached via a ford (almost exactly halfway along the straight line route) at Dalpatrick (NN 888185). Closer in, air photography has shown a small knot of roads immediately to the north of the fort (*colour plate 14*). These seem to form a triangular pattern and it is possible that they made up the skeleton of a civilian settlement, or *vicus*. There is also a series of irregular, ditched enclosures a little to the south-west (*colour plate 14*), which seem to be linked by tracks. One particularly clear air photograph (CUCAP neg: CHM8) shows that these represent a cluster of what are often called 'Celtic' fields and, whilst there can be no guarantee, without excavation, they do not seem to overlap with the fort, which means that they just might be contemporary (and even associated) with it.

4

THE GASK LINE:
STRAGEATH TO BERTHA

As we have seen, the eighteenth-century antiquary Roy believed that the Roman road crossed the Earn to the north of Strageath, and only then turned east, via a crossing of the Pow Water. Air photography has, however, shown that it turned well short of the Earn, ran parallel to the fort's north side and crossed the river at an old ford and ferry (where stone can be seen in the bank), opposite the famous chapel and library at Innerpeffray. The east bank of the Earn here is an eroded drumlin, into which the river is still cutting. As a result, there is a long line of river cliffs, on whose summit the library itself stands. Just to its south, however, the high cliff is broken by a slight nick where the ground, although still steep, is no longer sheer. The road heads straight for this feature and it is here that the single greatest engineering achievement on its entire line can be seen. This is a long, deep cutting, massively more impressive than those seen at Shielhill North and South: although it is now largely obscured by woodland. The feature (NN 902184) is over 130m long (*48*) and runs right up the slope from a point just metres east of the river. It still survives as a surface feature, 12-15m wide (*colour plate 15*), and recent excavations by ourselves showed it to have reached depths of 4.5m below the natural surface. It has been skillfully constructed to produce a fairly even gradient of 7.7° (1:5.7), on what, in places, would otherwise have been a near vertical incline, and this should have been gentle enough to allow the passage of wheeled traffic.

The excavation (Woolliscroft 2005) found that the cutting had been dug into a subsoil of pure glacial sand, of which over 2,000 tons had been removed. The sides

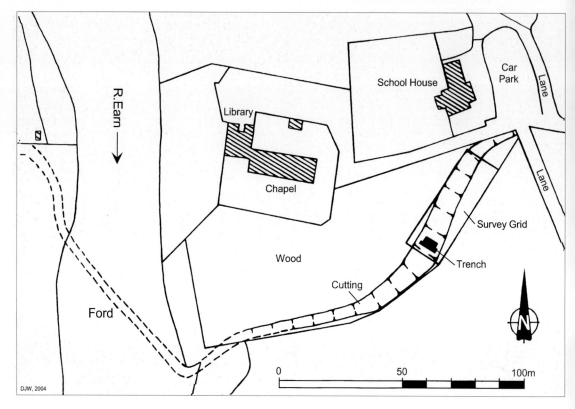

48 Plan of the Innerpeffray road cutting

and base had then been protected from erosion by means of a thick revetment of rammed or puddled clay, which was not native to the site, and so must have been brought from elsewhere. This had been so well laid that the feature remains in near pristine condition, despite the fact that the only outlet for rain water was to run down the cutting floor. The actual road surface was of gravel, laid on larger stones (which were themselves set into the clay base) and severe surface wear, including marked wheel ruts (49) showed that it had been in use for a prolonged period. The prime objective of the excavation was to check that the feature really was Roman. Roads are notoriously difficult to date, as they do not tend to incorporate datable material and the Innerpeffray cutting was no exception. It did, though, yield a fragment of medieval pottery, which at least showed that it had been in use well before the eighteenth century, which is the earliest period after the Roman occupation when properly engineered roads were constructed in Scotland. The Middle Ages tended to lavish any significant road engineering efforts on bridges, rather than the actual lines, and so a Roman date can probably

49 The road in the Innerpeffray cutting, showing wheel ruts

be inferred. Given that, the most surprising aspect of the cutting's design begins to make perfect sense: the fact that its 2.8m-wide road-bed was markedly narrower than any of the other known Gask road stretches, which range between 5.79m and 7.92m in width (Woolliscroft & Davies 2002, 56). For, interestingly, there are quite a number of parallels where other Roman cuttings show a similar narrowing of their roads. There are, for example, cuttings on the Stanegate behind Hadrian's Wall (Simpson *et al.* 1936, 188f), where the road can narrow to 2.75m. What are probably the best-known examples, however, have been found in and around the Alpine passes in Switzerland, where cuttings are known i.a. through the Great St Bernard Pass and on the Jura (Drack & Fellmann 1988, 367, 373, 390, 419 & 550). These too are often similar in width – with the road in the Great St Bernard cutting almost identical at 2.7m – and, although some are also a little steeper, all seem to have ruts to indicate use by wheeled vehicles. In all cases, the narrowing of the road is presumably a labour-saving measure to allow heavy traffic to move up and down a more gentle gradient – albeit only in

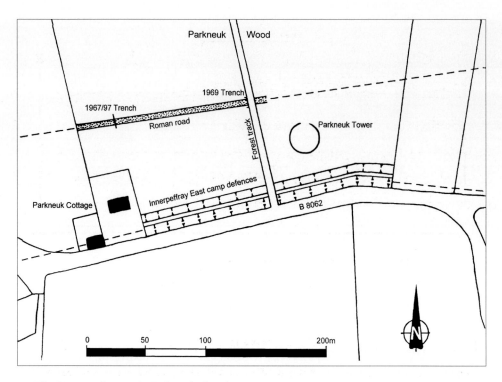

50 The Roman features in Parkneuk Wood

one direction at a time – without the need to excavate the full width of a two carriageway road. If so, the saving would have been considerable. For example, had the Innerpeffray cutting been dug to the full average width of the Gask road (*c*.6.8m), more than 1,000 tons of additional earth would have had to be moved. This would have been a 50 per cent increase in an already considerable workload, and so the design represents a good compromise between user convenience and economy of construction.

The cutting emerges beside the library car park, at NN 903184, and begins its ascent to the Gask Ridge proper. It is no longer visible on the surface, but has been traced from the air for 1,050m, running slightly north of east, as far as the modern B8062 (NN 912185). In the course of this stretch it cuts through the north-east corner of the Innerpeffray West temporary camp. This is a unique event on the line, and so deserves comment. For, although there are a good many other camps beside the road – including the major concentrations around Camelon and Ardoch – elsewhere, the camps and road always appear to respect one another. At Innerpeffray West it is not possible to say, from aerial evidence alone, whether the road or the camp was built first (although we are planning a small excavation to

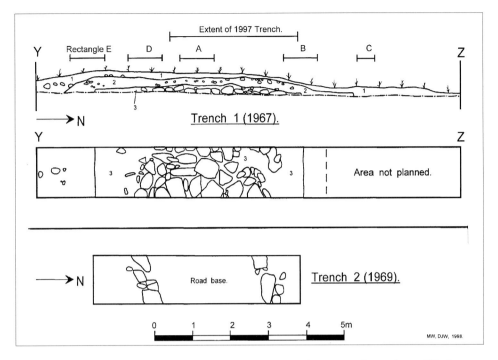

51 The Roman road excavation in Parkneuk Wood: 1. topsoil, 2. rammed gravel, 3. rubble in compacted pink clay

find out), and the camp itself is currently undated. The road does not enter or leave via a gate, however, which shows that the two cannot have been in use at the same time, and so we must assume that the road had either not yet been built, or had gone out of use at the time the camp was constructed.

After crossing the modern B road the Roman line becomes faintly visible at the surface for 100m. It then enters Parkneuk Wood, where a 250m stretch survives, still largely in use as a fire break (*50*). In 1967, Thomson and Lye cut a section across it at NN 915185. No report appeared, but notes survived and the trench was partly reopened by ourselves in 1997 and fully published (Woolliscroft & Davies 2002). It found the road to be 5.97m wide (*51*) and of slightly unusual construction. The road itself consisted of the normal rammed gravel surface, set on larger stones, but the entire structure was built up on a low turf *agger*. The ground here is level and so there would have been no advantage to road users of running on an embankment; but, even today, the surroundings drain poorly after rain, and it is possible that the bank was built to keep the line clear of what, in ancient times, was boggy ground. Even here, however, no side ditches could be found, despite a careful search via a trench stretching well over 7m from the road.

Elsewhere in the same wood, two other Roman features survive (*50*). The first is a long stretch of the north rampart and ditch of the huge Innerpeffray East temporary camp. These run immediately to the north of (and parallel to) the B8062 and can be followed with ease, for *c.*200m, along the wood's entire southern side. The Roman road lies some 70m to the north of the camp ditch, on a course which converges with it slightly towards the east and, halfway between the two (NN 917185), *c.*80 from the wood's eastern end, lies the next of the Gask system towers.

Parkneuk tower (*colour plate 16*) sits in a clearing, a little to the east of a modern forest track and, although it tends to become overgrown in summer, it is the first of the Gask towers to remain well preserved as a surface feature. Its circular ditch (partly flooded in places) is clearly visible, as is its entrance (which as usual faces the road), and there are even faint signs of an internal rampart. The site was partly excavated by Robertson (1974, 21ff), in 1968 and, although the work was relatively small in scale, some useful information can be gleaned (*52*). Although a single-ditched site, Parkneuk is noticeably larger in diameter than Westerton: at 22.5m. The ditch is also more substantial – at up to 3.6m wide and 1.3m deep – and its profile has a more regular V-shape. Inside, were the remains of a rampart, which was built mostly of clay, although it may have been turf revetted. In contrast to the ditch circuit, it may also have been sub-rectangular in plan, although insufficient area was excavated to make this certain. In the interior, three of the four tower posts were located, which were enough to show a rectangular structure, of *c.*3.05m (east–west) x 3.35m (north–south), set with its short axis facing the entrance. No datable material was found and there are no records of demolition debris. Nor were any signs of rebuilding or ditch recutting noted, but since no sections were recorded, this means virtually nothing. Parkneuk stands 1,750m to the east of Strageath, which is an usually long tower spacing (the average is around 1,130m), but as many years of search from the air (over what is fairly responsive ground) have failed to find an intervening installation, there may well not have been one. We cannot, however, rule out the possibility of a tower underlying Innerpeffray library, *c.*1,400m to the west, for this clifftop location offers a superb vantage point.

From the east end of Parkneuk Wood, the Roman road is lost from sight (even from the air) for over 1,100m: but the next visible section, at Raith (NN 929187), follows exactly the same alignment, and so the line must have continued straight on, uphill, under what is now Shearerston farm. Raith is also the site of the next tower. Nothing is visible on the surface, but the site sits on a hilltop, 170m to the south, at NN 93191852. This is an usually long distance from the road; indeed most of the other towers sit right beside the line, but an exception has

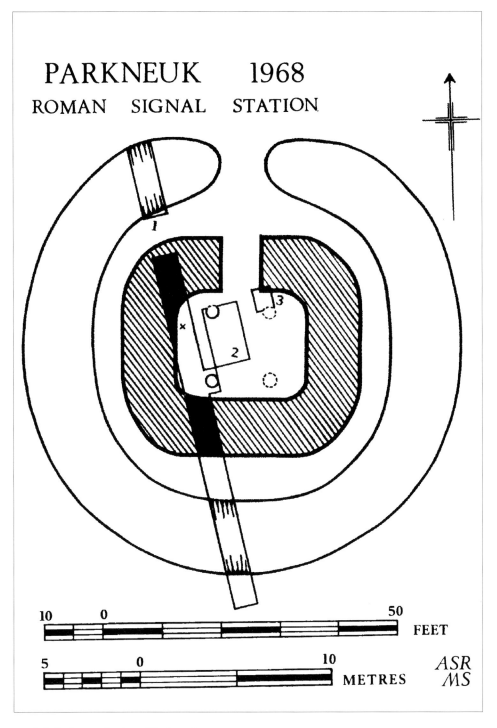

52 A.S. Robertson's plan of Parkneuk tower

clearly been made here, so as to exploit one of the best observation points on the entire system. The position has a spectacular field of view, taking in many miles of the Highland fringe to the north and west. To the south and south-east it looks right across Strathearn to the Ochil Hills beyond, whilst, to the east, from tower height, it has the entire ridge top in view and is intervisible with every Gask installation between the fortlets of Kaims Castle and Midgate. There have even been reports that it is intervisible with the Highland line fort of Fendoch, *c.*10km to the north: but the view is, in fact, thoroughly blocked by the, 351m-high, Stroness Hill. The site was discovered in 1900 when a pit sunk for the construction of a water tank revealed the four postholes of what appeared to be a watchtower, along with a quantity of unidentified red pottery (now lost). Fortunately, the features were noted by the antiquary: A.G. Reid, and published by Christison (1901, 28). His report is brief in the extreme, just two very short paragraphs, but it does tell us that the postholes survived to a depth of about 0.3m and formed a square with sides of 2.75m. Since 1900, the site has been accepted into the roll of Gask towers almost without question and, until recently, no further work had taken place. Indeed, it was assumed that the tower had been totally destroyed or, at least, rendered permanently inaccessible, by the water tank, which was covered by a considerable mound of earth. Objectively, however, the identification could not be regarded as proven. The excavation encountered no sign of a ditch. Nor has any trace of a ring ditch ever shown from the air: indeed the site is usually unresponsive to air photography. There is, however, one superb air photograph in the Cambridge collection (neg: AKD-96, see Woolliscroft 2002, 14, fig 1.9) which shows a number of cropmarks around the tank, which suggest a previously unsuspected level of complexity on the hilltop. These include a group of prehistoric cist burials (53, B) and part of a Roman temporary camp – with claviculate gates and an area of at least 1.47ha (3.6 acres). Perhaps the most interesting mark, however, was a playing card-shaped ditched enclosure (E), which surrounds the 1900 water tank (A). From the air, this feature resembles a single-ditched fortlet, in which case it could be relevant that it lies on the 6 Roman mile point, exactly halfway between Kaims Castle and the next fortlet: Midgate. We have already seen that Kaims and Glenbank were also 6 miles apart, and a Raith fortlet would provide further evidence for a regular spacing pattern. Given the lack of evidence for a tower ditch, this raised the possibility that the structure found in 1900 was not a free-standing tower at all, but part of a fortlet gate, like that found at Glenbank; and the first author is on record suggesting such a scenario (Woolliscroft 1993, 297f). Since that time, however, we have been able to conduct a geophysical survey of the site and the supposed fortlet enclosure proved to measure just 27m x 32m over its ditch, which is far too small

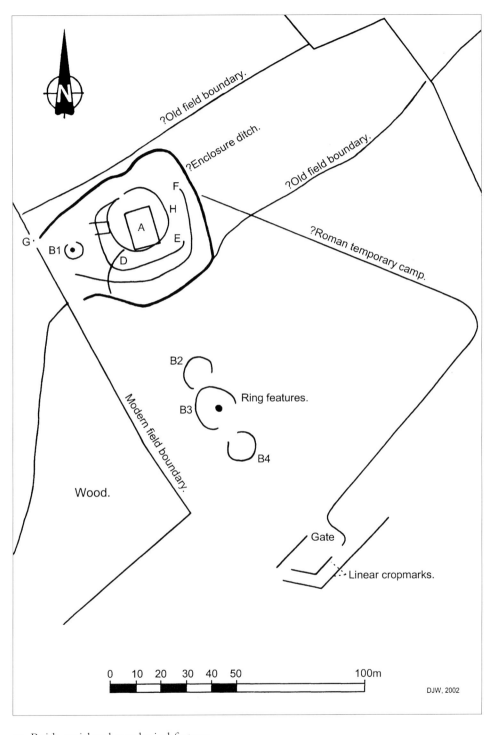

53 Raith, aerial and geophysical features

(Kaims Castle measures 49m x 58m). Instead, the survey located a sub-circular ring ditch, *c*.23m in diameter (H), which is all but identical to Parkneuk. The ditch surrounds the 1900 posts and has a single entrance, facing the Roman road. The survey thus appears to have confirmed the century old evidence for a tower, and there seems little further reason to doubt its identity.

From Raith a full 9.5km (6 miles) stretch of the road survives, almost all of which is still in use. The section starts as a 200m-long running mound along the southern edge of a field. From NN 931187, the line is (sometimes faintly) discernible for 650m in fenced off woodland, before emerging, at NN 938187, beautifully preserved and still in use as a farm track (54). This can be followed for a further 700m – still on the same heading begun at Innerpeffray Library, although the last 300m are overgrown. To the south of this stretch, around NN 943186, two overlapping rectangular enclosures with rounded corners have been seen from the air (RCAHMS neg: B5176). These measure 2.33ha (5.76 acres) and at least 1.96ha (4.86 acres) respectively, and resemble Roman temporary camps; however, excavation by the Roman Gask Project in 1999 showed that they were probably fairly modern enclosure boundaries (Woolliscroft, Hughes & Lockett 2002, 31f).

At NN 945188, the road crosses a fence line to run on the northern side of a wood, and continues as a green lane for the next 1,500m, initially partly choked by trees. Two hundred metres from the start of the wood is the next tower: Ardunie (NN 947188), which lies in a clearing, just south of the road (*colour plate 17*). The site was found in 1937 by Crawford (1949, 52), but no finds have been recovered and no excavation has ever taken place, so our knowledge is wholly dependent on the surviving surface feature. This is less clear than Parkneuk, but it still retains slight traces of an internal rampart, and the ditch circuit is fairly distinct. This measures 19m in diameter (which is closer in size to Westerton, than to Parkneuk and Raith) and the entrance break faces north towards the road.

From Ardunie, the road maintains its course as a green lane (55), now clear of trees and beautifully preserved. Moving 1,110m further east (NN 958189) there is a slight knoll to its north which marks the site of the tower of Roundlaw. Nothing is now visible on the ground, but the site was discovered from the air by St Joseph (1955, 87), and excavated by Robertson (1974, 24ff) in 1972. The combined results suggest an almost perfectly circular ring ditch, much the same size as Ardunie's (18.76m), and with its single entrance break facing south (56). The ditch has a 'Punic' profile, like Westerton's, but was rather deeper, at 1.22m, despite being cut through rock. No trace of a rampart had survived *in situ*, but the ditch contained plentiful turf which probably derives from its demolition and/or destruction by ploughing. Three of the four tower postholes were located, and

54 The Roman road on Ardunie farm

55 The road between Ardunie and Roundlaw

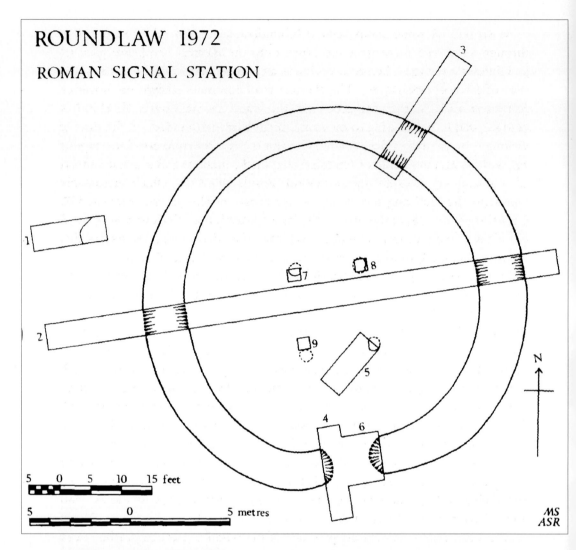

ROUNDLAW 1972

ROMAN SIGNAL STATION

5 0 5 10 15 feet

5 0 5 metres

N

MS
ASR

56 Robertson's plan of Roundlaw

also proved to be rock cut. They marked out a rectangular structure, of 3.05m x 4.27m, which was set south of centre within the internal area, with its short axis facing the entrance. No datable finds were recovered and, as at Parkneuk, no ditch or posthole sections were recorded, which means that nothing can be said regarding possible recuts or rebuilding. This site too has been said to be intervisible with Fendoch but, as at Raith, this is not the case. Fendoch cannot, in fact, see any point on the entire Gask line, and aerial surveys have produced no sign of an intervening relay tower on Stroness Hill to its south.

At NN 960188, some 200m beyond Roundlaw, a modern minor road swings through an abrupt, more than 100°, turn onto the Roman line (*colour plate 18*) and follows it for 300m before swerving away, equally sharply, to the north, at the start of a wood (NN 963189). The Roman road continues straight on, however, as a forest track. A little over 400m into the wood, the next tower, Kirkhill (NN 968188), stands in a clearing to the south of the road, surrounded – at the time of writing – by an area of fresh felling. The site is beautifully preserved (*colour plate 19*), with its 21.34m diameter, (circular) ring ditch, entrance and internal rampart all visible: along with an upcast mound outside the ditch, which presumably represents the spoil dug out during its construction. The site was excavated by Christison (1901, 28) at the turn of the last century, but no finds were recovered. No plans or sections were produced and little more detail was given except that a square, four-post, timber tower was traced which had sides of 2.9m.

At NN 972189, 475m beyond Kirkhill, the modern forest track swings off to the south, but the Roman road goes straight on, still on the same heading, and can be followed through the trees as a running mound for a further 150m, to the derelict farm of Muir O' Fauld. Here it is joined by another modern track (NN 977190), and the two lines continue to coincide for a further 1,200m. At NN 981190, some 700m after joining this track, the road makes an 11° turn to the north – which is its first real change of alignment since emerging from the Innerpeffray cutting – over 8km to the west – and 100m further on it passes the next tower: Muir O' Fauld (NN 982190). Until recently, this site lay in dense forest and it is still marked by tree stumps, but it can now be seen in a heather-covered clearing, just south of the road, accompanied by a Historic Scotland information board. Considering the violence modern forestry can inflict on the ground, the remains have survived remarkably well (*colour plate 20*) with the ditch, entrance, upcast mound and internal rampart all clearly visible. Christison (1901, 27) found it impossible to excavate, however, thanks to the presence of the woodland and no further work has been attempted since it was cleared. Consequently, nothing can be said about the tower structure itself or its history, but the ring ditch is more or less circular, and almost as large as Parkneuk and Raith: at 22.2m in diameter.

Just under 400m further east (NN 986191), the modern road from Kinkell swings onto the Roman line from the south, and remains on it for the rest of the visible section. The next tower, Gask House, lies 450m later (NN 990192), in woodland to the south of the line. Although only *c.*30m from the road, it is difficult to locate amongst the trees, despite being deliberately planted with sycamores to identify it; however, once found, it is well preserved, with the ditch, upcast mound, entrance and rampart all visible (57). The site has been subjected to two different excavations: one in 1900 by Christison (1901, 26), and the second in the

57 Gask House Roman tower

mid-960s by Robertson. Christison's report is only seven lines long and includes no illustrations, so it is hard to be sure what he did: but he does record the fact that the interior was covered by what he calls 'black mould' which is a term he uses elsewhere for what sounds like burnt demolition debris. The Robertson report is also less detailed than one would like, but does at least provide a plan (*58*) and more useful feature descriptions. The V-shaped ditch is shown as being sub-circular in plan, 22.12m in diameter and wider in the south than elsewhere. This much agrees with the surface feature, but the plan also shows the internal rampart as a rectangle with rounded corners, whereas the visible remains suggest a more generally rounded, if still sub-rectangular, shape. The rampart was found to consist of clay, set on a base of turf, and it was 2.74m thick.

Three of the tower's four posts were located, and its size extrapolated as 3.05m (east–west) x 2.44m (north–south): although Christison, who found all four posts, gives slightly smaller dimensions. The tower seems to have been set slightly to the rear (south) of centre within the internal area, and its long axis faces the entrance. Timber fragments were found in the postholes, which may have come from the posts themselves, but these were not analysed for species. As before, no sections were recorded, so we cannot tell if there was rebuilding or ditch recutting activity, but the site did produce a Flavian pottery sherd (made between *c*.AD 70 and 95), which provides additional support for a late first-century date. Robertson again raised the red herring of intervisibility between the Gask and Fendoch, by suggesting that Gask House was oriented to face the supposed watchtower at the mouth of the Sma' Glen: but, once again, the two cannot see each other and there is no known intervening site that could have served as a signals relay between them.

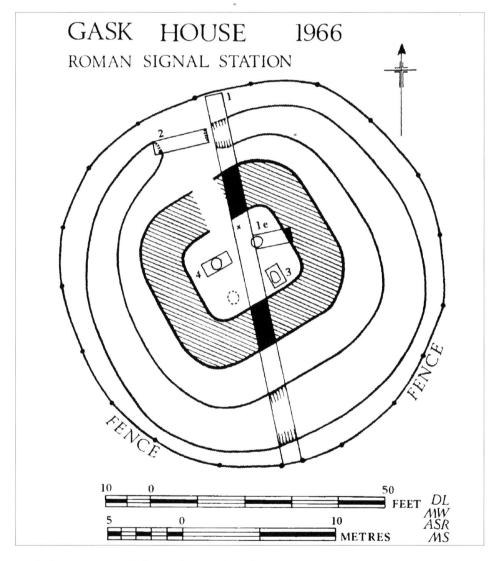

58 Gask House tower, Robertson's excavation plan

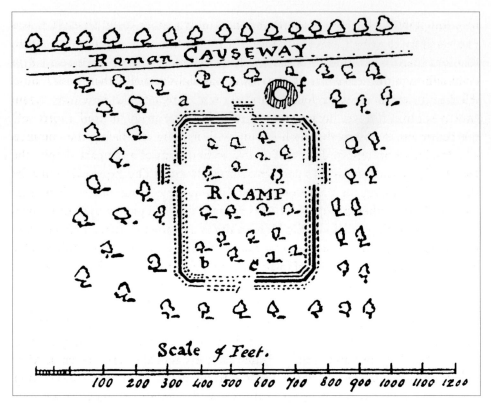

59 The Gask House temporary camp

The tower lies immediately north of a small temporary camp, which measures around 152m (north–south) x 129.5m (east–west) over the ditch, to give an area of 1.98ha (4.9 acres). This was clearly visible in the eighteenth century, when an anonymous plan was produced (59), but by Christison's day it was much erased, and it is now almost impossible to spot in the modern wood: although it does project into a field to the south, where it occasionally shows as a cropmark. The camp had four titulate gates and lies with its short axis facing the road, with which it is nearly parallel.

The road now continues on the same heading, and 800m further on we meet the next tower: Witch Knowe (NN 998195), which lies *c.*70m to the north of the road, in woodland. This is the last of the well-preserved Gask towers, but also one of the best: with the ditch, upcast mound, entrance and rampart all clearly visible at the surface, and with the entrance facing south. Until recently the site lay in a thicket, which made it very hard to see, but this is has been dying off in recent years (causing a degree of tree-fall damage) so that, although it is still hard to photograph well (*colour plate 21*), it is now much easier to understand. It was excavated in 1900 by Christison (1901, 26f) who, this time, did produce a plan (*60*). The ditch was found to be unusually substantial, at 4.27m wide and 1.83m deep, although the actual circuit, at 21.95m, was slightly smaller than Gask House. All four tower posts were located and showed a rectangular structure, 2.74m (north–south) x 3.35m (east–west), which sits fractionally behind (north of) the centre point within the ditch circuit, with its long axis facing the entrance. Oddly, Christison reported himself unable to find signs of a rampart, despite the fact that it appears on his plan and remains visible today. The explanation may be that he was looking for the wrong thing. By this stage in his career, Christison, and the distinguished group of scholars around him, had grown used to Roman ramparts consisting of laid turf, which produces a distinctive striped effect when sectioned. It is possible, however, that the Witch Knowe rampart was built of clay, like that of its neighbour Gask House, in which case he may not have recognised it as such. No finds were recovered and no sections recorded of sufficient detail to tell us much about the site's building (or rebuilding) history.

At NO 000196, 200m east of Witch Knowe, the road makes another slight (8°) turn to the north to head east-north-east: a heading it maintains for the rest of the visible sector. Nine hundred and twenty metres later, it passes the next tower, at Moss Side (sometimes: Mayfield), which lies 90m to the north of the line, at NO 008199. The site was ploughed out in the early twentieth century and now shows only from the air: but, a century ago – although the ditch had ceased to be visible – the internal area survived, which allowed Christison (1901, 29f) to excavate it whilst still relatively well preserved (*61*). The results were intriguing, although no datable finds were recovered. He found the rampart still surviving, almost 1m high x 4.3m thick, and described its material as '10 alternate layers of black mould and yellow or red clay'. The thickness is probably something of an exaggeration, as the feature had obviously spread, but the context description and his drawn section clearly show a rampart wholly constructed of laid turf. It was the tower itself that showed the most interesting features, however. It was square, with sides of 3.35m, and lay a little to the front and left (south-west) of centre within the rampart circuit. Uniquely, though, the tower posts were linked by slots for wooden beams. These could be interpreted as an attempt to provide greater stability, or as an anchor for wattle and daub side cladding. But Christison states that at least one of the tower postholes had been filled in to allow the beams to be installed, which would imply that the slots belong to a secondary structure, possibly some form of timber block house. Christison did not extend his trenches to investigate the ditch, but air photographs show it to have been circular in plan, *c*.21m in diameter, *c*.3m wide and with its entrance break facing south, more or less in line with the excavated rampart entrance.

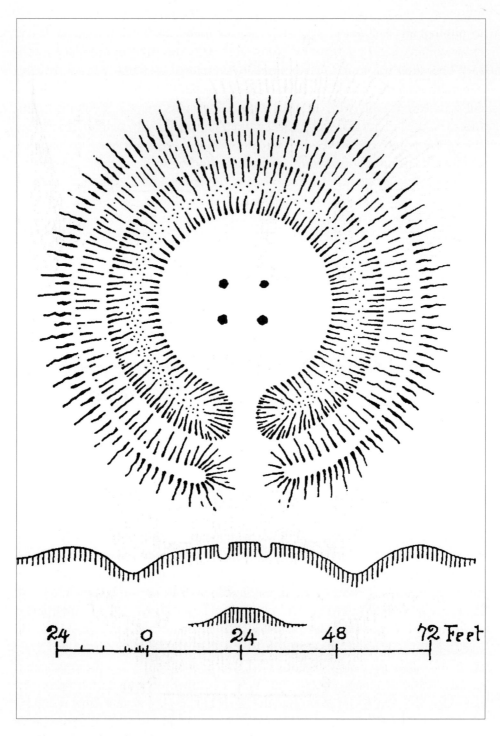

60 Christison's plan of Witch Knowe

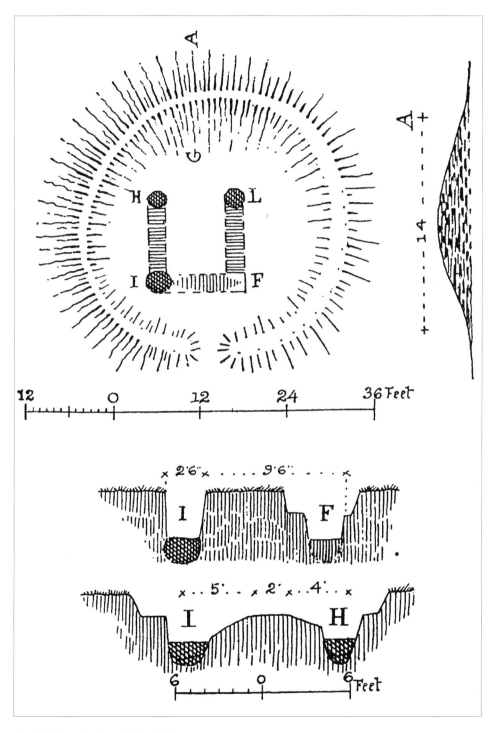

61 Christison's plan of Moss Side

Fourteen hundred metres further on (NO 021204) the road passes immediately south of a distinct knoll, which is topped by the site of Midgate (sometimes: Thorny Hill). This lies just at the edge of a wood, and is one of the most curious installations on the entire Gask system: for it is a double site. Today, the hilltop is dominated by the remains of a fortlet, very similar in size and design to Kaims Castle, if a touch larger at 20m x 23m over the rampart (as opposed to 20m x 22m). Until well into the twentieth century the site was just as well preserved as Kaims, albeit its eastern half is somewhat obscured in the woodland; but it was damaged during the Second World War by the imposition of a (now ruined) anti-aircraft position, in its interior, to protect the nearby Findo Gask airfield. Nevertheless, the site is still clearly visible on the surface (*62*), although Crawford (1949, 54) claims not to have been able to see it during a visit in 1940. Its rampart and ditch circuits remain almost completely intact, although the entrance, which probably lay on the long axis in the south, is now obscured. Just to the west of the fortlet, however, the faint remains of a ring-ditched structure, that looks to be one of the Gask towers, can also be discerned (*63*), with the two installations' ditches coming to within 13m of one another.

62 Midgate Roman fortlet

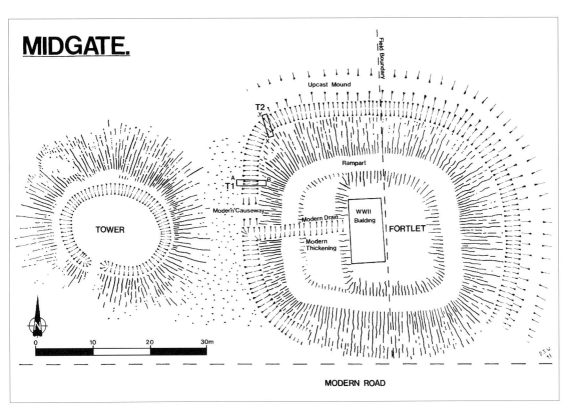

63 Midgate tower and fortlet

Both sites were excavated in 1900 by Christison (1901, 32ff), and we have
done further work (Woolliscroft 1993, 302ff). As with Kaims Castle and Glenbank,
no internal buildings were found in the fortlet, only an area of rough paving
and, as the entrance area remains undug, we cannot confirm the (albeit likely)
presence of a gate tower. The ditch was V-shaped, 2.5m wide, and up to 1.27m
deep. The ring feature is strongly oval in plan: measuring 21.34m (east–west),
but only 15.5m (north–south). Its single entrance break faces south-south-
west, towards the easiest way down to the road, whilst its ditch is 3.05m wide
x 1.52m deep and V-shaped. No datable material was found on either site, but
we can probably assume that both belong to the Flavian occupation and this
presents something of a problem because, obviously, the two features cannot
be contemporary. No defence system needs watch posts at 13m intervals, and
there would be simply no point in putting a fortlet and tower so close together.
Sadly the ditches do not intersect, and they remain just far enough apart that
their upcast does not seem to overlap, so that it has, so far, proved impossible

to determine which was built first. But, whatever the case, this dual installation should be another sign that Gask sites were often rebuilt in service: except that here, instead of a simple tower rebuild, we would have a site being replaced by one of an entirely different type. The only alternative is that one of the sites might not be Roman at all, and it has recently been pointed out (Hanson & Friell 1995, 514) that, whilst the fortlet is unquestionably real, legitimate objections could be levelled at the tower: for it does show a number of atypical features. There is, for example, its odd ovoid shape, and no internal rampart has been detected. Most importantly, however, Christison found no postholes in its interior, only a roughly rectangular (1.22m x 2.13m) area of paving. Instead, therefore, Hanson and Friell suggest that it might be a barrow with the paving representing the base of a burial cist.

Some of these objections are easily dealt with, for the oval ditch circuit is more or less dictated by the shape of the narrow hilltop. We sometimes exaggerate the standardisation of Roman military structures, but it is actually not uncommon for the plans of what are usually fairly generic installations to be radically adapted to the terrain. The classic example in Britain is the Hadrian's Wall outpost fort of Bewcastle, which is hexagonal in shape, again to meet the shape of the hill on which it stands (Jones & Woolliscroft 2001, 139ff), but there are other examples that could be cited. Likewise, the apparent absence of a rampart might be an illusion. The site is very poorly preserved, and so the fact that it cannot be made out on the surface is hardly surprising. Furthermore, as we have seen, Christison failed to notice the far clearer rampart at Witch Knowe, so his inability to record one here (even when excavated) may just be par for the course. The absence of postholes is more worrying, however. Christison's team had proved themselves perfectly capable of finding timber features elsewhere. Indeed, as we have seen, they pioneered timber archaeology in Scotland. We ourselves can affirm from experience that the site's loose, sandy subsoil makes it very difficult to see subtle, timber features but, even so, that particular group should have been capable of finding them. On the other hand, the 'paving' is rather large for a cist floor, whilst local barrow ditches tend to be very much smaller. They were, after all, dug only to produce the upcast for a burial mound, not because they were wanted in their own right. As a result, they tend to be shallow, saucer-shaped features and, although they can be somewhat intermittent, they do not, as a rule, have distinct entrance breaks. This deep, V-shaped ditch, with its one clearly defined entrance, is thus totally out of keeping with the local barrow tradition. At the same time, it is fully consistent with Roman work, albeit some residual doubt must remain until the site's identity can be properly re-examined.

64 Westmuir tower from the air

Four hundred and fifty metres beyond Midgate, at the east end of Midgate Wood, the modern road swings north, away from the Roman line (which continues straight on) and, from here to the Tay, the system has entirely vanished from the surface. Nevertheless, more sites are known from the air and, 465m further on, we meet the next tower, which lies *c.*40m to the north of the road at Westmuir (NO 028207). Nothing whatever can be seen on the ground and no archaeological work has been done, but the site was found from the air by St Joseph in 1943, and has since shown fairly regularly (*64*). At its best, the cropmark can be extremely clear and shows that the ditch is circular in plan, and smaller than its near neighbours, at *c.*15m in diameter. As might be expected, the single entrance faces south towards the Roman road. There is even one extraordinary air photograph (RCAHMS neg: B5100) that shows the four internal postholes, and so allows us to measure a tower of around 4m (east–west) x 3m (north–south), which had its long axis facing the entrance.

The top of the Gask Ridge is relatively flat; but the road has been rising since it left Innerpeffray, and Westmuir lies immediately south of its 154m-high summit. Here, the line runs just to the north of (and a little above) a steep-sided, natural amphitheatre in the Ridge's south side, known as the Cairnie Braes. It thus enjoys a superb field of view over Strathearn, although at present this is more potential than real, thanks to tree cover. Strathearn has always been a major strategic corridor and this was already the case in Roman times, when it served as a major invasion route. There are two large temporary camps in the valley bottom south of Westmuir: a 25.5ha (63-acre) site at Forteviot (NO 040175) and a still larger, 46.5ha (115-acre), example at Dunning (NO 025148). Others are known elsewhere in the Strath and, in 1999, we conducted excavations at two suspected, much smaller camps (3.3ha (8.16 acres) and c.1.63ha (4 acres)) at Upper Cairnie. These stand on top of the Braes (NO 038192), well above the valley floor, which made them seem more likely to be linked to the Gask: in fact, the excavation showed that they were probably fairly modern enclosures (Woolliscroft, Hughes & Lockett 2002, 32ff).

Beyond Westmuir the line begins its downward path towards the Tay and becomes much more difficult to follow. The next 4km are particularly confusing: this is not helped by the fact that much of the ground has been in arable cultivation since time immemorial, but is not particularly productive of cropmarks. A simple projection of the road's last known heading would have it re-cross the modern road at NO 031209, and an air photograph taken by T.Berthon (who kindly provided a print) does show a linear cropmark on the correct heading, running from here into Cultmalundie Wood (NO 034210). Further east, though, we are almost completely in the dark and it is even possible that there are two road lines over the next 3km: possibly with the Antonine route taking a different course to the original Flavian line. One of these branches may have taken a northerly course, via Tibbermore. There is, for example, a war-time air photograph (now in Perth Museum), taken by E.Bradley, that shows a linear parch-mark running approximately north-east, for c.275m, through the field immediately west of Tibbermore Manse (NO 049231-052233). This lines up with a series of possible quarry pit cropmarks (RCAHMS neg: PT10620), which run for c.320m, on a more north-north-easterly heading, at Blackruthven cottages (NO 060240-063241), and these, in turn, line up with a possible parch-mark (photographed by Berthon), which runs for a further 200m through the next field to the east, as far is its boundary with Blackruthven House (NO 065243). On the other hand, various air photographers, including ourselves, have recorded a series of at least four linear parch-marks further south, although these lie on a jumble of headings which do not appear to form a logical sequence. The first of these is a c.100m-long parch-mark seen immediately east of Cultmalundie Wood (NO 043211), and running approximately north-east, in a slight dip in the ground which might be a hollow-way. This is followed by a rather longer, c.300m, parch-mark which runs east-north-east to the north of Crossgates: from NO 048215-051216. Next, immediately to the west of West Lamberkine Wood, comes a *c.*200m parch-mark, which heads north-east from NO 054220-055222 and, finally, to the north of West Lamberkine Wood, a possible hollow-way shows regularly from the air, running north-north-east, from NO 056225-057228. As already stated, however, these isolated marks would produce a strikingly zig-zagged course, which seems unnecessary, given the easy terrain, and distinctly out of character with the rest of the line.

There is, though, a possible alternative. There is a long, straight series of field boundaries running north-east for almost 1km, to the south of Newbigging farm (NO 048216-053223). This lines up well with the section to the north of West Lamberkine Wood and, interestingly, the original 1866 6in Ordnance Survey map of the area shows the boundary of Tibbermore parish exactly following the two features (it has since been partially adjusted), which might thus mark something very old. The two also line up with the mark east of Cultmalundie Wood and, together, the three features would suggest a straight line, running on a north-easterly heading. If so, it might be worth noting that this, when extrapolated, points towards Blackruthven House and so, if there really were two lines, they may well reunite at this point.

It might even be possible to suggest that it was the southern branch that belonged with the Flavian system: for in 1986, the RCAHMS (neg: PT15159) found what looks to be another watchtower, immediately south of the projected line, at Peel (NO 060232). The ditch is circular in plan, with the usual, single entrance, facing north towards the possible road line. It also seems to intersect the less regular ditch of a native feature, although it is not yet possible to say which came first. No internal postholes appear in the air photographs and no excavation has taken place in the interior, so the tower identification cannot yet be regarded as certain: but there is already strong positive evidence. In 1999, the Gask Project conducted a geophysical survey, which was followed, in 2000, by a small excavation (Woolliscroft 2002, 62ff), although, thanks to partial flooding of the site, this was only able to section the ditch (65). No datable material was found, but the combined results do show a typical, V-shaped Roman-military-style ditch (0.84m deep x 2.04m wide), with a circuit almost identical to Westmuir's: at 15.7m in diameter. Moreover, the ditch fill was largely made up of deliberately deposited clay and turf, which may have derived from the demolition of an internal rampart. Very little silt was found in the ditch, which might suggest a short life for the site, but there was some evidence for recutting, so it is more probable that the ditch had been cleaned out shortly before its abandonment.

In addition to the evidence from the site itself, its position might also be significant: it lies almost exactly 2⅔ Roman miles from Westmuir, and 1⅓ Roman miles from the next tower to the east: at Huntingtower. These numbers are suggestive in themselves, but they might also be a sign that the towers had returned to a regular spacing system in this sector – probably of ⅔ of a Roman mile (987m) – similar to the ⅓ Roman mile spacings detected between Greenloaning and Shielhill North. If so, we might expect three more sites between Westmuir and Peel: one in Cultmalundie Wood (*c*.NO 039210), one to the north of Crossgates (*c*.NO 047216) and one to the east of Newbigging (NO 053223). We might also expect another close to Blackruthven House, at *c*.NO 064241, although at present, there is no evidence for any of these sites.

To the north and south-east of this sector, two tiny temporary camps have been found from the air, and subjected to small-scale trenching by ourselves (Woolliscroft, Hughes & Lockett 2002). The first, Easter Powside (NO 056245), takes the form of a slightly irregular parallelogram, and has one (asymmetric) *titulus*-style gate in the north. The site lies, bisected by a disused railway, 1,370m north of Peel, and measures just *c*.0.45 ha (1.12 acres). The second, East Mid Lamberkin, is a more regular rectangle, and is even smaller, at 0.41ha (1.02 acres), which makes it one of the smallest camps known in Scotland. It lies at

65 Peel, the ditch section

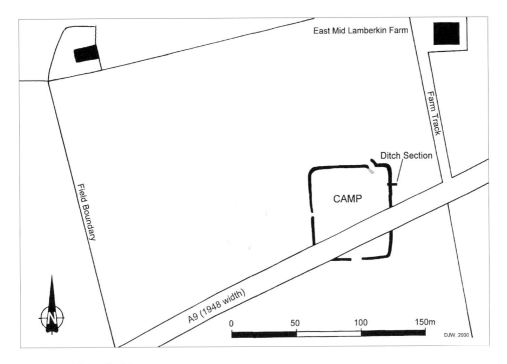

66 East Mid Lamberkin temporary camp

NO 074225, 1,520m to the south-east of Peel, and when first found it had already been damaged by the modern A9, which bisects its southern half. Since that time, massive additional damage has been done by the conversion of the road into a dual-carriageway, which here runs in a broad cutting and has destroyed the entire southern part of the site (apparently without prior archaeological investigation). Fortunately, a number of superb air photographs survive in the Cambridge collection (e.g. negs: CKO57 & AAG40) which show the site before this mutilation took place, and so it remains possible to reconstruct plans of virtually the entire ditch circuit (*66*). The site is unique in the region, because the three known gates (the east gate was destroyed, unrecorded, by the road) are each of a different, although still recognisably Roman, type. The west gate is a very narrow postern, whilst the south gate was of the wider *titulus* type (CUCAP neg: AAG40). The north gate shows an outward curving *clavicula* on its eastern side, of a type best known in Scotland from the Stracathro camps: but this is not a pure Stracathro gate, since it lacks the usual straight, outward turn on its western side. Instead, a single air photograph (now in Perth Museum), taken by W. Fuller, shows signs of what seems to be an answering inward curving *clavicula* on the gate's western side, which would produce a more symmetrical gate type previously known from sites such as Cawthorn: camps 'B' and 'C', in Yorkshire (Welfare and Swan 1995, 12). So far as the writers are aware, the presence of three different gate types in one Roman camp is unique: although sites, such as Cawthorn 'A' are known with two gate types (Welfare and Swan 1995, 12, No 72). The most attractive explanation is to see the site as a Roman practise camp, rather than as a work camp or as an overnight bivouac for some small detachment and, although it cannot be proven, it is tempting to wonder if a group of Roman recruits might have received training here in constructing a range of different gate types.

To the east of Blackruthven House, the Roman road has been picked up with more certainty from the air. It runs north-east, from NO 070246, as a parch-mark at the base of a low, but steep ridge, which itself heads into the outskirts of modern Perth. Two hundred and fifty metres further east (NO 072248), after crossing the drive to West Mains of Huntingtower, it makes a 22° turn to the south to run east-north-east and, just to the south of this turn (NO 073247), lies the last known Gask tower: Huntingtower. This stands on the ridge top, from where it enjoys an excellent field of view, especially to the north. It was found from the air by the RCAHMS, in 1985, and excavated by ourselves in 1999 (Woolliscroft 2000b). The circular ring ditch has its entrance facing north-north-west towards the road (67). It was 16.44m in diameter, which is very close to Westmuir and Peel, and the V-shaped ditch profile also resembled Peel's, at an average of 2.45m wide and 0.76m deep. Inside, turf-work from the internal rampart had survived, and all four tower posts were located, along with traces of internal metalling. The tower itself was irregular in shape; for, although the east and west sides were both 3.1m in length, the south side was markedly shorter than the north: at 3.1m, as opposed to 4.3m. This was a result of the site's most unusual feature: for the tower was set right at the back of the internal area, with its southern posts actually set in the rampart and, consequently, its southern side had effectively been squeezed to fit within the curve of the ditch. As so often, the tower structure had been rebuilt in service and there were signs that the ditch may have been recut: but the only find recovered was a single piece of pottery which, although probably Roman, could not be more closely dated.

To the east of Huntingtower, the aerial indications of the Roman road strengthen markedly: with a 970m-long, double line of quarry pits showing regularly as cropmarks, as far as NO 081251, to the west of Huntingtower Castle. Somewhere around this point we might expect the next tower, and there is a vanishingly faint trace of a ring ditch on an air photograph taken by the late Prof G.D.B. Jones that might be of relevance. It lies, at NO 079247, still on the ridge-top to the south and, although this puts it almost 200m from the road, it also gives it a much enhanced field of view. It might thus be a parallel for Raith, which was also set well back from the line for the same reason. It must

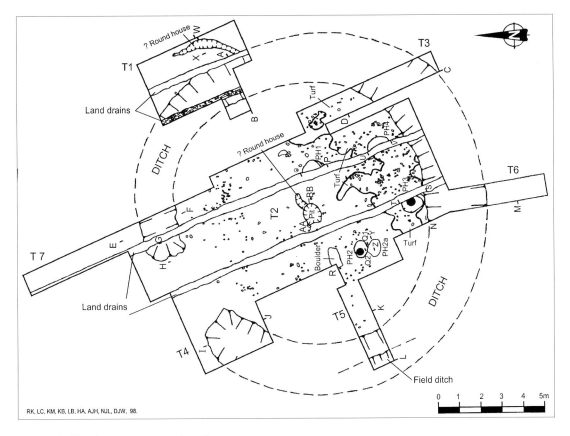

67 Huntingtower, excavation plan

be stressed, however, that we currently know next to nothing about this site, and it may well not be Roman. No entrance can be seen on the very faint air photograph and no surface work has yet been conducted. It is also just 730m from Huntingtower, which is almost 260m below the area's supposed ⅔ Roman mile spacing interval. Indeed, this would be the shortest spacing yet known on the system, albeit by just 70m.

At Huntingtower, the road fades from sight again, and the final 2km to the Tay remain something of a mystery. To the north of Huntingtower Castle, the ground slopes steeply into the flood plain of the River Almond, and the best route down is that now followed by a modern minor road to Inveralmond (NO 082252). The Roman line may well have taken a similar route, in which case it would have run on its last seen heading for a further c.100m, before turning to run due north down the slope. It would then, presumably, have turned back to the north-east, towards Bertha, and there is one small piece of aerial evidence that might support this. The flood plain is an impressive cropmark resource and was still more so before the construction of the Inveralmond Industrial Estate: but a bewildering array of paleochannels tends to obscure archaeological traces. Nevertheless, there are a number of man-made features to be seen, including some impressive formal garden features and a number of old trackways. One of the latter is marked by parallel side ditches, and can be seen running north-east, for around 150m (from NO 086255-087256), just south of a disused railway. This is more or less the line we would expect, and it may well be the Roman road, although there are potential doubts. No quarry pits have been detected, despite the valley's gravel-rich subsoil and, as we have seen, side ditches are not a common feature on the Gask road: although they are present occasionally and have sometimes been added during later reuse. The aerial traces also, however, make the line appear narrower than the Gask road's average 6-7m, and so it may have a more recent origin. Whatever the case, the Roman road presumably crossed the Almond, possibly just upstream of the old Almond Bridge (NO 094265), where the banks are less gorge-like than elsewhere in the area. It would then have turned east, towards the line's final fort at Bertha (NO 097268).

BERTHA

For centuries, the fort of Bertha had something of the status of an archaeological phantom. Everyone knew it was there, and all were agreed that it lay close to the Almond's confluence with the Tay; but no one was sure exactly where. Maitland (1757, 198) seems to have got it more or less right, although he may have mistaken the northern rampart for the road. Roy (1793, PL 12) and Stuart (1852, 204) had it bisected by, and largely to the south of, the Almond, whilst in 1799, the Rev. D. Moncrieff placed it correctly, to the north of the Almond, but so close that it was being eroded away (OSA, 15, 527f). Only in the early twentieth century was a reasonably accurate plan produced (Callander 1919, 145ff): but even this shows the fort as a trapezium, narrowing markedly towards the east; when it is really a regular rectangle, albeit narrower for its length than the other forts in the region. Even today the site is only poorly understood: but air photography, fieldwalking and an excavation have provided at least some significant information (68).

On the surface, part of the southern rampart can still be seen, running on strong ground, immediately to the north of the steep Almond valley. There are also faint signs of a ditch in places, and the south gate is marked by a gap in the rampart, now used by a modern field gate. In low angled sun, the north-east corner, along with parts of the north and west ramparts, can be seen as faint ripples in the ground, on either side of a railway. The east side has been virtually obliterated but must, again, have run on strong ground, near the steep bank down to the Tay. Indeed the position is generally well protected: there is even a slope to the west, so that only the northern side faced wholly open ground. The fort was unusually large, at around 3.9ha (9.6 acres) inside the ditches, but almost nothing is known about the interior. Indeed we cannot even be sure which way it faced: for the short axis road, which is usually (if not always) the *via principalis*, ran almost exactly across the fort's centre line, and no gates are visible on the east and west sides.

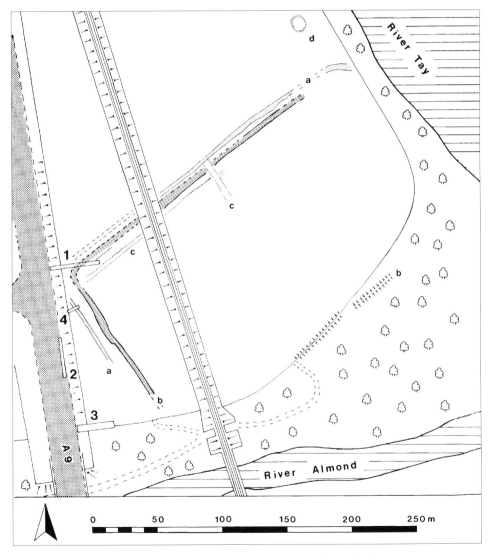

68 Plan of Bertha Roman fort. *Reproduced by kind permission of D. Gallagher*

The one excavation on the site took place in 1973, and concentrated on the north-west defences, in advance of encroachment into that area by a widening of the modern A9 (Adamson 1979 and Adamson & Gallagher 1986). It found (unusually) just a single V-shaped ditch (up to 2m wide and 1.7m deep) which, in one trench, was found to be clay revetted. Behind the ditch lay a shallow trench, filled with water-worn stones, which acted as the base for a (c.5.1m-thick) turf rampart, behind which was a gravel-built *intervallum* road. The ditch showed slight indications of a recut but, otherwise, the defences seemed to be of just one building period. It is probable, however, that there is greater complexity to discover, because the finds from the site show clear evidence for both Flavian and Antonine occupations. Even before the 1973 excavation, a Flavian dish had been found (Hartley 1972, 5), and an (probably post-Hadrianic) inscription to *Discipulinae Augusti* (the emperor's discipline) had been recovered from the Almond (Keppie 1983, 402). To this, the excavation added a small corpus of material of mixed date, and this has since been augmented by fieldwalking finds, most of which proved to be Antonine (Woolliscroft 2002, 40ff). It is a pity that the site is not more productive of cropmarks, which might have helped to clarify matters, but it is to be hoped that further surface work will be done in the near future.

Outside the fort, a number of features are known, and others have been suggested. The 1973 excavation found an area of cobbling a little to the fort's south-west, which may or may not be the incoming road. There are also antiquarian descriptions of what was probably a mix of cremations and ritual deposits, being eroded from the north bank of the Almond, a little further to the west. Some of these features took the form of c.5ft 6in (1.68m) deep pits which, when eroded in section, were described as 'pillars' of different soil colour, at the bottom of which were pots that sound like small amphorae (none have survived). The vessels contained ashes, and one also held a corroded helmet, part of a spear and a lead ingot (Stuart 1852, 206), whilst another held a glass phial (Cant, in Adamson 1774, 52). There are also native Iron Age features around the fort. One probable roundhouse has long been known from the air immediately to the north of the fort's north-east corner (*68*, d; NO 09782697), whilst, in 2003, a knot of similar houses was photographed from the air by Torrance, some 300m further north, at NO 096272 (neg in the Roman Gask Project archive).

The possible continuation of the Roman road beyond the Tay will be dealt with in the next chapter, but a number of antiquarian writers report seeing the remains of a bridge across the river at Bertha, which they claim (without presenting evidence) to be Roman. Moncrieff offers the following description (*OSA*, 15, 528):

The foundation of a wooden bridge thrown over the Tay at this place still remains. It consists of large oak planks, from six to eight inches in diameter, fastened together by long skairs, but coarsely jointed and surrounded with clasps of iron, frequently twisted. [...] I caused one of them to be raised some years ago at the request of Dr Hope, who assured me that the fabric of the wood was not in the least decayed.

By the time of the *New Statistical Account* in 1845, the Rev. W. Liston still claimed to be able to see these remains (NSA 10, 169), as did Stuart, shortly before (1852, 208). They had vanished by the early twentieth century but, in the 1960s, local amateur archaeologist, D.M. Lye, persuaded a sub-aqua club to examine the river bed hereabouts in the hope of finding surviving evidence (correspondence in Perth Museum). Nothing seems to have been found, however, and we can only admit that we have no idea whether the structure was Roman, or even exactly where it was.

The Tay is a major river at Bertha, but it still has something of the quality of an overgrown mountain stream, being relatively shallow, fast flowing and with occasional rapids. It would have been possible to get small river boats up past the fort, perhaps even as far as Inchtuthil: but ocean-going vessels, even the fairly small ships of Roman times, could not have progressed beyond Perth. In the first years of the third century, however, the area was reoccupied by the Emperor Septimius Severus (193-211), and a much larger (12ha (30-acre)) fortress was built at Carpow (NO 207179), which may have been designed to hold half a legion (*colour plate 28*). This site lies 13.6km (8½ miles) downstream, on the south side of the Tay Estuary, just below its confluence with the Earn. Here, it would have been accessible by much larger vessels and so could have acted as a logistics base and, although no trace has been found, it would come as no surprise if an equivalent Flavian fort was eventually to come to light, that might have acted as a transshipment point. That said, there is a curious little (*c*.0.51ha (1.27 acre)) enclosure at St Madoes (NO 209196), on the opposite shore of the estuary. This is usually described as a temporary camp and is currently undated. It also now fronts onto a marshy area, which denies it easy access to open water: but it is remarkably small for a marching camp and it is possible that it served as some sort of fortified harbour installation. If so, there is a similar, if slightly larger, site some 40 miles further to the north-east, at Dun (NO 689595), on the north shore of the Montrose Basin, which might have fulfilled a similar role.

Quite how Fife fitted into the Flavian occupation still remains uncertain: no great effort seems to have been made to monitor movements into and out of the area, and no permanent Roman installations have yet been found there. Some Roman activity is attested, because there are known, if undated, temporary camps

69 The Newton enclosure from the air

at Auchtermuchty (NO 242118) and Edenwood (NO 357116), and a probable third at Bonneytown (NO 546127). In 2003, the Roman Gask Project detected a large enclosure from the air, at Newton, Collessie (NO 291132), which did initially look like a fort (69). It was certainly a good location, since it sat right at the junction of two major north–south and east–west routes through the peninsular. Nevertheless, a large-scale geophysical survey disproved the identification, and so we are still lacking any evidence that the area was occupied. Some have suggested that its inhabitants, the Venicones, had allied themselves with Rome, and so did not need to be occupied militarily (e.g. Hanson 1987, 157): but, although this is perfectly possible, it cannot yet be confirmed. Indeed, it might be equally valid to argue that the lack of forts shows that the Romans were unable to conquer the area (or had just not yet got round to it) and we will have to wait for additional information before we can discuss the matter with more confidence.

5

THE STRATHMORE FORTS

No temporary camps have yet been found at Bertha, but at least two are known on the opposite side of the Tay. The first is the 48.6ha (120-acre) enclosure of Grassy Walls, which lies on higher ground, c.750m to the north-east of Bertha (NO 105280). The other is the somewhat smaller camp of Scone Palace (NO 104272), which lies east of the fort, on lower ground, beside the river. The latter is probably around 25.5ha (63 acres) but, as it is partially overlain by Scone race course, much of it has never shown from the air. Neither of these sites has been closely dated, but both have *titulus*-type gates. In addition to the confirmed camps, Maitland (1757, 198f) recorded an enclosure which had supposedly yielded a gold coin, and was consequently known as Gold Castle. This structure has since been seen from the air (RCAHMS 1994, 54f) and sits right on the bank of the Tay, 1,100m to the north of Bertha (NO 096278), with ditches on only the three land-ward sides. It seems to occupy an area of c.1.5ha (3.7 acres), but its nature and date remain uncertain.

As yet, there is no firm evidence that the Gask chain of towers and fortlets resumes beyond the Tay, although the possibility that the road may continue will be dealt with below. Certainly, no more Kaims Castle-type fortlets have been found, and only one more watchtower is known with certainty: but hope still endures (e.g. Breeze 2000, 56), and more sites may yet await discovery. Indeed, one may already have come to light, in the form of a double-ditched enclosure at Woodhead (NO 144347). The site is only known from air photographs and, at present, it remains unclassified (*colour plate 22*). It sits beside a small prehistoric settlement, but does not appear to belong: for, in contrast to the light, roundhouse foundation slots, it shows the much clearer cropmarks of fairly heavy ditches. Nor does it look like a barrow; but it does closely resemble the double-ditched, southern Gask towers, such as Shielhill North and South. It has a fairly circular outer ditch, *c.*25m in diameter, and probably *c.*1.5m wide. The inner ditch is more sub-rectangular; it measures *c.*16m in diameter and appears to be a little narrower. The site occupies a high point, with a breathtaking field of view, particularly to the north and west, over the Tay. It is intervisible with many miles of the Highland fringe and, perhaps most importantly, with the fortress of Inchtuthill. At the same time, it stands at the top of a steep, north-west facing, slope which would leave it fully exposed to the prevailing west winds and the worst of the winter weather. In these circumstances, one would expect a native site to follow the normal local preference towards an east-facing entrance: but the ditches are unbroken on this side and, although the cropmark evidence is tenuous, it is probable that the entrance faced north-west. As yet, there is no evidence whatever that the site is Roman, other than its suggestive shape: but if it is, it is a long way from a fort and so seems unlikely to have stood alone. It might, thus, be an indicator that there are more – possibly many more – towers still to find and, as always, it will be interesting to see what future flying might reveal.

CARGILL

Thirteen kilometres (8.2 miles) to the north-north-east of Bertha, we reach the twin Roman forts of Cargill, where a small fort, that might more properly be called a large fortlet (NO 163377), and a full-sized auxiliary fort (NO 166379) sit just 270m apart (*colour plates 23* and *24*). They lie atop a slight rise on the southern side of the Tay-Isla confluence, with useful views in all directions. The site is 4.8km (3 miles) downstream (south-east) from Inchtuthil, and its strategic potential, at the mouths of both Strathmore and Strathtay, is obvious. Indeed, its continued importance in later periods is marked by the presence of Castle Hill Motte a few hundred metres to the west, and the former royal castle of Kinclaven on the opposite side of the Tay. Neither of the Roman sites can be seen on the ground, but both were discovered during the Second World War by Flt Lt Eric Bradley, who was then an RAF flying instructor, stationed at Scone airfield. Bradley himself seems not to have taken photographs, because of the war-time shortage of film, but fairly accurate sketches of both installations survive in a 1941 correspondence with O.G.S. Crawford (now in Perth Museum), and both have since been photographed many times.

The fortlet (*70* and *colour plate*) stands above the Isla, with the ground to its north sloping down steeply towards the water. It is approximately playing

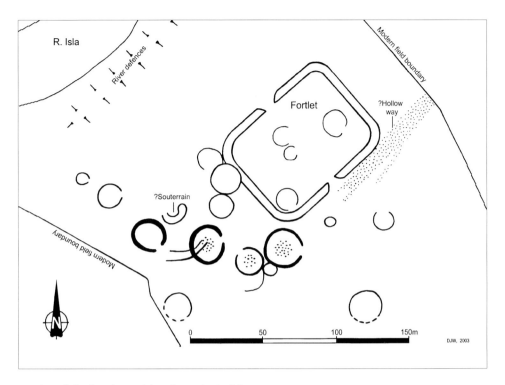

70 Cargill fortlet, the aerial and geophysical features

card-shaped, and has a double ditch with parrot-beak entrance breaks for just two gates: in the centre of the north-west and south-east sides. The rampart position is uncertain, but the site measures 63m (south-east to north-west) x 83m (south-west to north-east) over the inner ditch. This gives it an area of 0.5ha (1.24 acres), which is close to 1 *heredium*: a standard Roman land surveying measure. A small excavation was conducted by St Joseph, in 1965, and, although this was never fully published, a brief note did appear in print (DES 1965, 30). This records the ditches as V-shaped in profile, with the inner ditch larger than the outer: at 2.59m wide x 1.37m deep (as opposed to 1.5m wide and 1.07m deep). No trace of buildings was uncovered by the single trench dug in the interior, which may mean that the foundations have been ploughed away. The field has certainly been long under cultivation but, as the size and location of the trench remains unpublished, this might also reflect an element of bad luck on the part of the excavators in the positioning of their work, and the site might still reward future study.

In 2003, the site was subjected to a geophysical survey by the authors. This provided greater precision to the known plan of the defences and, in particular, showed that the south-east gate (which had never shown well from the air) was, as expected, a mirror image of its north-western counterpart. The survey's main contribution, however, was to provide far more information on a group of native roundhouses, to the fortlet's south and west. Seven such structures were already known from the air, but the survey more than doubled this number, to at least 19, which ranged from 8.2-22.6m in diameter. In addition, a curved stone feature was detected, which is probably a souterrain: an underground storage building, characteristic of the Roman period Iron Age in this area. Moreover, fieldwalking carried out during the survey picked up Flavian material from this settlement, which suggests that at least parts of it were in use during the Roman occupation.

The fort (*colour plate 24* and *71*) stands above the Isla, further along the same ridge, with the ground sloping away steeply to the north and west, but more level to the south and east. It measures 170m (north-west to south-east) x 115m (south-west to north-east) over the rampart: an area of 1.94ha (4.8 acres). On its south-west side it has the usual double ditch, with a parrot-beak entrance break. But, on the tactically weaker north-east side, and at least the eastern half of the south-east side, the fort had a triple ditch, reminiscent of Doune, with variant parrot-beaks in which the middle ditch simply stops where it meets the inward swing of the outer, rather than making its own inward turn. The *via principalis* shows from the air, running across the fort's short axis, slightly to the north-west of the long axis centre point, which should mean that the fort faced north-west, towards the river. If so, its front gate faces into what is probably a large annexe, which also shows a triple ditch. The exact size and shape of this enclosure remain unknown, despite a geophysical survey of the fort by the authors. At present a 166m length of the north-east defences is known, which runs at a slightly more westerly angle than the fort's defences. These end on the edge of an obvious erosion terrace, just short of the modern river bank: which means that the north-west defences may have been washed away. Alternatively, the annexe might originally have run right down to the water, but been left open at the bank, to use the river as a defence, or even to act as a defended landing area. For the Isla is easily navigable by small craft at this point, and so supplies could have been brought in by water.

As yet there is nothing to say whether or not the annexe had a rampart, although this seems highly probable. Likewise, the course of its western defences also remains a mystery. The ground to the west of both the fort and annexe is now badly disturbed by the modern A93, and the ditches may have been destroyed, or obscured, by its construction. The road does, though, follow an erosion scarp, so it is possible that the defences were washed away before it was even built. Assuming there ever was a complete circuit of defences, the annexe would have covered at least 1.1ha (2.7 acres) but, depending on the age of the

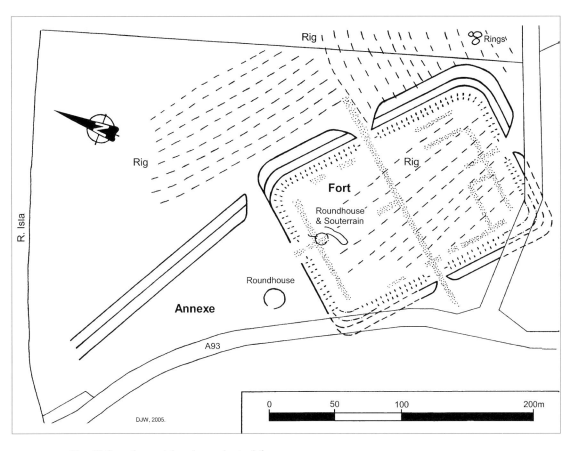

71 Cargill fort, the aerial and geophysical features

erosion scarp, it could have been significantly larger. The entrance arrangements, both between the fort and the annexe, and between the annexe and the outside world are also interesting. At the fort's north-east corner, the geophysical survey showed the triple ditches running together to form a single line, which appears to run along the whole of the north-west side, except for a simple gate break. The only external entrance through the surviving annexe defences also lies at the fort's north-east corner. Here the coalescing fort ditches produce the effect of one half of a parrot-beak and one might have expected the annexe ditches to mirror this. Instead, they form what is in effect a reverse parrot-beak, in which the inner ditches swing out to joint the outer, rather than, as is usual, vice versa. The result is an entrance, *c*.11m wide but, even assuming the presence of a rampart, the nature, and even the existence, of any gate structures can only remain speculative.

As with the fortlet, an excavation has been conducted by St Joseph and, although this work too remains unpublished, short notes, again, reached print. Much of the dig seems to have concentrated on the area of the north-east defences, just behind the *via principalis*. It sectioned a turf rampart, up to 6.4m wide, whose front and rear rested on a timber foundation. Other work found a similar picture on the south-west and north-west ramparts, and showed that the latter had undergone substantial repairs on at least two occasions, which suggests a reasonably long life. In the north-west, facing the annexe, the excavation failed to find a ditch, which contradicts the geophysical results, but it is not known how extensive a search was made. In the south-east, however, the V-shaped inner ditch began 2.4m out from the rampart, and measured 3.2m wide x 2.2m deep. The middle ditch lay 6m further out and was almost identical in size, whilst the outer ditch lay 8.2m further still and was 3.7m wide x 1.8m deep. Only a little work was done in the interior, but this too revealed evidence of multiple phases. In the south-east area, part of a large beam-founded granary was found beside the defences, south of the *via principalis*. This was 9.1m wide and at least 24.7m long (the full extent was not traced). Seventeen parallel sleeper beams were found (six more than in a complete Fendoch granary), and a posthole at the *via principalis* end might represent part of a covered loading bay. Closer to the rampart was a 4m-wide building that appeared to be secondary, since it impinged on the (4.3m-wide) *intervallum* road. Small-scale trenching in the annexe found three construction trenches, for a timber building, close to the fort. These too were secondary, as two of them had been dug through fallen rampart material: but they, in turn, had been burnt before the last of the rampart repairs. The excavation produced few finds, but what there was suggested Flavian only occupation, probably ending in the mid AD 80s. The dating picture has, however, been questioned by coin finds made during our own geophysical survey. These include coins from early in the reign of Vespasian (69-79), one of which showed little or no wear, so that it was probably lost soon after being issued. As might be expected, there were also coins of Domitian (81-96). More surprisingly, however, the site also produced a coin of the Emperor Trajan (AD 98-117) and two of Hadrian (AD 117-138). All three of these were found in worn condition, suggesting lengthy circulation before loss and, as this might be a pointer to Antonine (or even Severan) occupation, it will be interesting to see what future excavations might reveal. The site also produced two mid-third-century radiate copies (official forgeries), one of which may date to the reign of Claudius II (AD 268-70). At present we have no indications of a Roman military presence in Scotland at that time and so these coins may well come from the nearby native settlement.

No temporary camps are known in the vicinity but, like the fortlet, air photography has detected ring features, likely to be roundhouses, around the fort. In this case, however, the features lie mostly inside the defences and so will not be contemporary with the Roman occupation. Two are known with certainty: one in the annexe, close to the fort's north-west corner, and one just inside the fort's north-west gate. For the most part, the geophysical survey merely confirmed the aerial evidence, but it did add two additional details. The first is a knot of ring features, to the east of the fort's south-east corner, which may be a group of small roundhouses. Perhaps more importantly, however, a c.19m-long curving feature, which might be a souterrain, was found attached to the north gate roundhouse. Without excavation, the chronological relationship between these features and the Roman fort must remain uncertain, although the strength with which they show, both on air photographs and through geophysics, might suggest that they post-date the occupation.

Although both Cargills at least began with the Flavian occupation, they seem unlikely to be exact contemporaries: if only because it is hard to see the point of placing two significant garrisons so close together. In fact, a very few examples are known, elsewhere in the empire, of contemporary forts in very close proximity. For example, Osterburken, on the German Limes has two forts which are actually joined; whilst Welzheim, on the same frontier, has two only 500m apart. There, Baatz (1997, 14ff) has suggested that the arrangement may have been meant to allow long range strategic mobility for the cavalry unit known to have been stationed in the larger fort: by leaving a smaller infantry contingent in the small fort to continue with frontier watch duties during times when the *ala* was absent. The site does, after all, lie between the Rhine and Danube frontiers, either of which could need reinforcement in a crisis, and the long distances involved might mean that the larger unit could be away for prolonged periods. Whatever the case, the situation at Cargill is likely to have been very different: for the operational area in northern Scotland is vastly more compact and we, anyway, have no idea what type of garrisons the forts held. The likelihood is, therefore, that one of the two Cargill sites replaced the other, in some reworking of the area's defences, although which replaced which is currently impossible to say.

BLACK HILL

Cargill has an associated watchtower, which sits atop a steep-sided hill, 1,500m to the north-east (NO 176392). It is still clearly visible as a well-preserved earthwork (*72*), in woodland on the hill's northern summit: and takes the form of a square

72 Black Hill tower

rampart, with rounded corners, surrounded by a ditch and with a single entrance facing the north-west. The site now lies in trees but, without them, it would enjoy superb views in all directions, that would stretch for miles up Strathmore. Both Cargill forts are in full view and, from the likely height of a Roman tower, Inchtuthil might also have been in sight, so the installation could have served as a signals relay, as well as an observation post.

Black Hill has been subjected to two excavations. The first, in 1903 (Abercromby (1904, 82ff), concluded that it was an Iron Age house, albeit one containing Roman nails, and with a Roman-style V-shaped ditch (2.75m wide x c.1.4m deep). But, in 1939, a second examination by Richmond (1940, 37ff) was able to make more sense of the site, despite the considerable damage done by the earlier work (*73*). In particular, three large postholes (for (30cm)^2 posts) were found inside the rampart, which seemed likely to have formed parts of a square building with sides of 4.27m. This fits well within the size range of the Gask towers, although no closely datable finds were made. There was, though, one slight design difference, in that one of the posts was located a third of the way along the structure's south-east side, rather than at a corner. Richmond, who was only used to four-post Roman towers, explained this as a door post, and he may well be correct. Indeed Abercromby refers to the discovery of a stone in the same vicinity which might be a pivot block. But the post seems unduly large for such a non-structural role, so it is worth pointing out that Roman towers have since been found (on exposed positions) with 12 posts (Woolliscroft & Swain 1991): and, given the damaged state of this site when Richmond dug, he can hardly be blamed if he failed to recognise another.

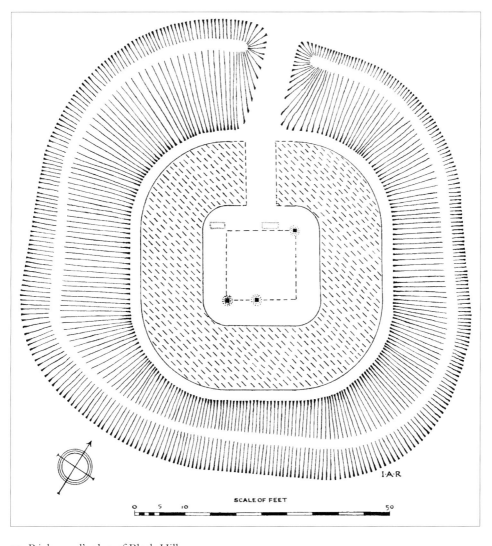

SCALE OF FEET

73 Richmond's plan of Black Hill

At the time Richmond's report was written, neither of the Cargill forts had been discovered, and so the tower's true context could not be discerned. As a result, Richmond produced a theory that, although perfectly understandable at the time, was to influence and mislead scholars for decades as to the workings of the Roman occupation of this area. Five hundred metres to the north of the tower, a long earthwork, called the Cleaven Dyke, had long been known (*colour plate 25*). A 1.8km-stretch remains visible today, running in a linear clearing through woodland (NO 156408-172399) and air photography has extended the confirmed length to *c*.2.2km (1.4 miles). The monument consists of a broad, but low, central bank, flanked on either side by a shallow ditch: to create a feature 54m wide. The Dyke was too insubstantial to be a defence, but it would have been difficult to cross without noticing and Richmond hypothesised that it might have been intended as a highly visible demarcation line for a Roman military zone. He also suggested that the known stretch might be just a small part of a much longer system, from the Isla, perhaps as far as the hills around Dunkeld: a total of *c*.10km (6 miles). In this model, Black Hill would have acted as a security feature, supervising the Dyke: and he anticipated the discovery of other towers to form a series along the line. The idea seems to have appealed, and it soon became established as what has come to be known as a 'factoid', in other words something generally accepted as fact, but for which there is actually no real evidence. Indeed it was still being retailed by serious scholars over 40 years later. In the 1990s, however, the feature was shown to be a very much older Neolithic cursus (a site type not known to exist in Scotland in Richmond's day), which has no connection whatever with the Roman period (Barclay & Maxwell 1998).

CARDEAN

The fort of Cardean (NO 289460) lies 14.5km (9 miles) east-north-east of Cargill, and 1.3km to the north of the village of Meigle. It sits on a flat-topped, free draining promontory, between the Dean Water and the River Isla and is, at present, some 600m east of their confluence; historical records and old river channels make it clear that the junction was once much closer. To the north, south and west, the ground slopes down almost vertically towards the rivers, and the site enjoys good views in these directions, albeit now partly obscured by woodland. Only the east side is easily accessible, since the ground here is fairly level, and this is also reflected in a poorer field of view. The fort is, however, carefully positioned to incorporate a small glacial gully into its eastern defences and, with the help of this feature, its ditch system and annexes combine to cut off the entire promontory.

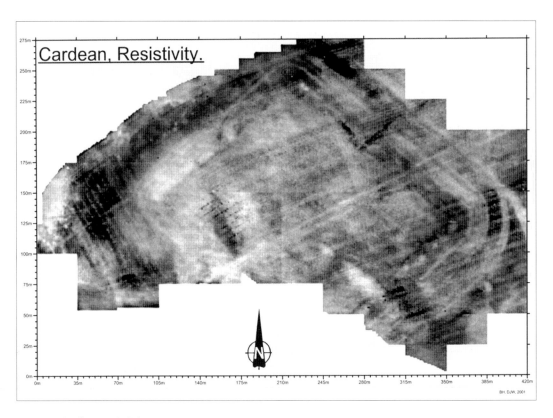

74 Cardean, resistivity survey

The fort has been known since the eighteenth century (Crawford 1948, 88) and must have been visible as an upstanding monument until the early nineteenth. Even today, parts of the site can still be made out, despite ploughing and the former presence of a road and country house, although the surface marks are extremely faint. It does, however, produce, sometimes excellent, cropmarks (*colour plate 26*), and has been photographed many times since its rediscovery by Crawford (1939, 287f), during a flight made in 1939. This aerial data, supplemented by geophysical work, by ourselves (*74*), allows us to say that the fort measured 209m (north–south) x 177m (east–west), over the ramparts: an area of 3.7 ha (9.14 acres). This makes it one of the largest forts in the region and, indeed, in the whole of Britain. Antiquarian sources mention finds recovered on the promontory, but very few survive, and most of our knowledge of the site's history comes from large-scale excavations (*75*), conducted between 1966 and 1975, by Professors J. and A.S. Robertson (not related). These confirmed a Flavian date (with no sign of Antonine reuse), along with Iron Age activity, both before and after the Roman occupation.

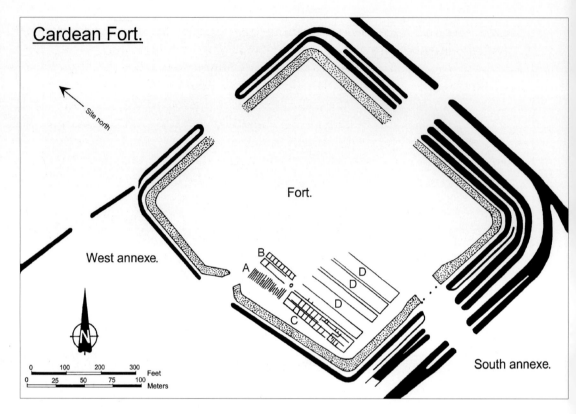

75 Cardean, excavation plan

The fort's ditch system is unusually varied, and only the north-west side has the normal double ditch, with parrot-beak entrance break (75). The north-east side has up to four ditches, whose gate arrangements are not clear: and, although not all of these have been sectioned, the geophysical evidence suggests that the outer is much larger than the rest. The south-west and south-east sides are both protected by annexes and, as at Cargill, the south-west side has only a single ditch. The south-east side, however, has up to six ditches, of which only the first two from the rampart form a parrot-beak. They also vary enormously in size. The average ditch profile for the fort is around 3m wide x 1.5m deep but, on this side, the second ditch can be as small as 60cm x 40cm, whilst the fourth was a massive 8m x >3m.

The southern annexe ditch joins the outermost fort ditch at the south-east corner, and seems also to have been unusually large: for a partial section, cut in 1967, produced a depth of over 3m. Part of this annexe has been eroded away by the Dean Water (as has part of the south-west corner of the fort's ditch), so it is not possible to estimate its original size. Nor do we know what access it had to the outside world, except to say that no entrances have been detected through the surviving part of the defences. The west annexe, on the other hand, had a lighter ditch and, although it was not sectioned, it seems likely from the geophysical evidence, to be more akin to the fort average, already cited. It has an entrance break, *c.*45m west of the fort but, although it starts at the fort's north-west corner, it seems to leave another slight break at the junction. The extent of this annexe too remains unknown: for the southern defences, assuming they ever existed, have again been eroded by the Dean Water. Indeed, it is not impossible that the two annexes are actually one vast enclosure, covering two whole sides of the fort. Even its western limits are open to question, for no defences have been found on that side. We have usually assumed that it would have continued to the edge of the plateau (*c.*100m from the fort) and that the western defences would also have been lost to erosion. There is, though, one air photograph (RCAHMS neg: A64833) which hints that its northern ditch might have stretched beyond the plateau, down to the bank of the Dean Water. This is a possibility worth testing, for the river is navigable to small boats at this point, as is the whole of the Isla down to Cargill; if the annexe did reach this far, it may have lain open-ended to the water, and acted, at least in part, as a fortified landing area.

The *via principalis* runs between the south-west and north-east gates, which themselves lie a little north of centre on the long axis sides, to leave the fort facing north-west. At the south-west gate, the turf ramparts swing in to form a somewhat asymmetrical version of the recessed gates seen elsewhere. Little is known about the north-west and north-east gates, but the south gate has no re-entrant, although there were signs that the rampart may have thickened here. Virtually nothing is known of the gate structures, because neither of the two excavated gates provided data. The south-west gate had been disturbed by an early modern road (erroneously marked as Roman on O.S. maps), whilst the work at the south-east gate yielded only a few pits, which were too small to have held tower posts, and may well belong to a later phase of activity. In the *intervallum*, the excavations found what may have been an interval tower on the north-west defences, virtually the only one seen in the area, whilst the geophysical survey detected a series of probable rampart ovens. Air photography has long detected what appeared to be parts of the fort's internal road system but, on excavation, these features proved to lie well above the Roman levels, often overlying Flavian buildings and abandonment deposits. They are thus post-Roman in date and may relate to the gardens of the much later country house.

The internal buildings were mostly founded on posts, set in construction trenches. In the south-west corner, a series of long, rectangular buildings were located (75, D) all of which seem to be barracks. Only one was excavated in detail (75, C and 76), but this showed clear signs of two construction periods. The primary building was at least 50m long and consisted of 10 *contubernia*, separated by a 1.2m-wide alley from a substantial centurions' quarters. Areas of dark staining in the floors of some of the *contubernia*, combined with finds of horse equipment, might suggest the presence of a cavalry or *equitata* unit. The structure was later rebuilt from the ground up (very slightly to the south of its original position), as a narrower building of similar length. This contained at least four rooms, but there is no sign of a centurions' quarters or of the longitudinal division that would normally be expected in a barrack. Its function is thus uncertain, but a further poorly understood building was constructed across a 3.65m-wide alley to the north-east.

To the north of the barrack, and separated from it by a road (8.54m wide), was a granary (75, A and 77) and, again, two phases can be distinguished. Both front onto the *via principalis* (although the smaller, earlier structure was set well back from its side), but neither shows evidence for a loading bay. The first was a post-founded structure, just 11.90m long and 9.8m wide, built in the centre of a larger plot. This was later replaced by a post-trench founded granary, 29.30m long, but still 9.8m wide. Despite the large size of the secondary building, comparison with the similar sequence at Strageath would suggest that there would still have been at least one more granary at Cardean. This has not been located, but it may have lain at the other end of the *via principalis* or even facing the known example, on the opposite side the road.

To the east of the granary, but also aligned on the main street, were two further rectangular structures (75, B). The first seems to have been early, for it was partly overlain by an alley which flanked the granary. At the rear, it ended short of the road which separated it from the barracks, and thus left a small yard, in one of whose corners a possible well was encountered. The building itself was only partially excavated, but it was at least 21.25m long x 3m wide. It seems to have been open-ended towards the backyard, whilst the one room partition found lay towards the front. There was no conclusive evidence for its use, but similar structures at Corbridge and Ribchester served, respectively, as a storage area and a workshop (Hanson *et al.* 1979, 78 and Buxton & Howard-Davies 2000, 105–15). The latter is a particularly close parallel, so it is tempting to see the Cardean example as a *fabrica*: such a building must certainly have existed somewhere in the fort, because workshop debris, including a large number of copper-alloy working crucibles, was found dumped, just outside the south gate.

The area to the east of this building was originally left empty, and apparently fenced off from the rest of the fort, but later another long, rectangular building was constructed here. This was at least 30m long (with projecting rear end-walls)

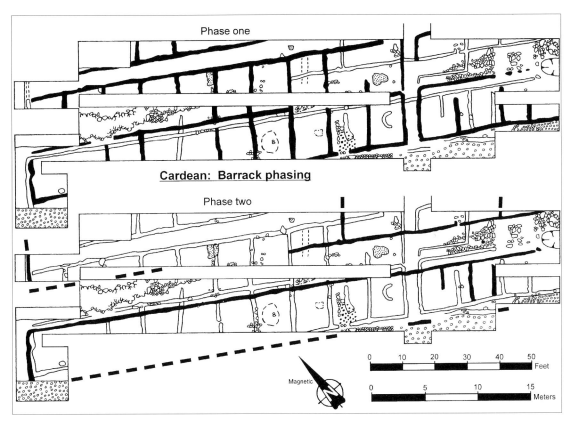

Phase one

Cardean: Barrack phasing

Phase two

0   10   20   30   40   50
Feet

Magnetic

0   5   10   15
Meters

76 Cardean, two-phased barrack plan

by 4.3m wide, and was divided internally into eight, roughly equal-sized (4.27m x 3m) rooms. These contained areas of burning, which might indicate hearths built against the walls, but the evidence was such that demolition bonfires remain a possibility. This may be some special type of barrack (Robertson 1979, 44), one wing of a larger building, such as an extended *praetorium* (Johnson 1983, 137f), or one of the so-called 'hospitals', seen elsewhere. Whatever the case, the building produced an usually rich finds assemblage, including Samian pottery, glass, a bust of Minerva (possibly a decoration from a chest), a tinned copper-alloy spoon, and a silver coin. Even the coarse wares (e.g. *mortaria*) found here were different from those from the rest of the fort: being from northern Gaul, rather than from Britain. This sets it firmly apart from the neighbouring structure, which contained none of these exotica, but did contain a substantial number of iron objects. It is probable, therefore, that the building had a high-status, residential or storage function, and there is certainly nothing to support an interpretation as a medical facility.

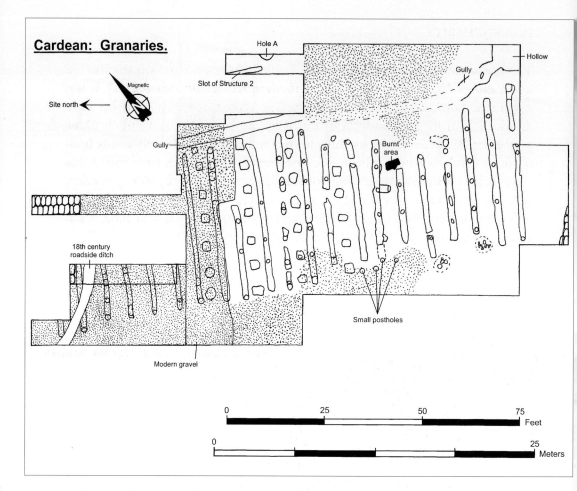

Cardean: Granaries.

Hole A

Slot of Structure 2

Hollow

Gully

Magnetic

Site north

Gully

Burnt area

18th century roadside ditch

Small postholes

Modern gravel

0   25   50   75 Feet

0   25 Meters

77 Cardean, the two-period granary

Four hundred and fifty metres to the east of the fort is a large temporary camp, at least 49.6ha (122.5 acres) in area, which might have a smaller camp inside it. The fort also has a great deal of native settlement around it (*89*). The western ditches cut a number of roundhouses, which must thus be earlier in date, although they produced first-century pottery and so must have been in use until shortly before the fort was built. There were also roundhouses overlying the granary which produced first- and second-century pottery, and are thus post-occupation in date, but a so-called 'complex roundhouse' in the western annexe might be either pre- or post-Roman. There are more roundhouses immediately north of the fort, and a souterrain to its east, which might even be contemporary, although as yet there is no dating evidence to prove the point either way.

INVERQUHARITY

The next Strathmore site, Inverquharity (*colour plate 27*), lies 16.7km (10.4 miles) north-east of Cardean, to the north of modern Kirriemuir (NO 404581). It was discovered from the air in 1983 (Maxwell & Wilson 1987, 15f) and lies on a distinct (*c.*1km-long) promontory, formed by the South Esk and Prosen Water, on the north, and the Quharity Burn to the south. It slopes relatively gently from north to south, but its northern side ends in an almost sheer river cliff. It has reasonable views in almost all directions and provides a tactically strong position, well placed to monitor traffic along all three river valleys. Nothing can be seen on the surface, but the site has shown repeatedly from the air and, in 2002, it was also subjected to a geophysical survey by the authors (*78*).

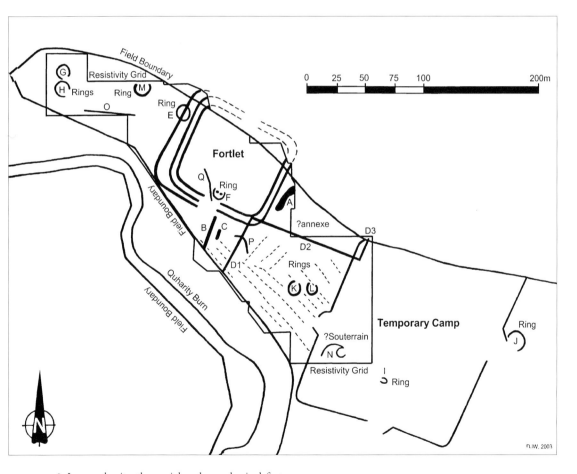

78 Inverquharity, the aerial and geophysical features

The site is often described as a fort, but it would probably be more correct to call it a large fortlet: for it is very similar in size to the smaller of the two Cargill sites. Most of the northern defences have been eroded away, but the geophysics located the north-west corner, which makes it possible to project that the site measured 68m (north–south) x 79m (east–west) over the inner ditch, to give an area of 0.52ha (1.28 acres). As at Cargill, there were no entrances in the short axis sides, but the one surviving gate, on the south side, would probably have been mirrored in the north. The site has a double ditch around its entire surviving circuit, with a third around the west side, and the western half of the south. Unlike other Flavian forts in the area, however, the ditches appear to remain completely separate at the gate, rather than forming parrot-beaks. A trench dug across the southern defences, but not yet properly published (Frere 1984, 274), found the two inner ditches to be 4.9m apart (centre to centre) and V-shaped. No width, depth or phasing data were provided, but rectified air photographs would suggest ditch widths of around 2-3m, with the third ditch perhaps a little larger. The excavations also found the postholes for the southern gate tower but, again, no more detail is available. No dating evidence was recovered, but the other forts in Strathmore were only occupied in the Flavian period, and Inverquharity also seems more likely to be Flavian than Antonine. If nothing else, it would be hard to imagine such a small installation standing alone here in the Antonine period: for it lies 45km (28 miles) to the north-east of Bertha, which is the nearest site known to have been active at the time (Woolliscroft 2002, 40ff). The possibility of Antonine activity at Cargill should be remembered, but even this would still leave it 32km (20 miles) from support. That said, Antonine sites of this size do exist: for example Rough Castle on the Antonine Wall, and so, on current evidence, such a dating cannot be flatly ruled out.

Outside the fortlet, a number of linear cropmarks have been sighted (*78*, B, C & D) which have generally been interpreted as annexes (Maxwell and Wilson 1987, 16). There has been no excavation on any of the features, however, and no certainty is possible: but Feature D seems unlikely to be Roman, since it makes sharply angular turns and crosses the fortlet ditches. The status of Features B and C is less certain. Feature C is reminiscent of a temporary camp *titulus*, but there does not seem to be a corresponding entrance break in Feature B so, although it is still possible that one or both may be Roman, there is no convincing evidence either way.

Further to the east is a small, Stracathro-type, temporary camp. As with the fortlet, the northern side has been eroded away but, again, part of the north-west corner has survived, making it possible to extrapolate the full circuit. There are signs that the camp was slightly irregular, however, so the reconstruction can only be approximate. The surviving west side, with both corners known, is 144m long, but the east side, with only one corner surviving, is already 159m long. If the full north-west corner turned an exact right angle, so that the north-east corner would have lain immediately north of the current erosion line, the camp would have covered *c*.2.2ha (5.5 acres): but this can only be regarded as a minimum. A section cut across the east ditch in 1984 (DES 1984, 35) showed it to be V-shaped, 1.8m wide x 0.9m deep, but no other details were published.

As elsewhere, there is a considerable knot of native structures around the Roman site, but none have been excavated, and we have no evidence for their date (*78*). Two, however, cannot be contemporary with the Roman occupation: for Feature F lies inside the fortlet and F's E is cut by its outer ditch. Two more sites (I & N), lie inside the temporary camp, which probably rules out occupation during the camp's own (possibly very short) usage, whilst another (J) lies uncomfortably close to the camp's east gate. Nevertheless (although it is speculation), it is not impossible that Features G, H and M, to the west of the fortlet, and F's K and L to its south-east, might have been contemporary with the occupation, whilst F's I, N and J could still post-date the camp, but still be contemporary with the fortlet. Perhaps the most interesting of these features is N. Air photography had already detected a *c*.25m curving structure at this point, which is thought to be a souterrain: but the geophysics added a 7-8m diameter roundhouse, which seems to be attached to it. Armit (1999) has suggested that souterrains may have been a specific native response to Roman military supply needs in the Flavian and (more particularly) Antonine periods. He suggests that they were built to store agricultural produce intended for the army, and then abandoned *en masse* in the late second and early third centuries. Aspects of this model have since been challenged (Coleman & Hunter, 2002, 95ff), but excavation on a site such as this, so close to a major Roman installation, might well provide a valuable expansion to our understanding of the role of these structures: and it is thus very much to be hoped that work will some day take place on either this site, or its close parallel outside the fortlet at Cargill.

The small size of the Inverquharity fortlet, coupled with the presence of a (probably) non-contemporary fort and fortlet at Cargill, has led to speculation that there may be a full-sized auxiliary fort still awaiting discovery in the neighbourhood: probably further downstream on the South Esk. Indeed, considerable aerial effort has gone into locating this putative site. Much of the search has concentrated on Finavon (NO 495575), a good bridging point on the river, now used by the modern A94, and the location of a known, titulate temporary camp. Flights over the area by the authors have also monitored a promontory inside a loop in the river at Tannadice (NO 473579), further to the west, but despite years of coverage, along many miles of the river, no new fort has been discovered and, although it may still eventually come to light, it may equally not have existed.

STRACATHRO

Twenty-two and a half kilometres (14 miles) east-north-east of Inverquharity, to the north of modern Brechin, lies the northernmost Roman fort yet found: Stracathro (NO 617657) (79). The site lies on a plateau south of the West Water, close to its confluence with the North Esk. To the north it tops a steep river cliff, which has encroached on the site since Roman times, but the south-west and south-east sides are fairly open and face onto level ground. The fort has good views in all directions, stretching for miles to the north, towards the Highland fringe. It is thus in a good position to control the North Esk valley and the main north-east to south-west route through Strathmore, whose modern embodiment, the A94 dual-carriageway, passes only 1,200m to the south.

Almost nothing is visible on the ground, but the site was discovered from the air in 1957 (St Joseph 1958, 91) and has shown again regularly since. The north-east corner has been washed away by the river, and the interior is partly obscured by a church and a minor road, which means that even the best cropmark years produce relatively uninformative images, but some useful data can still be gleaned. The north-west and south-west sides have a double ditch, but, like the larger of the Cargill sites, one of the tactically weaker sides, here the south-east, has a triple ditch. The situation on the north-east side remains unknown, thanks to erosion, tree cover and poor cropmark development, but there are faint signs that this side too might have a triple ditch. The visible gates have parrot-beak ditch breaks and, at the triple-ditched south-east gate, the middle ditch follows the same pattern as Cargill, by simply stopping where it meets the inward swing of the outer ditch, rather than making its own inward turn. The one visible short axis gate (the south-west) is located centrally but, on the long axis, the south-east gate appears to lie a little east of centre, suggesting that the fort faced north-east. In all, the fort measures *c.*183m (north-east to south-west) x 144m (north-west to south-east), inside the inner ditch, to give an area of *c.*2.6ha (6.4 acres).

Some excavation has taken place, but none of it has been properly published and both of the excavators involved are, sadly, now dead. In 1958, soon after the site's discovery, St Joseph sectioned the outer (third) ditch on the south-east side. This was found to be V-shaped, 4.27m wide x 2.1m deep, but no further information was given. Later, in 1969, A.S. Robertson conducted slightly larger-scale rescue work, ahead of the expansion of the church's burial ground. Short notes on her findings reached print (e.g. Robertson 1977, 72f) and we have been able to see the typescript of another short report, but we have not seen copies of her drawings or photographs, without which the written descriptions are ambiguous. To judge from the gate positions, the churchyard should lie in the *praetentura*, and this does

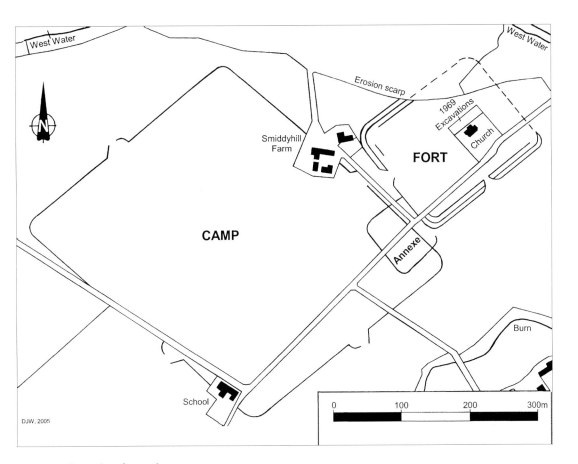

79 Stracathro fort and camp

seem to have been confirmed: for Robertson found a long, narrow building, founded on sleeper trenches, which appears likely to represent a barrack block. The building was orientated with its long axis running south-west to north-east, so that its short axis would have faced onto the *via principalis*, like the barracks at Fendoch. The building was not traced for its entire length and no width was recorded, but it was at least 27.4m long. The structure was subdivided into rooms, *c*.3m wide, and may have had a verandah along its long axis side. A piece of late first-century pottery was recovered, along with a Domitianic coin of AD 86 (lost in mint condition), all of which supports a Flavian date. The fort has a single-ditched annexe on its western side, with a south-east-facing entrance. Its ditch crosses that of a *c*.15.5ha (38-acre) temporary camp, but which came first remains unknown.

No more permanent installations are known with certainty to the north: for, although a number of sites in Moray have been suggested as forts by Jones and Daniels, the idea has since been largely dismissed (Gregory 2001). There are, however, quite a few more temporary camps, which extend at least as far as Auchinhove and Muiryfold, on the edge of Moray (NJ 463516 & 489520). Indeed, they may even reach Bellie (NJ 355611), just 2 miles from the Moray Firth, although the identity of that site is disputed.

There are a number of antiquarian reports of a road which may once have linked the Strathmore forts to Bertha. Most of these are extremely vague, however, and there is little hard evidence to support them. There are five fragments of old road which have been suggested as potential parts of this line, but one can be dismissed out of hand and the others have no dating evidence associated with them. For example, the Ordnance Survey shows a possible Roman road starting at NO 101269, just across the Tay from Bertha, and then running north-north-east towards the temporary camp of Grassy Walls (NO 105280). The evidence for this line was antiquarian reports, mostly from the eighteenth century, but nothing had been seen in modern times. In 2003, however, A.S. Torrance photographed a clear road line showing as a cropmark in oil seed rape (*80*), which was later confirmed by ourselves (Gask Project neg: 04CN2-8). This reaches the Tay *c*.200m upstream of the O.S. line (at NO 100271) and runs north-east to meet the O.S. line, just short of Grassy Walls, on the edge of Sherifftown Wood (NO 103276). An intensive search has so far failed to find any further lengths of this line, however, and there is currently no way of dating it.

Further to the north-east, air photography has picked up what looks like a road line, running for *c*.850m from Mains of Cargill (NO 161374), past the south side of the Cargill fortlet, to line up with the *via principalis* of Cargill fort. A number of field gates have been set on this line, which suggests that it was still used as a field road until relatively recently. Indeed one part remains visible as a slight hollow-way in the fortlet field, and others emerged on the geophysical survey (*70*). Again, however, its date remains unknown. The first series O.S. 6in map (of 1867) shows the local road and field systems essentially as they are today, with not so much as a track crossing the fortlet field. But Stobie's 1783 map of Perthshire shows the road to Coupar Angus running a little to the north of its present course. This would fit perfectly with the air photograph line, which lies 200m to the north of the modern road at this point: and the hollow-way certainly seems to have been in use after the fortlet's occupation, as it has encroached on the eastern end of its outer, south ditch. It is, of course, possible that the line came into use at a time when the large fort, although long abandoned, was still upstanding as an earthwork, and so forced any track running through it to pass through the Roman gates: but the air photographic and geophysical evidence show a perfectly straight alignment, at least 500m in length, oriented on the

80 Possible Roman road to the north of Bertha. *Photograph A.S.Torrance*

81 The possible Roman road in Caddam Wood

fort's main street. This would be rather more unusual for a medieval trackway and raises the possibility that the hollow-way might represent a reused section of Roman road. Nevertheless, this can only be speculation, until further work can be mounted, and the road may well date to the eighteenth century when straight roads, often modelled on Roman examples, were again being built in this area.

Two miles to the west-south-west of Cardean, at Bankhead of Kinloch (c.NO 260443), air photography has revealed a series of pits, which run for c.300m on either side of a linear cropmark (Gask Project neg: 05 CN10#17). The feature heads in the general direction of the fort and it is not impossible that it represents a Roman road flanked by quarry pits, but again, this cannot be stated with confidence until more is known.

Air photographs of Cardean show short spur roads emerging from each of the gates, but nothing linking up to them. There are, though, aerial indications of an 870m, straight section of road, running from the fort on a north-westerly heading, before uniting with a modern minor road at NO 297465. The Ordnance Survey marks this as 'Roman road, course of' but, in fact, this is impossible: for, although the road passes through the fort's south-west gate, it is stratigraphically later. It also crosses the eastern defences through the rampart, rather than by a gate. The route is, in fact, recorded as the old turnpike road to Forfar, running up from the old Bridge of Dean: a route that was later adjusted onto the line of the modern road with the construction of the new Dean bridge (Hoffmann forthcoming b).

The fourth road section lies in Caddam Wood, to the north of Kirriemuir. The 800m-long stretch runs straight (from NO 379554-386559), first as a running mound in thick woodland and then as a metalled forest track (81). Excavations in the 1960s by Mechan and Wilson (now being prepared for publication by ourselves) found a raised (5.8m-wide) causeway flanked by two flat-bottomed ditches. The construction was not unlike the Gask road in Parkneuk Wood, with a surface of rammed gravel and clay, set on a low turf *agger*, and the road heads in the general direction of Inverquharity. There is a long-standing folk tradition that the line is Roman, but the excavations produced no dating evidence and, as there are many early modern roads in the area with similar construction, we can only reserve judgment until additional data comes to light. That said, work by G.D.B. Jones in the 1990s (DES 1995, 94) might link it to a final possible road section, a little way to the west at Reedie (NO 357518-374562), to make a c.4km stretch. The latter sector was already reported as being old, and possibly Roman, in the eighteenth century (Maitland 1757, 200 & Roy 1793, 108), when modern road engineering in the area was in its infancy, and so a Roman date can certainly not be ruled out.

PART II

INTERPRETATION

6

THE HISTORY OF THE FIRST-CENTURY OCCUPATION

In 1425 a single manuscript of three hitherto lost works of the Roman politician and historian Tacitus surfaced in the library of the monastery of Hersfeld in Germany. These were the *Dialogue on the Orator*, the *Germania* and, most importantly for our purposes, the *Agricola* (Hoffmann 2004). The latter is a short, posthumous, account of the life of Tacitus' father-in-law, the ex-Consul, Gnaeus Julius Agricola; its fascination for British historians and archaeologists lies in the fact that Agricola was a former governor of Roman Britain. Indeed he served an unprecedentedly long, seven-year term of office. Tacitus credits him with leading the first-century invasion of Scotland; and his story has thus dominated studies of the occupation ever since. This little book is our only narrative source for this period of British history and has been studied and dissected more than almost any other non-religious text. Scholars have attempted to tease out ever more subtle nuances of meaning, as though this was all that was needed for some ultimate truth to be revealed. Unfortunately, the account is notoriously vague, especially when it comes to geographic detail, and the exact dating of the events described is also somewhat uncertain. Nevertheless, the sequence of events described can be summarised as follows.

Agricola was appointed as governor by the founder of the Flavian dynasty of emperors, Vespasian (69-79), who had himself served as a legionary commander during the original invasion of Britain under Claudius (41-54), in AD 43. The date of his appointment remains disputed. Most scholars now follow a chronology proposed by A.R. Birley (1976), which would put it in AD 77; but some still follow an older time-scale based on 78 (e.g. Fraser, 2005, 47). We tend towards the 77 start-date, although in practice it makes little difference. Agricola is said to have arrived in his province late in the season (*Agricola* 18), but showed resolution by immediately taking to the field to deal with the Ordovices: a tribe based in what is now north Wales, who had exploited the interregnum between governors to attack a cavalry *ala* stationed in their territory. The result, according to Tacitus, was a virtual genocide, with Agricola pursuing the tribe into the hills and all but exterminating them, to act as an example to others. He then went on to take Anglesey, which had been assaulted some years before by Suetonius Paulinus, but perhaps not properly consolidated, since that governor had had to withdraw to put down the revolt of Boudica.

Tacitus' account of the next campaigning season is a triumph of applied waffle. Agricola is portrayed as the soldiers' soldier: appearing everywhere, to encourage and cajole his men, choosing camp sites himself, building forts and bringing peoples to provide hostages. In the past, this has often been taken as an account of the conquest of northern England, and the tribe of the Brigantes (Salway 1982, 141): but, in fact, not a single place name is provided and we are given no real idea where these activities took place. The third season supposedly saw him advancing as far as the estuary of a river called the 'Taus', which is usually identified as the Tay (Rivet & Smith 1981, 470), although, in fact, there is no evidence to confirm it. This was followed by a year's consolidation, and then a fifth season for which Tacitus seems to describe an amphibious operation into an area facing Ireland (*Agricola* 24): possibly Argyll or Galloway. Agricola is even described as contemplating using a refugee Irish chieftain as an excuse for mounting an invasion of Ireland and Tacitus tells us that, in later years, his father-in-law often said that it could be taken and held by a single legion and a modest force of auxiliaries. The sixth season saw a return to campaigning in earnest, with combined operations of the army and fleet, north of the Forth and Clyde. At one point during this campaign Agricola made a serious mistake which almost cost him a legion. The enemy had been operating as three separate columns and Agricola divided his own forces to match: but the natives then united and, before Agricola had responded, the combined Caledonian army made a night attack on the sleeping camp of the IX legion. Agricola cannot have been far away, for he heard of the danger and rushed to their aid. The IX legion had been selected as the target because it was said to be the weakest of Agricola's legions, and this does seem to have been true, for we have an inscription (ILS 1025) that tells us that part of the legion was away on detached duty in Germany at this time. Whatever the case, however, the result was a rout, as the natives were caught in the jaws of a pincer movement, between the relief force and the occupants of the camp. Indeed, Tacitus states that if the enemy had not been able to escape into forests and marshes, the action might have ended the whole war. This was not to be, however, and Agricola's seventh and final season in Britain, AD 83 (or 84), culminated in the battle of Mons Graupius: the first recorded major battle in Scottish history. The battle site remains unknown, although hunting for it has become something of a cottage industry, but Tacitus tells us that Agricola's army faced at least 30,000 Caledonians, who had occupied strong positions on the hill. Yet, we are told, such was the quality of the Roman army, and Agricola's generalship, that the natives were defeated by the auxiliaries alone, without the legions needing to engage. The victory claimed was cataclysmic, with 10,000 natives dead, against just 360 from Agricola's army, of which only one was a Roman citizen: a somewhat impetuous auxiliary prefect called Aulus Atticus, who allowed an over-spirited horse to carry him too far into the enemy ranks.

All in all, Tacitus presents his father-in-law as the consummate provincial governor. Outside the campaigning seasons, he is pictured as a firm but fair, and above all honest, administrator: keen to weed out abuses, especially in the tax system, and to promote the adoption of Roman culture by the Britons. In the field he is presented as the greatest general yet to operate in the province, and as its ultimate conqueror. To judge from its temporary camps, the Roman army never got further than the fringes of Moray, and most of the Highlands remained untouched. Nevertheless, after the end of Agricola's term of office, Tacitus felt able to claim, in another work (*Histories* 2), that all Britain was now conquered, although he then goes on to add, rather cryptically, that it was then 'immediately thrown away', suggesting that the new territories were abandoned shortly thereafter.

Not surprisingly, archaeologists have long seized on this text, because it seemed to explain so much of what we find in northern Scotland. For here we have a fortified road, a remarkable collection of over 70 temporary camps, a full legionary fortress and numerous auxiliary forts, much of which seems to date to roughly this period. We also have coin evidence to suggest that it was, indeed, all abandoned in the mid-80s. There has been much argument over detail, but it has been increasingly assumed that the northernmost forts, including the Inchtuthil fortress, were built after Mons Graupius by Agricola's as yet unknown successor, and were thus only in use for perhaps a maximum of three years. On the other hand, some of the forts to the south of the Tay might be the work of Agricola himself, and so occupied for a little longer: albeit still perhaps no more than seven years. The Gask line itself was often seen as being shorter lived still: perhaps lasting for as little as a single year. This was partly because it was thought unlikely that it would have coexisted with the Highland line forts to the north and partly because, although the Gask forts had shown signs of two Flavian structural periods, which suggested a long enough occupation for repairs to become necessary, only a single period had been recognised in the towers and fortlets. This led to a number of suggestions for stages within the Flavian incursion where a short chronology of Gask might be fitted: of which the most popular was that it represented an attempt to hold onto Fife, in the late 80s (e.g. Breeze 1982, 65). The entire story seemed beautifully neat, and a model of the way in which archaeology and historical texts could be used in combination. All of today's Roman scholars grew up with it, and the present authors, like most, believed it implicitly. As we have seen, however, excavations on the Gask over the last decade have complicated matters immensely because, to our great surprise, we now find ourselves, at least potentially, with too much archaeology to fit.

It must be admitted that recent work has done only a little to fix the absolute dating of the Gask. Only two datable finds had been recovered from the towers before the mid-1990s, and our own work has added just four more: of which two come from the still rather mysterious site of Cuiltburn. Roman timber towers are notorious for their lack of finds, however, so this should come as no great surprise; and the latest material does at least provide additional support for the traditional Flavian date. This means that only the system's three fortlets remain undated: for no dating evidence has been recovered from any of them. The possibility exists, therefore, that they were not part of the Flavian system at all, but belonged to the Antonine period when the Gask forts came back into use as outposts to the Antonine Wall. Small fortlets of this type, although known in the first century, are much more a second-century phenomenon: the possibility of a Flavian system of forts and towers, and an Antonine one of forts and fortlets (rather than just forts as has usually been envisaged), seems a better balanced and so attractive scenario. There are, however, two strong counter arguments. Firstly, Glenbank, like the towers around it, had a double ditch, whilst the northern fortlets, like their towers, had single ditches; and, secondly, the fortlets seem to fit well into the pattern of tower spacings. These do appear to be strong indicators of integration between the two site types, and thus of a Flavian date for both.

If nothing else, the lack of finds from the Gask towers and fortlets may allow us to say something about the way they were occupied. For the absence of refuse makes it seem unlikely that the garrisons actually lived on site. This picture is further strengthened by the fact that, despite the excellent state of preservation of some of the sites, no Gask tower has yet produced evidence for hearths, which suggests that little cooking activity took place on site. The tower crews may, thus, have been outstationed on a shift basis from larger installations, most probably the forts. Any food eaten on duty might then have been in the nature of a cold packed lunch. Alternatively, it could have been cooked and eaten from metal mess tins, which would not have suffered the breakages inevitable with pottery and so will not have left fragments in the archaeological record. Cooking may have been done over braziers, which might, again, have left little archaeological trace: although the fact that no signs of pre-demolition fire ash have been found on any of the towers makes even this somewhat open to question. Indeed, the absence of hearths might even suggest that occupation was seasonal: for the sites would have been bitterly cold in winter without artificial heating. This does seem unlikely, however, and again braziers (perhaps at upper floor level) might have been used without leaving much trace, especially if the ash was dumped outside the ditch circuits (which usually represent the limits of excavation).

Where the most recent work has been of more help is in shedding light on the system's likely life-span; the single most serious complication for the traditional model is the discovery of multiple structural periods in some of the Gask towers. Of the 18 towers so far discovered on the system, two (Ardunie and Westmuir) have yet to see any excavation, and a further 10 were not excavated, or at least recorded, to a standard where such phasing might be expected to show. But, of the remaining six, four (Greenloaning, Blackhill Wood, Shielhill South and Huntingtower) show definite evidence for at least two (and, in some cases, three) tower builds, whilst the remaining two (Westerton and Moss Side) have produced features that could certainly be interpreted as rebuilding. In other words, of the sites dug to a standard where phasing might show, all have yielded conclusive or suggestive evidence for it. The full excavation data is available in the relevant site reports (referenced in chapters 3 and 4), but the potential significance of these discoveries is such that it is perhaps worth giving at least a sample here. The most important data are signs that the towers' main structural uprights were replaced in service: and a good example is the south-west tower post at Greenloaning. Figure *82* shows a section cut through the posthole. Layer 9 represents the remains of a pit, probably an early post pit, overlain by a layer of rammed gravel, L1a, which is presumably the primary interior metalling. Both layers have clearly been cut by a second pit, consisting of at least layers 3, 4, 5, 6 and 7, which are fill layers, holding the pipe for a now vanished post (L2) against the pit side. The pit has then been overlain by a second layer of metalling (L1) which extends up to the sides of the post itself. There are thus two clear phases present. This still leaves one slight difficulty, however, for layer 4a, which also cuts layers 1a and 9, appears to have been cut in its turn by the secondary post-pit. It is, of course, possible that this layer represents the remains of a backfilled demolition pit, dug to extract the primary post; but this would imply that this hypothetical feature had then been filled in prior to the second post-pit being

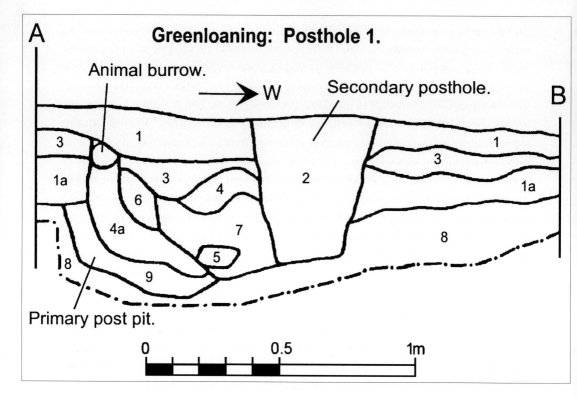

82 Greenloaning, section through the south-west tower posthole

dug. This may be a perfectly plausible scenario, but it is equally possible that the layer represents the remains of yet another post-pit: giving us no fewer than three structural phases on the site. Meanwhile, the tower's north-west post was represented by two separate postholes, with both post-pipes visible in plan (*34*). In other words, after the initial construction of the system, the tower was rebuilt from the ground up, at least once, and possibly twice.

If only one tower was involved it would not be hard to think of circumstances in which a single installation might have required rebuilding, with no implications for the rest of the line. There were no signs that any of the first-phase towers burnt down, but any number of factors, from poor materials to faulty initial construction or even storm damage, could have necessitated remedial work on just one site. Six sites, however, spread over the entire length of the line, are far more difficult to explain in terms of some localised accident or building error. Yet the alternative is that the towers were rebuilt simply because they had reached the end of their usable lives, and this would certainly suggest more than just a brief occupation. Alternatively, it could perhaps be argued that the rebuilds might indicate that the Gask towers, like the forts, were reoccupied 60 years later in the Antonine period: but, on current evidence, this does seem very unlikely. For, although Shielhill South yielded one of the new first-century dates; the minor installations have yet to produce a single Antonine find. Moreover at Greenloaning, where the interior surfacing survived well, there was no significant accumulation of soil or other rubbish that might have served as an indication of a prolonged abandonment between the tower phases. Instead we find just a thin band of loamy material (*82*, L3) between the primary and secondary metalling layers, which probably reflects nothing more than dirt trampled into the site during its rebuilding. The fact that the replacement posts at all three sites were set in almost exactly the same positions as their predecessors (whose locations must thus presumably still have been known) would also suggest that there was no significant break between occupations: especially as the tower at Greenloaning is set in an unusual off-centre position which is unlikely to have been repeated by chance. We would, therefore, appear to have evidence for a quite prolonged, but still wholly Flavian, occupation. Just how prolonged, though, still remains open to question and much probably depends on how long the towers' big timber uprights (up to 40cm in diameter) could be expected to last before needing replacement. This in turn depends, at least partly, on what they were made of; for, as Hanson (1978) has pointed out, the Romans did sometimes use far from ideal timber in their military structures: alder, for example, which rots fairly quickly once set into the ground. Environmental analyses from sites on the Gask, and elsewhere in the area, have suggested that virtually the only trees growing in this landscape in Roman times were water-loving species, such as alder, around the rivers; with the rest of the area virtually treeless and devoted to grazing. This might have severely restricted the Romans' choice of timber if only local trees could be used. Yet even if such material was employed, we might still expect such large diameter timbers to be at least reasonably durable, and so not likely to need too frequent replacement. There is evidence, however, that timber may, indeed, have been imported from elsewhere for use on the Gask: our own analysis of wood fragments found by Robertson in the postholes at Roundlaw, coupled with earlier evidence from Raith (Christison 1901, 28), would suggest that the timber actually used was good solid oak. This could have been expected to last for many years before needing to be replaced, especially if it was treated with pitch; the likely life-span of the installations would increase accordingly.

Tower rebuilds are not the only evidence for a longer than expected occupation, however, for a number of other factors can also be brought into play. One obvious issue is the presence of a fortlet and tower on essentially the same site at Midgate. As we saw in chapter 4, there are possible doubts over the identity of the tower, and it is also conceivable that the double site reflects a design change to the system made during its construction. This would not be unusual. Hadrian's Wall, for example, underwent a massive redesign whilst it was still being built, with the addition of the forts and Vallum (e.g. Jones & Woolliscroft 2001, 79), and there is evidence that the Antonine Wall was also modified under construction (Gillam 1975 & Swan 1999, 429ff). Nevertheless, it remains possible that again either the tower or the fortlet were only built when the other reached the end of its useful life. Much more direct evidence, however, comes from the fact that a number of the sites had to have their ditches re-dug in service. Moreover, this was not just routine cleaning, for it was not done before a considerable depth of silt had formed in the ditch bottoms. By way of an example, *83* shows all of the ditch sections dug during our own excavation at Shielhill South, and it is readily apparent that in places the silt deposits in the primary ditches had become so deep that the recutting was a far from simple operation. Indeed it has missed the original ditch bottoms in places, presumably because they were no longer identifiable. Perhaps the clearest example is section K-L, across the tower's inner ditch. Here the primary cut is represented by a classic, if small, V-shaped ditch, which had filled (layers 7 & 11) almost to its full original depth before being cut by a second, broadly similar, ditch (L2). Yet rather than simply re-emptying the original profile, the recut has been driven right through its northern (outer) side, so that the two ditch bottoms lie some distance apart. Again, such deep silting must have taken quite some time, and another Gask site, the fortlet of Glenbank, had its ditches cut no fewer than three times.

Finally, we have been able to find ancient pollen trapped in the turf used in Roman ramparts (which derives from the immediately pre-Roman landscape) and compare it with pollen from the Roman-period ditch silts: and there is evidence that farming intensified during the occupation (e.g. Ramsay 2002). This was may well have been in response to Roman supply needs, which would probably have been fed by some mixture of taxation and purchase. But, as the pollen also shows that native farming in the area was almost wholly based on stock rearing, rather than arable farming, this is again something that could not have happened overnight. Building stock numbers significantly takes years, especially at a time when the farmers had also acquired as voracious a new consumer as the Roman army, and so, again, a fairly lengthy occupation seems to be needed. There are, of course, counter arguments which might be raised to at least limit the length of occupation we would be forced to envisage. For example, Midgate seems to have been abandoned whilst in the course of a ditch recut, and it is possible that the Roman pull-out came shortly after the bulk of the system had been refurbished. We thus do not have to assume an occupation

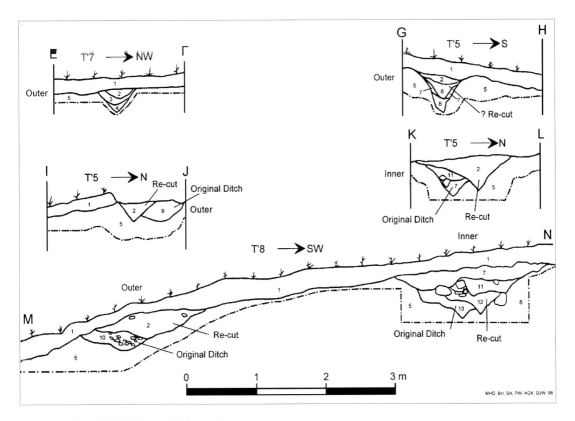

83 The Shielhill South ditch sections

equal to the full maximum operating lives of all of the known installation phases. Nevertheless, it should still have taken a significant time for the towers to need replacing at all, especially if some really were rebuilt twice. In short, we find ourselves in something of a dilemma: for our much cherished historical text, which tells us to expect between one and seven years of occupation, is suddenly faced with archaeological evidence for perhaps 15-20 years, or even more.

So much for the life-span of the Gask itself, but things get even more complex when we look again at the forts in Strathmore. These lie north of the Tay and so, on the current chronology, they should only have been in use for, at most, two to three years. Yet, again, we find multiple building periods. For example, the excavated granary and barrack at Cardean had been completely rebuilt during the Flavian occupation. Still more impressive is the fort of Cargill. Here we have seen that a large fortlet, only an acre in area, sits just a few hundred metres from a full-sized auxiliary fort. The two seem unlikely to be exact contemporaries, so we probably already have two building periods, in which one site replaced the other (in whichever order). But the large fort itself has multiple phases in certain areas. The details that have made it into print were described in chapter 5, but we are told by one of the surviving excavators (pers com, G.S. Maxwell) that certain areas might have had up to six construction phases. In other words, at least parts of this fort could have been built, and then rebuilt or repaired, five times. The recent discovery of Trajanic and Hadrianic coins on the site might imply that some of this activity could be Antonine: but the fort is still very definitely a Flavian foundation. This means that we have a minimum of two structural periods, one for each fort, and the chances are that at least some of the other large fort phases are also first century in date.

Because it remained unfinished when it was abandoned, the site most often cited in support of a short Flavian occupation is the legionary fortress of Inchtuthil. A recent study by Shirley (2001) has calculated that the fortress could probably have been finished in around three years, given the labour available: so the fact that it was not, might imply a distinct time shortage, even if we assume that it was not begun until after Agricola's recall. Yet this site, too, may present greater complications. Firstly, it was by no means unknown for Roman military installations to remain apparently incomplete for long periods, even though in full operation. For example, the granaries of the Hadrian's Wall fort of Birdoswald seem to have sat unfinished for decades after the rest of the fort came into service (Wilmott 2001, 70 and 83), whilst parts of the legionary fortress of Chester may have stayed incomplete for over a century, surrounded by a fully working site (Mason 2001, 128). As a result, it is not inconceivable that the missing Inchtuthill structures were simply not yet considered necessary, at least with any great urgency. Interestingly, Inchtuthil is the only site in first-century northern Scotland to have a stone wall inserted into the front of its defensive rampart, and it is worth noting that Chester acquired a similar wall at much the same time. The Chester wall shows exactly the same masonry style as that used in the so-called 'elliptical building' in the same fortress, and the two were probably contemporary. If so, this would date it to Agricola's governorship, because water pipes used in that building are stamped with the names and titles of both Agricola and Vespasian and can be dated exactly to AD 79. It is possible, therefore, not only that Agricola (rather than his successor) was active in the construction of Inchtuthil, but that he was modifying a plan begun by a predecessor. It is even possible that the *praetorium* and the final version of the *principia* were also going to be in stone. If so, they would have taken longer to build and may have been left until last, simply because getting the base as a whole up and running would probably have been a higher priority than making it impressive. There is also archaeological evidence for a longer and more complex site history than is often thought. For example, there is the extra ditch and rampart defence discovered to the east of the fortress in 1901. Oddly, this was ignored in the report of Richmond's post-war excavations, as were the two long rectangular buildings which could be associated with it, but these might well represent a completely different phase. Likewise, we have two phases in the barracks of the so-called 'officers' compound', which is itself not guaranteed to be contemporary with the fortress, however likely that may seem. There may even be signs of Roman activity on the site after the fortress was given up. For the 1901 excavation found ovens set into its ditch, whilst Richmond himself found what he thought was a Roman ditch cutting one of the demolished tribune's houses, although Pitts and St Joseph (1989, 131) dispute this. In short, the fortress might only be one of a number of periods of military activity on the Inchtuthil plateau, and so just part of a longer sequence. If so, this would mean that only the Highland fringe auxiliary forts have so far failed to produce evidence for major site rebuildings, and even this might mean little, since almost none have been excavated well enough to reveal them. We have seen that there are features at Fendoch which seem to have been replaced, and there are signs that Bochastle's north rampart was modified in service: but given our current ignorance, this could well be just the tip of an iceberg.

We thus seem to have evidence for prolonged Flavian occupation, even as far north as Strathmore, and this makes it still more difficult to force the archaeological findings into the straight-jacket of our current, very brief, historical model. Of course conquest periods do involve a degree of military flux, and deployments can be rapidly altered, but to produce such a high rate of adaptation and modification on individual sites within the traditional time-scale, would require something more akin to chaos. An obvious possibility, therefore, is that there is something wrong with our history, and that we really do have a longer first-century occupation than we had thought possible. The problem is: where can we push the present chronology? Obviously the AD 79 start-date imposed by Tacitus' 'Agricola' seems to be writ in stone, so the natural assumption is that the Romans must have stayed on rather longer that we had thought and, if so, this would be a very useful addition to our knowledge: for the 20-30 year period between the mid-80s and the early years of the second century is something of a dark age in Romano-British studies. By the end of that time we find the Roman army firmly ensconced on the Tyne–Solway isthmus, beginning work on the Stanegate frontier, which was itself to evolve into Hadrian's Wall (Jones & Woolliscroft, 2001 33ff) in the 120s. What happened in between still remains somewhat mysterious, however, and it would certainly be attractive to be able to agree with Macdonald (1937) that they were actually still in northern Scotland. There is, however, a serious problem that would appear to rule out such an option.

Current theory on the end of the Gask rests largely on an analysis of the coins from northern Scotland by Hobley (1989). Roman first-century coinage did not, it seems, enter Britain in a steady flow. At this relatively early point in the life of the province, the principle route for coinage to enter Britain was probably through government expenditure, mostly on the military. But it seems that new coins were only provided by the central mint when they were needed for some reason, perhaps to top up a government pool usually reliant on the taxes of a province which may still have been running at a loss. There were thus 'surge' years when large numbers of coins arrived, followed by dearth periods (which could last for many years) when new coins were rare, and probably only entered through trade and other non-governmental flows. The years AD 86 and 87 happen to be particular surge years, so much so that it is unusual for a site of any significance occupied during those years not to produce their coins. There was then a pause in the coin supply lasting until after the death of Domitian in 96. The forts of northern Scotland have produced quite a number of coins of 86, an unusually high percentage of which show little or no wear: which means that they were lost soon after issue. Yet none are known with certainty from 87, to the north of the Southern Upland fort of Newstead. There is a single coin of 88 recorded at Camelon (Christison *et al.* 1901, 415), but its significance is debatable, as such coins were rare in Britain in their own time and the site also has Antonine occupation. The coin's state of wear is not described, so it is impossible to estimate how long it had been in use when it was lost, but it was not unusual for Roman coins to stay in circulation that long. Indeed, coins from the Roman Republic (which ended in 31 BC) have been found on Hadrian's Wall and at the Strathmore fort of Cargill. Under these circumstances, the absence of coins of 87 would suggest that the area was abandoned at some time after the coinage of 86 arrived in the province, but before the arrival of coins of 87, which might be well into that year. This is extremely strong evidence, especially as other datable find types, such as pottery (Hartley 1972) and glass, can also not be pushed beyond *c.*AD 90. Moreover, this early abandonment date fits well with what we know of the wider history of the Roman Empire during this period.

We will look at the reasons for Rome's failure to permanently conquer Scotland in more detail in chapter 7, but there is general agreement that the trigger for the first-century withdrawal was not trouble in the area itself, but a series of Roman defeats, suffered in the mid-80s, in the Danube lands, at the hands of the Dacians, from what is now Rumania. This area, just a week or 10 days' march from Rome, was strategically vital and, as a result, troops had to be withdrawn from wherever they could be spared to protect the imperial heartlands. Britain, as a peripheral, and perhaps ultimately expendable province, was an obvious target. It thus (as it turned out, permanently) lost a quarter of its entire garrison, including one full legion: *Legio II Adiutrix* (Ritterling 1924, 1441-4, but see also Bérard *et al.* 1995, 203-6 & Kurzmann 2005, 243). The redeployment worked. The Danube frontier was stabilised and, in the early years of the second century, the Emperor Trajan (98-117) went on to conquer and annex Dacia as a Roman province. In Britain, however, the troop reductions meant that the provincial army no longer had the manpower to hold its northernmost conquests safely, and a withdrawal in 86/7 would fit perfectly. It would also fit with the next change of governor, assuming that Agricola's successor had the normal three- to four-year term in office. Moreover, however long the occupation was, we have plentiful evidence that the abandonment, when it came, was a matter of deliberate Roman policy, rather than the result of at least direct hostile pressure. There is no evidence from any of the sites for the sort of destruction that might have been caused by enemy action. Instead we find a general picture of careful demolition, and the destruction, removal or burial of useful material. At the same time, however, the withdrawal might also have been rather sudden and unexpected by the men on the ground. Because, as we have seen, the Gask fortlet of Midgate seems to have been abandoned part way through having its ditch cleaned out. This would not have been a particularly long job on a site of this size, and, even allowing for the potential of professional armies for bureaucratic mix-ups and orders for pointless activity, it was surely something that would not have been started, had the garrison known that they were about to pull out. We are thus left with something of a dilemma. If we have too much archaeology to fit the accepted chronology and cannot push the abandonment date later, we are left with the possibility of an earlier than expected invasion. Yet this obviously brings us into conflict with the AD 79 start-date given by Tacitus for Agricola's first foray to the Tay.

Somewhat nebulous doubts about Tacitus' veracity are hardly new, and more specific scepticism has been aimed at our traditional, glowing image of Agricola's military talent (e.g. E. Birley, 1976, 10-19). In particular, a most courageous book was published by Hanson in 1987, which raised serious questions over parts of Tacitus' narrative, despite being denied much of the archaeological evidence which has since come to reinforce his doubts. More recently, Tacitus' credit was given a more concrete blow by tree-ring dates for a series of timbers from the rampart of the earliest fort at Carlisle (Caruana 1997, 40f & forthcoming and Groves 1990). As with Scotland, Tacitus has at least been read (in practice somewhat unfairly) as assigning the conquest of northern England to Agricola, and so Carlisle had usually been assumed to be an Agricolan creation (although see Bushe-Fox 1913, 299f & Birley 1951, 56, contra Haverfield 1922, LI). It thus came as something of a shock that the dendrochronology dates provided a firm foundation date of late AD 72.

These were not seasoned timbers, so we cannot simply argue that they had spent time in storage before being used. Likewise, this installation was no temporary camp that could be safely assigned to some minor, unrecorded excursion. It was a permanent Roman fort. Yet it had been founded five years before Agricola's tenure of office even began, in the time of his predecessor but one as Governor: Q Petillius Cerialis (Gov AD 71-73/4). Since then, similar datings have appeared for other forts all over the north of England (most recently at Roecliffe, Bishop 2005, 214) and there now seems little doubt that the Roman army had occupied the entire area by the end of Cerialis' time in office. Such a serious contradiction of the accepted wisdom has forced us to re-examine the history of this period, and evidence can now be put forward to suggest that Cerialis' activities may have extended well to the north of Carlisle, and perhaps as far as Strathmore.

We have already seen that the new structural evidence might argue for an earlier occupation, but there is growing support from finds analyses. For example, Caruana (1997, 46f) has suggested that enough Neronian (54-68) and early Flavian material has been found to suggest pre- or very early Flavian occupation at Camelon, and possibly even Strageath, along with more southerly Scottish forts such as Dalswinton, Castledykes and Newstead (6). Similarly, a correspondence analysis of the glass assemblages from sites such as Newstead, Camelon and Inchtuthil, suggests a very close chronological relationship with forts as far south as the Lunt, in Coventry. In particular, there is a marked tendency to use coloured and cast glass, and a range of early drinking vessels, which were very much in vogue in the early seventies (Hoffmann forthcoming a). Meanwhile Shotter (2000a, 194f) has pointed to the presence of disproportionately large numbers of Neronian and early Vespasianic coins from a number of Scottish sites, many of which show little wear and so had not been in circulation long when lost. These are, again, sufficient to point to possible Cerialan activity at Strageath and Camelon, whilst Cardean and Cargill might also now follow this pattern. Indeed Shotter even goes so far as to suggest a Cerialan origin for the Gask line itself.

So much for the archaeological evidence but, although they have been much neglected, there are also Roman literary sources to back it up. For example, in retirement the senior politician Silius Italicus wrote a massive epic poem on the Punic wars. This includes a series of what purport to be prophesies of the achievements of the Flavian dynasty emperors (*Punica* III, 597-629), but written with the benefit of hindsight at some point well into the reign of Domitian. Amongst the achievements he lists for Vespasian is that he will be 'the first to raise battle against the Caledonian forests'. There then follows a series of achievements for Titus and a much longer and more fanciful list for the still reigning Domitian, but none of these so much as mention Britain, which might imply that the island was regarded as conquered by Vespasian's death. Moreover, this must surely have been the official line at the time, since it would have been dangerous, bordering on the suicidal, for anyone to publicly deny, or even ignore, any conquest to which the capricious Domitian himself made any claim. Yet Italicus' family continued to prosper under the emperor, with his son and probable adopted son both receiving consulships in Domitian's later (and supposedly most paranoid) years (Grainger 2003, 7). Indeed the latter was Consul at the time of Domitian's assassination. Next, Pliny the Elder makes a reference in his Natural Histories (IV, 102) to Roman campaigns against the Caledonians within 30 years of the invasion, i.e. by or before AD 73. This reference has often been misunderstood by modern scholars (e.g. Kamm 2004, 60), particularly those who lack Latin, because the relevant passage has been mistranslated in the standard English edition not as 'within 30 years' but as '30 years ago'. That would be manifest nonsense, for it would attempt to place an invasion of Scotland into the late 40s: but one in the early 70s no longer seems so implausible. Meanwhile, the poet Statius (*Silvae* v, II, 145) specifically refers to Cerialis' own predecessor, M. Vettius Bolanus (Gov 69-71) setting up 'watchtowers and strongholds' in Caledonia, which sound suspiciously like the Gask. Statius was a poet and his geography may be somewhat uncertain (as, notoriously, was Tacitus'). It might thus be argued that, to him, 'Caledonia' may have meant little more than 'up north somewhere'. Indeed it is even possible that he may be describing the otherwise undated line of early watchtowers on the Roman road over the Stainmore pass, between Brough and Bowes (now the A66) in northern England. That said, however, it is interesting that the term he actually uses is the 'Caledonian plain', which fits well with the central belt region, including the Gask (but not with the Stainmore chain), whereas the normal Roman stereotype for Scotland was of mountain country. Western historians are notoriously suspicious of the use of poetry as a source, because we tend to classify it as fiction. It is, thus, salutary to be reminded that Latin literature defined historiography as the closest literary art form to poetry, so that, in the ancient world, the two were seen as less diverse than we might think. Whatever the case, however, Pliny was a very different animal. He was a scientist and a friend of Domitian's father, the Emperor Vespasian. He was also a senior Roman official who knew his geography and might be expected to use political language with precision. Under normal circumstances his 'within 30 years' might, even then, be taken as somewhat vague, with a margin for error which might perhaps be pushed as far as Tacitus' AD 79 date for Agricola on the Tay. But Pliny died in 79, in fact, in the same eruption of Mt Vesuvius that destroyed Pompeii and, as his book's dedication suggests that it was published a year or two earlier, in 77, there can be little doubt that he is referring to operations before Agricola became governor. By itself, even this might not be enough to prove permanent occupation, rather than occasional campaigning, but, as we have seen, archaeology might now be bridging that gap.

TACITUS

At first sight the evidence of the *Agricola* should be unassailable. It was, after all, an account of a man's achievements written by a close relative who should have been in a matchless position to establish his facts. But is this necessarily so credible a work? Indeed, to what extent can we trust it at all? The *Agricola* is all too often treated as an objective biography, or even as straightforward history, but in reality it is no such thing and was never meant to be: Tacitus says so (*Agricola* 3). Instead, it falls into a number of standard Roman literary genres. Firstly, it is a eulogy to his late father-in-law, modelled on the orations in praise of the dead given at Roman funerals and, as such, strict historical truth may have taken a poor second place to the glorification of the subject. Agricola's achievements can thus be expected to have been lauded to the maximum, possibly well past the point of exaggeration, whilst those of others may have been ignored or belittled, not necessarily out of malice, but simply because they were irrelevant to the writer's theme. The work is also what is known as an *apologia*, which means a justification, rather than an apology; and it is as relevant to Tacitus' own situation as to Agricola's. The Emperor Domitian went down in history as a brutal tyrant who, in particular, was given to executing political figures with little if any justification. Yet Tacitus, himself first and foremost a politician, had progressed very smoothly during the reign.

The *Agricola* seems to have been published in AD 98 and Tacitus was writing in what was politically a very fraught situation. After the assassination of Domitian, the Senate elected as Emperor, Nerva (96-8), an elderly and ailing Senator. He may or may not have been the first choice of the assassins, but although he tried to restore good governance, after the dark years just gone, he never seems to have been wholly in control. He was also conspicuously vulnerable to being deposed by the commanders of the large armies that Domitian had assembled in Pannonia and on the Rhine, and may have remained safe only because these were both engaged in (or about to engage in) major warfare across the frontiers.

The emperor's failing health and his lack of a military power-base meant that a viable successor needed to be appointed urgently and, within 13 months, Nerva adopted Trajan his own appointee as governor of Germany as his son, and then promoted him to be his heir and co-emperor. Unlike many other imperial candidates, however, Trajan did not move immediately to Rome, but stayed on in the provinces with a large army at his back, diffusing the situation on the Rhine but, perhaps more importantly, providing military backing to the regime. Meanwhile the Senate was repositioning itself, and prosecuted a number of Domitian's informers and compromised Senators. The Senate must have been relieved, and perhaps actively surprised, that there was no overt attempt at a coup, with the only likely contender, the governor of Syria, being brought to Rome to celebrate a second consulate and so separated from his power-base. It is perhaps hard for us to appreciate the political atmosphere in Rome, but any Senator over the age of 40 would have had all too vivid memories of the rapid descent into civil war that followed a similar attempt by Galba to nominate a successor in AD 69. For the massive bloodshed that followed cut a swath through the governing class. Under these circumstances, Tacitus probably found himself in the potentially dangerous position faced by many representatives of discredited regimes, and needed to rehabilitate himself. He may even have feared a purge of Domitian's supporters, although in fact this never materialised. Consequently, one of his themes is the argument that good men can thrive even under tyrants and still retain their principles: something that was no doubt intended to reflect on himself as well as Agricola. That said, he reached the consulship in the autumn of 97, probably shortly after Trajan's nomination. As Consul, he delivered the eulogy for Verginius Rufus, who had been Consul Ordinarius with Nerva earlier in the year. This speech was a highly political act, for Rufus had been offered the purple by the armies of Lower Germany during the chaos of AD 69. He had declined the offer and yet, amazingly, survived to tell the tale. He could thus be held out, by a still unstable regime, as a model of restraint, who put country before personal ambition, and whose example should still be followed, so that Tacitus might now have been acting as a government spokesman. By the end of January 98 Nerva was dead, and Trajan, still in Germany, was sole emperor, but the situation may still have been tense. Which means that, as Tacitus wrote the *Agricola*, the tenor of its introduction, with its hope for a return of happier times, must have been genuinely poignant. Another possible motive for the work is that Tacitus might have wanted to glorify himself by boosting the status of the family he had married into. In other words, he is a far from impartial observer. He had quite a number of axes to grind, ranging from what we would call political spin, to filial loyalty and personal vanity. It is also worth noting that he was not particularly highly regarded as a historian in the ancient world; in fact one ancient writer, Tertullian (*Apologeticum* 16), straightforwardly calls him a liar, and much of his standing today rests on the fact that he is often all we have.

Of course, it is easy to argue that Tacitus could not have strayed too far from the truth, or he would no longer have been taken seriously by his audience. But the exact same point could also be made about Statius' reference of Bolanus: for the events described by both were still well within living memory when their books were written. Nevertheless, there would still have been men alive in Rome who had served on Agricola's staff, or as subordinate army and naval officers, so it would have been readily detected if Tacitus' account strayed too far into the realm of fantasy. This does, though, presuppose that Tacitus intended the work to be taken seriously, at least as literal truth. Some alternatives here are perhaps worth raising only to be dismissed. For example, satire was an established Roman literary form and the prospect of portraying a figure known for his passivity, as a great military leader would certainly fit the genre. This would have been extremely dangerous, however, in a society where the performance of the individual was seen very much in the context of family networks, and where to satirise a relative (albeit one by marriage) would have been looked on, at the very least, as being in extremely poor taste. Nevertheless, there are examples that come close, most notably Seneca's *Apocolocyntosis* which was written for his tutee, Nero, yet satirises that emperor's predecessor, father-in-law and adoptive father: Claudius. It might also be argued that we cannot be sure that the book was originally written for public consumption, and that what would have been unacceptable in a published work might have been taken as a mere joke when read at some private (perhaps alcohol-fuelled) function. Likewise, the education of a Roman gentleman revolved around rhetoric. The ability to marshal evidence and argue a convincing case was vital in politics and the courts: one of the exercises frequently practised by young aristocrats was to attempt to argue the unarguable. The object was not so much to win, but to practice the ability to make a case at all, and the portrayal of a comparative nonentity as a military hero would be a perfect example. Again, however, these scenarios would have been beyond the pale of good taste when used against a relative and can thus, probably, be discounted. Perhaps more plausibly, however, the work may have been intended as a general parable, in which Agricola was made to stand for a generation of Domitian's Senators. He (and so by implication they) had been a virtuous man in the true Roman tradition. He had carried the torch of Rome's imperial mission, under near impossible conditions; and, as this example might have been designed to reflect on virtually the entire Senate, including the new emperor, it would have been difficult to challenge in public. Certainly the work is a literary and oratorical tour de force and Tacitus was a master rhetorician. Pliny the younger (ep. 1,20 and 2,1) calls him 'the greatest of orators', and he could have trounced most of today's so-called 'spin doctors'. He used language like a film director would use music: to build atmosphere. He could switch his writing style at will, for effect, often adopting that of another well-known writer and, incidentally, bringing in actual passages and events from their works. He was also a genius when it came to linguistic slight of hand, being particularly adept at making the reader believe that he has said something which in fact he has not: something which has misled some modern translators. In short, the *Agricola* is a great, if tendentious work of literature, most of whose effect is lost in translation; but as a historical source it needs to be treated with the deepest suspicion.

What all of this boils down to is something that would have seemed utter heresy just a few years ago. For it is looking more and more likely that Agricola was not, as we have always believed, the first governor to occupy Scotland. The Romans were already there when he arrived. The issue is still open to question; but a life-span for the occupation from, say 72-87 no longer seems unlikely and, at the very least, we need to stop trying to explain away what would otherwise have been perfectly valid literary and archaeological data, simply because they conflict with Tacitus. Likewise, we may find that we need to re-examine the basis of some Scottish small find datings, since the material itself may have been dated in the first place through being found on what had been assumed to be Agricolan forts. Indeed, in extreme cases, we must even be careful not to mistranslate Tacitus himself because he too conflicts with our established model. For example, in his account of Agricola's fourth season, Tacitus (*Agricola* 23) uses the words *praesidiis firmabatur* in connection with garrisons on and around the Forth–Clyde isthmus. This is generally translated as 'established garrisons', which is what we would expect for a period of conquest. A number of scholars (e.g. Ogilvie & Richmond 1967, 192) have pointed out, however, that, elsewhere, Tacitus always uses that expression to mean 'strengthened garrisons'. This would obviously change the picture completely: it would imply that there were already Roman garrisons in the area when Agricola reached it, and that he merely uprated them.

None of this, of course, is to deny any role for Agricola, for we know from inscriptions (RIB 2434, 1-3) and other written sources that he did govern Britain at this time. Indeed he probably did notch up military achievements. This reinterpretation of history would, however, solve a number of other questions that have puzzled scholars in the past. For one of the strangest things about the whole Agricola story is that he was simply not the sort of man who was given the job of governor of Britain: at least at a time when serious campaigning was contemplated. One recent book has made the bizarre claim that the governorship of Britain was 'no great prize' (Fraser 2005, 47) but nothing could be further from the truth. Britain always remained a rather odd province for the Roman army because, as an island, in an age of unreliable sea transport, it was difficult to reinforce quickly. As a result, it had to be able to stand alone in a crisis, and so always had a disproportionately large Roman garrison: in fact the largest of any province in the empire. This meant that its governorship was one of the most senior available, and almost always went to one of the leading generals of the day. Yet this is something which Agricola, most emphatically, was not. It is strange, but although enormous effort has gone into analysing the account of Agricola's doings in Scotland, comparatively little attention has been paid to Tacitus' description of his early career (*Agricola* 5-9). The only exception is that some have claimed that the fact that Agricola served for two brief periods in the army, marked him out as a military man. In fact, however, Roman public service careers mixed civil and military posts almost without distinction, so that these were normal, indeed necessary, steps in the career of a Roman politician. Indeed, the only unusual thing about these interludes was the fact that both were spent in the same province, Britain, which might at least have given him a claim to local expertise. Normally, however, a governor of Britain would already have governed at least one other military province and would probably have seen active service under his own command. We can take as examples Agricola's three predecessors, any one of which might have been the real invader of Scotland. Vettius Bolanus (Governor 69-71), who Tacitus attempts to portray as ineffectual, had campaigned successfully in Armenia. Cerialis (Governor 71-4) was possibly the most able general of his day, as well as being a relative of the emperor, and he had come to Britain shortly after putting down a near disastrous revolt of the Batavian tribe in the Rhineland. Meanwhile, Julius Frontinus (Governor 74-7) had also played a prominent part in the suppression of the Batavian revolt, and wrote books on military science. As for what Agricola had done: Tacitus gives us quite a catalogue, but, although he does his best to make it seem impressive, it boils down to little more than this: firstly, he served as a tribune (*laticlavius*) in the army, something that virtually everyone who wanted to stand for senatorial office had to do. Next he was an assistant to the governor of the wholly civilian province of Asia: but the only thing Tacitus could find to say about his term of office was that he wasn't corrupt! Next, he was one of the Tribunes of the People in Rome, but Tacitus effectively says that this was under Nero, when no one ever did anything, so Agricola did not either. He was then appointed to the old republican judicial office of *Praetor*, but Tacitus says that he wasn't actually assigned to a court, so he spent his year in office organising games and carrying out ceremonial and administrative duties.

There then came the turning point of his career. In AD 68 the Emperor Nero was deposed and committed suicide. He was briefly replaced by Galba, an aged, rather straight-laced aristocrat who had been governing Spain. In 69, however, in what has become known as the 'year of the four Caesars', Galba was murdered by an erstwhile supporter called Otho (who had been passed over as Galba's chosen successor) and the empire dissolved into a three-way civil war. Firstly, the Governor of Lower Germany, Vittellius, rebelled against Otho, invaded Italy and eventually made himself emperor. Then, Vespasian, who was governor of Judea, declared against both and became the eventual winner. Agricola's personal involvement stems from a senseless incident of the kind that can happen under civil war conditions, when military discipline becomes weakened. An element of Otho's fleet went on a plundering rampage in part of Liguria, and one of the looted estates belonged to Agricola's mother, who was murdered in the process. Out of vengeance, Agricola rebelled, but instead of taking what might have seemed the more logical step of backing Vittellius, whose forces were nearer at hand, he declared support for Vespasian, who was still far away in the east. It is possible that he had been friends with Vespasian's eldest son, the future Emperor Titus, who was almost exactly the same age. Whatever the reasoning behind it, however, he recruited troops for the cause (there is no mention of him actually commanding them): a bold move that would not be forgotten once the Flavian regime was established. The initial result was a tour as commander of the xx legion in Britain, ironically under Cerialis. Tacitus says that he was given the post because the legion had been slow to declare allegiance to the new emperor, and so needed to be brought round. Whatever the case, this was his first real military post. Tacitus does his best to prevaricate over the events of Cerialis' governorship, but he does let slip that there were military successes in the province at the time. What these were and what, if any, role Agricola played in them was kept vague, however. Tacitus claims that his father-in-law was so modest that he put down these successes to the generalship of the governor, as if this was not really fair. Nevertheless, it is hard to imagine him missing the opportunity to trumpet any notable action on Agricola's part, had there been much to report.

Next, he was finally given the governorship of a province, but this was still far from an independent military command: for he was sent to *Gallia Aquitania* (modern Aquitaine), one of the few Roman provinces with no army presence whatever. The only other posts we hear of him holding were largely financial in nature; which means that he had had a career of almost wall-to-wall administration. Knowing the Roman aristocracy, he was probably a competent politician, lawyer and bureaucrat, but although he had enough military experience to know how the army worked, he was by no means a proven general. Yet this serial 'pen pusher' was next appointed to govern Britain: one of the most senior commands in the empire. At first sight, it seems little short of madness but, in fact, there are plenty of precedents and, timed well, it could be a perfectly sensible move. What usually happened is that once, and only once, a series of major campaigns was over, and any new territory was pacified, exactly such a figure would be sent in to create the proper machinery of Roman provincial government. This involved the foundation of complex institutions such as a tax system, a judicial system and efficient logistical arrangements for the army. It thus fell more obviously to the purview of an administrator than an established fighting general. Of course occasionally Rome got it wrong, the most famous example being Varus, in AD 8, who was sent into Germany after the province's supposed conquest and ended up loosing his life, his army and the province itself in the course of a native revolt. For the most part, however, this arrangement worked well and it is noteworthy that Tacitus stresses Agricola's work in Romanisation and taxation matters. Of course there may still have been trouble and there may still have been a battle of Mons Graupius, although it may actually have been little more than a skirmish. Nevertheless, fighting was probably not the real the reason Agricola was appointed. It seems more likely that he was sent to put conquests, actually gained by his predecessors, onto a proper administrative footing; and that what military experience the Roman twin-track, public career system may have given him was merely a useful safety feature.

More light might be cast by another ancient writer: the historian Cassius Dio (*Histories* 66, 20-21), who provides the only other account of Agricola's activities to have survived. Oddly, this has been almost totally ignored, but it may answer another of the strange aspects of Agricola's governorship: the very long, seven-year, term of office ascribed to him by Tacitus. For, the normal term was three to four years. As we have said, one of Tacitus' aims in writing the *Agricola* was to show that good men could still prosper under the tyrant Domitian: who came to power in 81. We have also said that this had implications for his own position, because if the now dead Agricola could be held up as a paragon, that would imply that Tacitus must also have been a good man. After all, in an age of dynastic, political, arranged marriages, why else would the virtuous Agricola have let him marry his daughter? There is a problem, however. Dio doesn't even mention Mons Graupius, although he does say that Agricola did a certain amount of fighting. The event he really noticed, was a circumnavigation of Britain by the fleet, which finally proved that Britain was an island. Both Tacitus and Dio discuss this event, and Tacitus (*Agricola* 38) says that it was the last of Agricola's governorship. That should put it in AD 83, but Dio gives a very different date. He says that, in celebration, the Emperor Titus took his fifteenth imperial acclamation. Titus, Domitian's older brother, ruled briefly, from 79-81, and took his fifteenth acclamation in AD 79, the year in which Agricola supposedly reached the Tay. Indeed Silius Italicus (*Punica* III, 597) says that Vespasian, who died in mid-79, achieved 'victory over previously unknown Thule' (which probably refers to the Shetlands), so that it is even possible that Titus took credit on his accession for something actually done under his father. Moreover, there is a tentative corroboration for this date, for the Greek writer Plutarch (*Oracles*, 410) describes a conversation with a man who seems to have been on the circumnavigation, but who was back in Greece in AD 82. The effects of all this could be shattering, because if Dio is correct in his dating, and this really was the last thing to happen before Agricola's governorship expired, it would mean that, in reality, he only had the normal three-year term of office, and that most of the time for his famous northern campaigns would evaporate. More amazing still, it would also mean that he never served under Domitian. Tacitus' account might thus be a fantasy, possibly one that conflates the three years Agricola spent as a legionary commander under Cerialis with the period of his own governorship. To invent four years of warfare does seem too tall a tale even for Tacitus, but there is a more plausible alternative. Imperial acclamations were major events. They involved the army saluting the emperor as a great general, and were so treasured that they were commemorated on the coinage. Having won Titus such kudos, Agricola could normally have expected to be rewarded by being given one of the very few even more senior commands in the empire, such as Syria, or one of the Danube provinces. However, there was already serious trouble brewing on the Danube which, as we have seen, was to explode in the mid-80s. There was also danger in the east, where a pretender impersonating Nero caused internal turmoil and almost triggered war with the Parthian Empire. Again, therefore, these provinces needed very experienced generals in command. Agricola probably still did not match up to the job description, and so Titus may have felt it safer simply to award Agricola a second term of office where he already was: in Britain, where, to put it bluntly, he was less of a risk. This term took him through into Domitian's reign, but as he was then never given an official post again, he can hardly be said to have thrived under the tyrant.

Another possible interpretation of the *Agricola* derives from its very structure, and might also follow on from Agricola's pre-Britain career. We have already mentioned the mix of genres within the *Agricola*. The work is not quite oratory, not quite an *apologia*, not quite history and not quite biography. Some classicists (although increasingly few) have seen this as a sign of an author who still needed to develop his writing skills, and who only came into his own with the *Histories* and *Annals*. Yet, at the time Tacitus was writing the piece, he was already considered an established authority on Latin oratory, as his contemporary, Pliny the younger, attests (*Plin.ep.* 1,20 and 2,1). Instead of seeing it as a sign of weakness, therefore, we should probably see the style of the *Agricola* as deliberate, and designed for effect. In other words as an attestation of well-honed language skills, with which Tacitus was able to walk between genres and so borrow from all. A further quality that readers of translated Latin literature often miss is the fact that the work does not stand alone, but is part of a lively literary and cultural scene in which the ability to imitate, or obliquely refer, to other writers, through quotations of their imagery, phrases or style was much praised. This was seen as a way of displaying one's own erudition whilst, at the same time, paying the audience the oblique compliment of assuming a similar level of learning. This form of literature reached its peak in the so-called 'Second Sophistic', in the mid-second century, which celebrated the ability to re-create the styles and vocabulary of long-deceased writers, often in improvisations, whilst commenting on current themes. This form of literary appreciation was, first and foremost, a pastime for the elite, as few others could have afforded the education, books and leisure required. Nevertheless, we can see from similar referencing in contemporary political art (Alföldy 1999), that some degree of understanding was probably widespread. Both types of work were designed to appeal on many levels, so that a basic story could be enjoyed by anybody able to read them, even if deeper levels of metaphor and allegory may have been out of the reach of all but a few intimates. Similar referencing is still practised today, often as a form of humour, with one prolific exponent being the cartoon series *The Simpsons*. This Russian doll approach to literature has one final surprise, because the innermost layers may hold a very different (and even contradictory) message from that apparently put forward on the surface. A good case in point is Tacitus' own *Germania*, which purports to be a geographic/ethnographic treatise on the northern provinces of the empire, but is really a moral treatise on Rome itself (Mellor 1993, 15). This approach was also used to make political statements, as is documented by Tacitus himself (*Agricola*, 1-2) in the *Agricola's* opening chapters, where he relates stories of writings on past heroes, such as Thrasea Paetus, being understood as indirect attacks on the emperor of their day (Domitian), and so as treason. Indeed the very inclusion of this passage by Tacitus' could be a coded caution that his own readers should look out for the subtext. The ubiquitous lectures on the nature of good kingship or government held in many Greek towns of the period can also form part of this tradition, as can the sometimes highly metaphorical, apocalyptic writings of the Levant: including the Biblical Apocalypse of St John.

If we apply this model to the *Agricola*, it would follow that the straightforward story of a Flavian official may be no more than a facade, like the proverbial cake that hides the file. We do, though, need a way of detecting the underlying layers, and one method may be to look for places where they force distortions on the surface story. In other words, we should be alert for points where the material presented (or even the way it is presented), does not appear to fit well as part of a normal biography. Research of this kind must be founded on detailed literary and historical analysis, which it would not be appropriate to discuss in full in a book on Roman Scotland. We will thus present a brief outline, but leave the more detailed work to a separate volume (Hoffmann forthcoming d).

The *Agricola* covers its subject's entire life, from his origins in *Gallia Narbonensis*, to his death in Rome. Yet a true biography (or a eulogy) might be expected to narrate the major points and achievements of a whole career: and, here Tacitus' text develops immediate problems. For the *Agricola* is carefully shoehorned into a rather odd, highly symmetrical, structure which seems to militate against its purported purpose. It has a double story-telling frame, consisting of its introduction and ending, between which is sandwiched a central section which consists of the following five, roughly equal parts:

1. Agricola's life up to his appointment to govern Britain (47 years) (*Agricola* 4-10).
2. An excursus on Britain's geography and past history (45 years) (*Agricola* 10-17).
3. The first six years of Agricola's governorship (*Agricola* 18-27), with an excursus on the defection of a cohort of Usipi (*Agricola* 28).
4. The final year in Britain, with the battle of Mons Graupius (1 year) (*Agricola* 30-8).
5. The aftermath and Agricola's death (*c.*7 years) (*Agricola* 39-45).

This division, by itself, makes it clear that Tacitus has no interest in providing a full and balanced biography. On the contrary, Agricola's actions before and after his governorship of Britain are seen purely as a frame: and it is Britain and the governorship itself that are important. To achieve such an even spacing, Tacitus has compressed much of the data for the first two parts, whilst expanding other sections, notably the final year. As a result, we are only given the starkest outline both of Agricola's youth and the characterisation of Britain, which has led to almost one-line descriptions of the activities of his immediate predecessors. Indeed, any particular detail given here should draw our attention, because it forces even more compression elsewhere. By contrast, the section on Mons Graupius, with just a single campaigning season, contains more detail than any of the others: a point we will return to later.

That the *Agricola* is not a pure biography is hardly a new revelation, and, as stated, it has also been looked on as an *apologia*. We have seen that one of Tacitus' goals may have been to deflect hostility from men, like himself, whose careers had prospered under Domitian. Yet there may also have been a countervailing subtext, because there are signs that Nerva's reign was somewhat bedevilled by the problem of satisfying the demands of powerful, and outspoken, Domitianic supporters: not least several army commanders. In fact recent histories of the period (Eck 2002, 7-21 & Grainger 2003) have stressed the importance of a group of so-called 'king-makers', who brought the Senate to appoint Nerva in the first place. These include figures such as the Consul Fronto (who chaired the crucial senatorial meeting), and the former governor of Britain, Julius Frontinus, and they were themselves Domitianic beneficiaries. One of the less overt themes of the *Agricola* is, thus, that the good man did not, in the end, get his due under the evil Domitian: for he was denied one of the prestigious pro-consulships which should have crowned his career. This neglect could equally refer to a number of the 'king-makers', who had also not held office for many years. Above all, however, it applied to Trajan, who had only held a legionary command under Domitian. This was in northern Spain, from where, in 89, he marched to the Rhine to support Domitian against the would-be usurper Saturninus, but although he received a consulship (in 91) as a reward for this loyalty (as did all who showed similar support), he was then given no further appointments.

In AD 100, two years after the *Agricola* was published, Pliny the younger, as Consul, delivered a speech to the Senate in praise of Trajan: which he too presumably meant to be taken seriously. In his published version, Pliny (*Panegericus* 15, 1-3) tries to paint a picture of a man of boundless military expertise, claiming, in particular, that the future emperor served for an unprecedented 10 years as a military tribune. Modern scholarship has, however, shown that this was probably a fantasy (Eck 2002, 11), and that Trajan actually had little military experience when he came to power. The *Agricola* thus provides a close parallel: for he too was given a major command with very little military experience but, according to the story, he was still able to rise to the occasion and fight successful wars. In the context of AD 98 one might thus raise the possibility that the *Agricola* was meant as an exhortation to the emperor, and perhaps as an optimistic parable for any senators doubtful of the wisdom of putting a comparative 'rookie' in charge of an empire with 30 legions, in the middle of a large Danube war. All this might be dismissed as interesting, but irrelevant, coincidence, were it not that Tacitus stresses Agricola's origins and family relations in Gallia Narbonensis. There would, of course, be nothing unusual in this in a biography, except that it is emphasised in a passage that is otherwise very compressed; and it may be relevant that a large proportion of Nerva and Trajan's early supporters came from the same province: some, indeed, from the same towns. This place-name dropping, might thus be less casual, and might well be a pointer to Tacitus' own position amongst the 'king-makers' of AD 97. Moreover his stress in the introduction, on a return to freedom of expression and the good old days of the Republic, reads like a regime manifesto. Nerva's coinage stressed 'freedom', 'justice' and 'equity', and the emperor himself called on the, otherwise defunct, people's assembly (the *comitia*) to pass a republican-style land reform bill (Grainger 2003, 47 & 57f). This may suggest that Tacitus was working to what amounts to an official 'party line', which might make at least parts of the *Agricola* a homily for a new age and its proponents, rather than an *apologia* for anyone specific. Likewise, Trajan, as governor of Germany, seems to have reorganised the civil structure of his province in much the same way that Agricola is said to have done in Britain so that the lengthy excursus on Agricola's civilian activities may in reality be a well placed compliment to the new emperor.

One final point to notice is Tacitus' neat adaptation of Caesar's Gallic exploits to a British context. The main section of *The Gallic War* deals with Caesar's own seven-year campaign, which culminated in the decisive battle of Alesia. The parallels are striking. Both generals reached their commands late in the season, but immediately took to the field. Both achieved two victories in quick succession. Both had to rescue a subordinate from a dangerous night attack. Both went further across the ocean than anybody before them (Caesar to Britannia, Agricola circumnavigated Britain). Both were foiled in their attempts to conquer distant islands (Caesar: Britain, Agricola: Ireland) and, in the end, both had to fight a decisive battle, against an alliance of tribes, before which someone in the enemy camp supposedly gave a long speech on the value of liberty. This might just be dismissed as coincidence, although the chances seem remote. Yet the very language seems to militate against it. For example, Tacitus (*Agricola*, 11) begins his British section by declaring that Britain is divided into three parts, in which the respective people look similar to Spaniards, Gauls and Germans: just as Caesar had with Gaul (*Bel Gal*, 1). Whilst, later on, near verbatim quotes can be found, especially during the battle of Mons Graupius and the night attack on *Legio* IX. The references are just too dense to be accidental. But the question is: why would anyone want to compare a relatively minor governor with Julius Caesar? We have already said that satire of a relative would be unacceptable, but in the light of the possible parallels between Trajan and Agricola, we might actually be intended to read Trajan for Agricola in which case the work could suddenly show a loyal well-wisher crediting Trajan with the ability of Caesar, who was himself regarded as one of the greatest generals of all time. It would also, however, make us view Tacitus' reliability as a historical source in a very different light, and the *Agricola* is not unusual in this respect. Tacitus' other historic writings have been much re-evaluated of late (e.g. Mellor 1993) and there is no reason why the *Agricola* should be any different. At the very minimum, however, the parallelism with Caesar must leave suspicions over the veracity of the basic narrative and this is doubly so as passages have also been borrowed from other writers. Indeed, even the story of Aulus Atticus charging too deep into enemy ranks, would appear to have been lifted from Sallust (*Catilinae*, 60). There is little doubt that the story would not have worked at all, had there been no fighting during Agricola's governorship, and perhaps one of the true events may have given Tacitus the idea for the Caesarian parallel. But without external corroboration we should be extremely wary of the likely truth, sequence and relative importance of the reported events. When dealing with the *Germania*, the recognition of its allegorical nature has been such that some researchers now express surprise when any fact given in the text is corroborated by archaeology. We would not suggest that such a level of hyper-criticism should yet be applied to the *Agricola*. Nevertheless, a healthy dose of scepticism does seem fitting, and it would certainly now be very difficult to justify our traditional tendency to assign Tacitus' story priority over other historical or archaeological sources.

7

ROME AND THE NATIVE POPULATION:

WHY DID THE CONQUEST FAIL?

For decades, Romanists in Scotland have been rightly criticised for showing too little interest in the effects of the Roman invasions on the native population. In a way, this is a continuation of the Romans' own attitudes. For the ancient accounts of military operations in the area also largely ignored the indigenous people, except as a fighting enemy. On the other hand, prehistorians have sometimes dismissed the Roman incursions as a virtual irrelevance, because they represent only a few brief periods in an Iron Age that lasted a thousand years. Fortunately, there are signs that the situation is changing and more effort is now being put into studying Roman/native interactions. Part of the spur in our own case has been the growing evidence for a longer than expected occupation, of perhaps 15-20 years, rather than seven. This might not seem that much of a difference in the great historical scheme of things but, if correct, it would provide time – and a greater need – for more complex relationships to develop, and it would also take the occupation past an important psychological point: for it would allow a generation of native children to grow to adulthood who could not really remember the time before the Romans came.

In the popular imagination, the story of Roman/native relations in first-century Scotland is straightforward, if bloody: the Romans invaded, they killed and destroyed and then left. Moreover, the model imagined by many Romanists has not been much more sophisticated: varying largely in that there has been speculation as to whether certain areas, such as Fife, might have greeted the Romans as allies. In fact, however, this hit and retreat model has never been wholly credible; this is doubly so now, given the longer time scale: if for no other reason than the Roman army's enormous supply needs. Assuming, as now seems likely, that all of the northern forts were occupied simultaneously, Rome maintained a garrison of up to 18,000 men north of the Forth and Clyde and, as there are likely to be more forts left to discover, the true number might be higher still. To maintain this force, the army would have needed vast amounts of food and clothing. It had a phenomenal demand for leather, for everything from tents to shoes, and indeed anything for which we would use plastic: and it also needed fodder, and replacements, for cavalry and transport animals. These materials and others, such as pottery, glass, timber and metals, would add up to thousands of tons a year. At the same time, however, many of the military sites were not set close to rivers that were navigable by anything larger than a canoe and, except along the Gask line, no inter-fort road network seems to have been completed, which means that it would have been difficult to import supplies from outside. It seems likely, therefore, that the army would have tried to source at least bulk, low-technology supplies locally wherever possible. Simple pillaging may have been feasible in the short term, but it is obviously not sustainable: for if an army starves the hand that feeds it, that hand will not survive to feed it again next year. We might thus expect some ordered mix of sustainable taxation and purchase to have developed fairly quickly, with all manner of other relationships, be they political, commercial or personal, evolving in train.

We should also remember longer-term considerations. Even at 15-20 years, the first-century occupation was still relatively brief: but there were also two more invasions that we know of. In AD 142, 55 years after the Flavian withdrawal, the Romans returned. This time there seems to have been no plan to conquer the entire country. In fact the whole adventure was probably a political move to bolster the prestige of the Emperor Antoninus (138-61), who had been a somewhat last-minute choice as successor to the childless Emperor Hadrian (117-38). The bulk of the occupation army stopped on a new frontier: the Antonine Wall, on the Forth–Clyde line; but the forts of Camelon, Ardoch, Strageath, Bertha, Dalginross and possibly Cargill were brought back into use as outposts (*84*). If it was politics that had brought the Romans back, however, it was politics that caused them to leave again, and the occupation lasted less than 20 years. Antoninus' successor, Marcus Aurelius (161-80), did not need this trophy conquest and returned to Hadrian's Wall. Indeed, the withdrawal may even have happened before Antoninus' death. Almost half a century later, in AD 208, the Emperor Severus (193-211) brought new forces to invade Scotland, this time

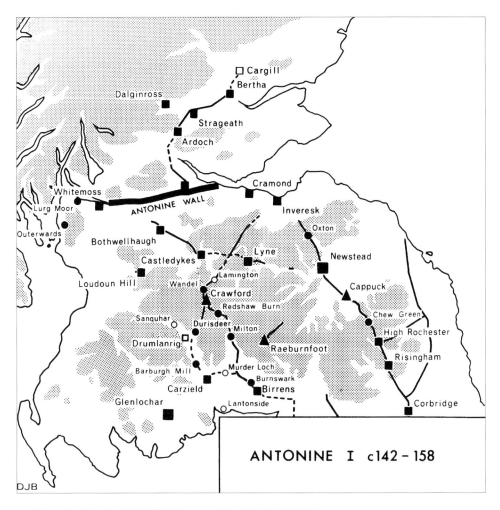

84 Antonine Scotland. *Modified from an original by Prof D.J. Breeze*

planning complete and permanent conquest. Severus' army was probably the largest force ever to invade Scotland. He penetrated Perthshire and Strathmore and built a 30-acre fortress at Carpow (*85* and *colour plate 28*), on the Tay estuary, which was large enough to hold half a legion. But the invasion ended in failure because the emperor died in 211 before the operations were complete. His sons, Caracalla (211-17) and Geta (211 (sibling rivalry)), made treaties with the Caledonian tribes, and rushed back to Rome to ensure their accession. At one time they might have left a subordinate to complete their father's conquest, but the military mood of the empire was starting to change, and major campaigns increasingly needed the emperor in command. Armies under lesser officers had

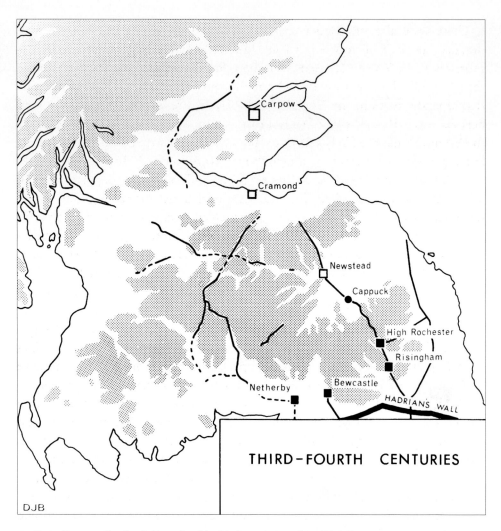

85 Later Roman Scotland. *Reproduced by kind permission of Prof D.J. Breeze*

been known to proclaim their commanders as rival emperors, triggering civil war. Indeed, Severus had come to power in this way, and his sons abandoned their father's achievements rather than take the risk. Moreover, the words 'that we know of' are used advisedly, as there may well have been other significant incursions. For example, there are vague, ancient literary accounts of northern campaigns throughout the fourth century, although we don't know how far they reached. There have recently been tantalising hints of reoccupation as far as the Tay under Commodus (180-92) in the late second century, and there may well have been others.

There were also still longer-term influences. Time seems to telescope with distance and it is all too easy to see the entire history of Roman Britain as relatively short. Yet the Romans were here for almost 370 years; which is more than five full, 'three score years and ten', human lifetimes: or as long as the time that separates us from the English Civil War. As a result, even during the long periods when Rome stayed firmly in the south, mostly on Hadrian's Wall, we should not forget the likely effects on the Caledonian societies of having a rich, but capricious superpower as a neighbour. Rome certainly had much to offer in terms of technology, culture, trade goods and economic opportunity: not to mention as a political model and occasional target for raiding. She always remained dangerous, however, and, in particular, always felt herself to have an absolute right to interfere at will, far beyond her frontiers. Just as importantly, the invasions were spaced in such a way that few Caledonians would have passed through life without experiencing Rome's military power at first hand. They would also know that she could re-invade whenever she chose, quite possibly for internal reasons (including the personal aggrandisement of emperors), rather than because of anything taking place on the ground. All of this is likely to have affected the region's politics, economics, culture and general mind set and, as a result, there may be much greater scope for Roman influence than we have sometimes tended to assume, even when no occupation forces were present.

We then face the problem of defining what exactly it was that was being influenced. In many ways our perception of the Iron Age population has tended to follow stereotypes put about by the Romans themselves: who describe them as long-haired, warlike, barbarians who lived in a state of endemic, often internecine, warfare. Even more serious, modern reconstructions have tended to portray a warlike and, incidentally, almost exclusively male, society: but although some seem to like this red-blooded, testosterone-fuelled image, no society can live by warfare alone. In fact, the Romans often tend to exaggerate accounts of the savage nature of their opponents: to make their victories seem more impressive and to portray their own imperialist adventures as civilising missions. So who were these people really? Firstly, they were not Scots. The Scoti were an Irish tribe which didn't settle in Scotland until after the Roman period. Nor were they Picts, at least at first. The Picts seem to have begun as a federation of existing tribes which united, perhaps as a response to Rome, but not until some point in the later third century, at the earliest. The Romans called them Caledonians, and they were probably a series of Celtic-speaking tribes which, archaeologically, show considerable regional differences. There are signs of hunting and fishing but, for the most part, they lived by farming. Until recently it was thought that much of Scotland was covered in dense, almost primordial forest at this time; but, over the last few decades, the increasing use of scientific techniques, such as pollen analysis, on archaeological deposits has radically changed this picture. It now seems that large-scale forest clearance began in the late Stone Age, perhaps as early as the third millennium BC, and continued apace thereafter, until by the time of the first Roman invasion, the Gask area had an almost treeless landscape, apart from a few water-loving species, such as alder and willow on the river banks. Cereal remains, mostly barley, along with vegetables and fruit are found on Iron Age sites; but the pollen would suggest that the economy was largely based on stock rearing, with the vast bulk of the land given over to grazing, interspersed with some small areas of cultivated fields and orchards.

Nevertheless, if we look at the surface traces, a first impression might seem to confirm the warlike picture: because by far the most visible of the surviving remains are hillforts (*colour plate 29*). There are large numbers in the region: partly on the Highland fringe, but especially in the Ochils and Sidlaws, and many are very impressive. We might thus get an impression of acute instability, with a patchwork of local communities or fiefdoms, all feeling such a need for defence that they were willing to live in very exposed, inaccessible spots, and to invest huge amounts of manpower in forts. There is, however, a major problem. Many of these sites are surprisingly little studied, but we know that many of them went out of use well before the Romans arrived, whilst others were not occupied until later, in the Pictish period. The Romans might, thus, have entered a world where large areas had few, if any, active fortifications (Hingley 1992). Instead, aerial photography has been gradually building a very different picture, in the form of literally thousands of roundhouse features (*colour plate 30*). Almost none can be seen on the surface, so they went largely unsuspected until recently, but their cropmarks can be seen from the air and, although the area has been flown for decades, more are still found every year. The sheer numbers are already prodigious. Figure *86* shows a survey of the area within 8km (5 miles) of the Roman fort of Cardean (Hoffmann forthcoming b), and every dot represents a known Iron Age site. There are already over 100 in this one small neighbourhood (many of which represent more than one structure) and more are still appearing (four in 2005 alone). Interestingly, large parts of this area would have been wetland or water meadow in ancient times, and by using excavation data and written records from before the start of the land improvement movement in the eighteenth century, it has proved possible to map where these were. Figure *86* shows the Iron Age sites superimposed on this map and it is immediately apparent that there is an exact correlation. The twentieth century may have been rash enough to build in flood planes, but the Caledonians were not. They had a rational comprehension of their landscape and, although they often built as close as they safely could to water, they kept very carefully to the firm, slightly higher ground.

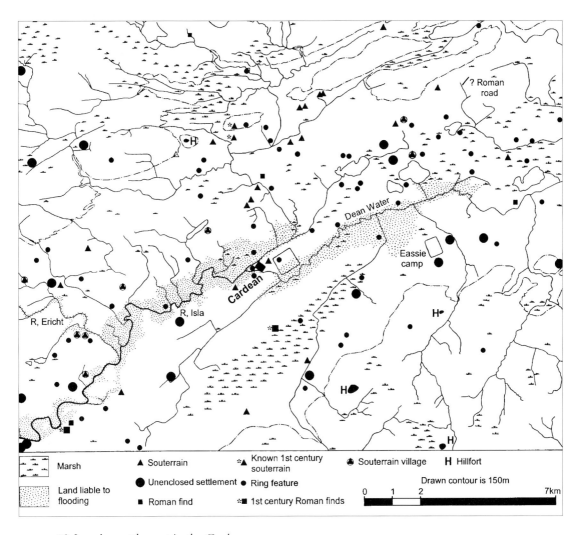

86 Iron Age settlement in the Cardean area

These numbers are probably just the tip of the iceberg, however, for a number of recent, large-scale geophysical surveys have revealed a much denser pattern, and excavations find yet more. Obviously not all of these sites would have been occupied simultaneously; but, even so, the evidence suggests a significant population. There were no towns, and few sites that could even be classed as villages; but the purely rural population may have been as large, if not larger, than that of the same area today. Perhaps the most important point, however, is the nature of these settlements: for many are isolated farmsteads (*colour plate 30*), whilst others are tiny groupings, just big enough, perhaps, to house a single extended family. This flies in the face of the traditional barbarian image, because given instability, let alone endemic warfare, people group together for security. Isolated farms are very vulnerable and they are usually an indication, not just of peaceful conditions, but that an area has enjoyed such conditions for so long that people feel able to take them for granted. Compare, for example, the modern British countryside, with its centuries of peace, and its isolated family farms, with the historically far less tranquil French and German landscapes of heavily nucleated, sometimes defended villages. A roundhouse, being a relatively simple structure, might represent less investment than a modern farm, and so might make risk-taking a little easier but, with lives at stake, the basic analogy still applies. The Iron Age picture thus seems far from compatible with a society of warlike, cattle rustling savages, especially as a lot of the sites are completely undefended. Many do have fences or palisades around them, but these were far too light to act as a serious military defence, and they were probably just designed to control livestock. Likewise a few substantial roundhouses (some up to 15m in diameter) had ditches around them, which may seem to make them more heavily defended: but even these might have been little more than status symbols, because their entrance breaks are too wide to be defensible. For example, the Roman Gask Project has recently excavated such a site at East Coldoch, near the Roman fort of Doune, which has a massive ditch: up to 2m deep and 6m wide. Around 500 tons of earth were dug out to create it, and yet it has an entrance break 9m wide. No sign was found of any kind of gate structure to make such a gap even vaguely defensible and just how accessible it would have been can be seen in a reconstruction drawing (*87*). There were a few, more defensible structures, called brochs, which were essentially stone-built roundhouses, but these are relatively rare in our area. There were also structures called crannogs, which were, again, usually isolated roundhouses, but built on piles or artificial islands in the lochs (Dixon 2004). Yet even these could have been taken by a small band of men in a boat, especially as the wattle, daub and thatch roundhouses would have been extremely flammable. Of course, none of this means that the Caledonians were military innocents, unable to defend themselves. After all, British and US armies have long proved highly effective, despite their peaceful homelands: and we certainly know that Iron Age societies had weapons. Nevertheless, the traditional savage image seems to be a major exaggeration.

The local political and social organisation still remains something of a mystery, and regional diversity in site types and other cultural traits, should anyway warn us not to expect homogeneity. The domination of the hillforts in earlier times suggest a warrior aristocracy or some other strong, if purely local, authority. But we have seen that by Roman times there was less in the way of a settlement hierarchy, and this might suggest a more egalitarian society, or at least one in

87 East Coldoch roundhouse. *Reconstruction by T. Davis*

which power, wealth and status were not displayed through buildings. There is a degree of variation in the size of individual roundhouses, which might represent wealth differences, and we also find variations in the levels of high-status goods (including Roman imports) on different sites, so we are certainly not dealing with perfect equality. Indeed, the Stirlingshire brochs might be the homes of local chiefs: whilst in Perthshire and Angus some, but by no means all, settlements had large underground storage structures called souterrains (*88*), which might also be a sign of greater prosperity. These were often stone lined, and roofed with large stone slabs that a single family would have been hard put to move. Their construction thus represents a significant investment, but whether they represent grassroots communal activity, or the stores of local notables, who could command the labour of others, we really don't know. Certainly, however, there are few of the signs of embryonic statehood that were emerging in southern England at the time of the Roman conquest. For example, we see no signs of tribal coinage or of individuals with titles equivalent to king.

Ironically, this apparent lack of political development might help to explain why the Romans never managed to permanently conquer Scotland: for the entire situation is distinctly peculiar. If Tacitus is still to be believed, we have in the battle of Mons Graupius a historic victory for Rome and a cataclysmic defeat for the Britons, from which there should have been no real chance of recovery.

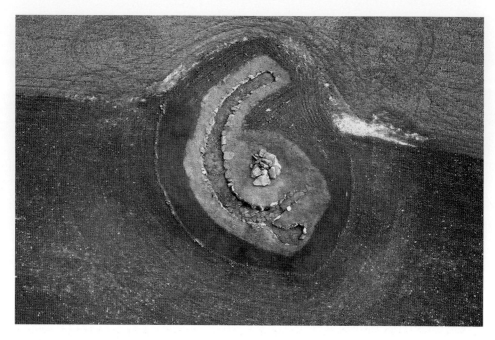

88 Shanzie souterrain, from the air

If he is not, then Rome had occupied the area, apparently successfully, for years before withdrawing. This was a time when Rome stood at the height of her power, and when many of her citizens still saw world conquest as their destiny and yet, by the mid-80s, they were suddenly in full retreat. To say the least, it is a situation that requires explanation.

We have already seen that there is little evidence that the Caledonians were exceptionally warlike or militarily effective: but even if they had been, the Roman army was used to conquering warlike peoples. Indeed, whenever the Caledonians met Rome in battle, from the first century onwards, they seem to have been beaten, and so can have stood little chance of expelling the Romans by force. The Highlands too were not especially difficult terrain. Rome had routinely annexed far worse: including the Atlas Mountains, the Alps and the Pyrenees. The Highlands' potential for guerilla activity can likewise be easily exaggerated. Guerilla warfare was practised in the ancient world, with occasional spectacular successes, but its effectiveness was weakened, in an age without firearms, because, even with archery, its exponents still had to come to quite close quarters with the enemy. Besides, the southern uplands and Pennines, which were retained, would both have been better guerilla country than the lowland areas and glen mouths which seem to represent the northern limit of Roman activity in Scotland.

The lack of a developed market economy in Iron Age Scotland, which has been suggested as a possible cause of Roman logistical difficulties (Groenman van Waateringe 1980, 1041), can also be exaggerated as a problem. The theory has been that the lack of local market mechanisms for managing surplus agricultural production would have made the army difficult to supply: but numerous societies, from Minoan Crete to the USSR, have found alternative methods of organising, concentrating and/or distributing surpluses, albeit with varying degrees of efficiency. Indeed, as Millet points out (1990, ch 7), it is probably anachronistic to look for a full market economy anywhere in Roman Britain. Likewise, Scotland may not have had the easily available precious metal resources that helped to attract the Romans into Wales (Jones and Mattingly 1990, 179-192), but the probability of low potential tax revenues from the area could also have been less of a problem than might, at first, be thought. For, as long as Scotland could be held by the existing army of Britain, it should also have involved little additional expenditure (Woolliscroft and Woolliscroft 1993, 56f). Indeed, given a sufficient degree of assimilation, money might even have been saved because, with no land borders with external powers to defend, overall force reductions might eventually have been possible in Britain. Besides, as Mattern (1999) has shown, Roman thinking when it came to retaining conquered territory was often driven far more by concepts of face, status and honour than by cost-benefit analyses: so much so that they often hung on with a tenacity which defied any such rational considerations.

In fact, the main reason for the pull-out at the end of the first century occupation was the force reductions caused by the need to shore up the Danube frontier against Dacia. Initially, at least, this may have been intended as a purely temporary expedient, and the army in Britain may have expected its missing units to return. In fact, though, this was never to be and, thereafter, the political will never again existed in a sustained enough form to permit a successful attempt at renewed total conquest. But is this explanation sufficient in itself? For, whilst one would not dispute for a moment that the loss of these forces was important, Britain was still left with the single largest provincial army in the entire empire: with a strength of perhaps 45,000 men (including three legions). Moreover, the growing evidence for a longer occupation means that the army had had years to consolidate its hold on the occupied parts of Scotland before the withdrawals began and, in many other parts of the empire, including parts of southern Britain, Roman control over regions, and even whole provinces, had been able to survive the running down of their garrisons remarkably soon after conquest. Scotland, however, may have presented an additional problem because of its apparently decentralised society.

An interesting idea, first put forward by Groenman van Waateringe (1980), with relation to Germany, may be relevant here. The Romans always tried to run an economical administration. Consequently, they sought to avoid the need to leave large numbers of administrators in conquered provinces, at least for any length of time, and the military presence was also kept to a minimum, especially in areas away from the frontiers. Instead, they tended to take the local administrative, legal and law enforcement systems largely as they found them and simply turned them to their own ends, under the overall direction of the provincial governor and his surprisingly minimal staff. This meant that, even after bloody wars of conquest, at least local elites were often left with their power and wealth substantially intact, and simply acquired responsibilities to the Roman state in taxation, judicial and law and order concerns, which, in any case, they might already have been discharging under their pre-conquest government. In other words, Rome ruled most of her provinces, not by the direct supervision or coercion of their populations, but by bending their governing classes to the imperial will. Even here, the empire frequently seems to have had a fairly light touch, so long as all went well: and the deal was reciprocal to the point of symbiosis. The local magnates not only survived; their position necessarily acquired imperial backing. They continued to run their communities, and they could profit from doing so well: not only by preserving their local status but, with time, the more able and ambitious might also hope for profitable careers on the empire wide stage. For an imperial power, Rome also showed an unusual generosity with her own citizenship, especially to provincials who had served in the army or local administration, so these people could even aspire to become fully one of the conquering people, rather than one of the conquered. And this was not just a polite legal fiction: by the time of the first invasion of Scotland, there were already Greeks, Gauls, Spaniards and others in the Roman Senate and, from the second century onwards, even the emperors were increasingly of provincial origin. For example, Trajan and Hadrian came from Spain, whilst Septimius Severus was North African. The provincial elites thus acquired a vested interest in preserving the imperial power, rather than, as might otherwise have been expected, becoming natural focuses for resistance. It was an inspired system and, on the whole, it worked superbly well. It made efficient use of (and eventually expanded) the scarce pool of Roman manpower. It was cheap. It made local people feel less under the imperial thumb; and the provincial elites, being small and readily identifiable, were more easily encouraged, communicated with and, if needs be, intimidated than entire populations. In short, it was a system that allowed Rome to govern an empire by, at least tacit, consent that she could never have ruled by force alone, and it was a major reason for her success. The problem was that it had grown up on the assumption of finding the sort of centralised societies which possessed the necessary political infrastructure to make them capable of being left to run themselves in this way. As a result, the Romans may simply have found the socio/political state of Scotland to be too incompatible with their established system of provincial governance to be either workable or, at least, worthwhile. For it is extremely difficult to coerce a society made up purely of individuals or small, near independent, family groupings. How, for example, do you even communicate your wishes to such people, let alone enforce them? And if military force is used, how do you strike against an enemy with no identifiable seat of power? In extreme cases, even basic concepts such as power (at least as wielded from afar) and, perhaps especially, taxation might have been difficult for the natives of such a society to comprehend, and still harder for them to accept. For, unlike other areas, where the Roman conquest might have meant little more than the replacement of one ruler by another (whose direct representatives they would, anyway, rarely have seen), a highly decentralised society would have been asked to accept rule and complex administrative procedures where none had existed before; which is a far more difficult transition to make. If we, therefore, assume the absence of any pre-existing local administration to do their job for them and, perhaps more importantly, of the habit of obedience to such authorities in the minds of the natives, the Romans could only have controlled and taxed Scotland by means of a large and sustained investment of manpower: which, thanks to the force reductions, they no longer had.

If the battle is not a figment of Tacitus' imagination, these ideas can be taken back to Mons Graupius and even slightly before. It is noteworthy that he does not refer to any other specific battles in Scotland before this action, except for a night raid on the camp of *Legio IX Hispana* in Agricola's sixth season. He does say that, in the fifth season, Agricola advanced through 'repeated and successful battles' (*Agricola*, 24), but apparently did not consider any of these to be worthy of individual mention. This could, of course, have been simply a literary nicety, as constant battle descriptions might have detracted from the work's current clean build-up to the climax of Mons Graupius: especially if some of them were not quite the successes claimed. Yet letting *Legio IX* get caught as it was hardly reflects well on Agricola's generalship, and Tacitus still refers to this, albeit whilst trying to present it in as good a light as possible. As a result, it is difficult to believe that Tacitus' apparent hero worship of his father-in-law would have allowed him to let any other significant engagements, let alone real successes, go unmentioned. Instead we have a rather curious situation. All military operations are conducted against people, not simply terrain and yet, as things are, Tacitus and, following him, many modern accounts, read as though Agricola was merely marching through an empty landscape, with the discussion centring almost entirely upon which landmarks he reached in which season.

The attack on *Legio IX* is interesting, however. Tacitus specifically says that the Britons attacked the sleeping camp in full force and that the IX legion had been chosen as the target because it was the weakest of the three columns into which

Agricola had divided his army: and yet it survived. Certainly, there was a rescue operation, which may well have saved the day, but the fact remains that, when the relief force arrived, Tacitus tells us that the ix legion was already up and fighting and seems to have been driving the Britons out of its camp unassisted. This obviously begs a question: what kind of army gets itself beaten with so many advantages in its favour? If this really was the full British force, it was either hopelessly incompetent, or remarkably small. Yet Tacitus specifically says (*Agricola*, 26) that once it was retreating from the camp: 'If it hadn't been for the forests and marshes that covered the fugitives, that victory would have ended the war', as if this force was all that the natives could have been expected to be able to muster. Chapter 27 of the *Agricola* does then go on to refer to further native recruiting and (only now) to a confederacy of action between the native tribes: but this was in preparation for Agricola's seventh season, i.e. shortly before Mons Graupius, whereas, even on the traditional chronology, the Romans had by then been operating in Scotland for several years. Assuming that Tacitus is giving us a true account, therefore: were the natives only now taking Agricola seriously, or had they only now developed, under stress, the political ability to do anything of any moment about him? Tacitus says (*Agricola*, 29) of the period immediately before Mons Graupius: 'For the Britons unbowed by the outcome of the previous battle [singular], seeing their options as either revenge or slavery and learning at last [again only now] that mutual danger must be repelled by common action, had brought into the field, by means of envoys and treaties, the cream of all their nations. Already more than 30,000 armed men were on view [at Mons Graupius] and still the stream flowed in.' This does not sound like the same army we have just seen attacking *Legio ix*.

Even allowing for the tendency of ancient writers to (sometimes grossly) exaggerate enemy numbers, in order to magnify their own side's achievements (no doubt amplified here by Tacitus' desire to portray Agricola to the full as a hero), it is hard to imagine any army even approaching this size being thrown out of a camp by one half-asleep, under-strength legion. We are told that the Britons were already occupying Mons Graupius before Agricola advanced to the site to give battle, and that warriors were still joining the native force when he arrived. It would seem, therefore, that somehow (and we can only guess at the political and diplomatic processes involved) Mons Graupius had been chosen as a rallying point at which the natives had assembled and, indeed, were still assembling when the Romans appeared. In other words there had not previously been any united Caledonian army as such. For the army now gathering at the battle site had never marched, fought or operated together in any way, as such, because it had simply never existed before. If we accept this as, at least, a reasonably fair appraisal of the state of the native army, the next question must inevitably concern its command structure. For who, if anyone, was in command of this impromptu assembly? The answer that has always been assumed is: Calgacus, but was he? Tacitus never says so. Calgacus is never recorded making dispositions, as Agricola was; nor is any action of his during the battle recorded. Indeed, we do not even learn his fate. The only thing he is ever said to have done is to make a (no doubt fictitious) pre-battle speech and thereafter we hear no more of him. Not only is he never said to be in command; he is never referred to by any term, such as 'king' or 'general', that would have allowed us to take this as read. He is simply introduced as 'distinguished by birth and valour amongst many chieftains was one called Calgacus'. Tacitus goes on: 'To the gathering host demanding battle he is reported to have spoken along the following lines', then comes the speech, and then nothing. This is unusually coy. If there had been a single Caledonian commander, the Romans would surely have found out who he was, even if only from prisoners after the battle. Even in an event such as the Varrine disaster in Germany, where hardly a Roman lived to tell the tale, Rome had no doubt known who she had been fighting: so why such uncertainty here? Furthermore, it was quite usual for Roman writers to take an interest in the actions and eventual fates of enemy commanders, such as Vercingetorix, Boudica, Caratacus and the like, so why not Calgacus? True, it was normally regarded by the Romans as both the prerogative and the duty of a commander to make a rousing speech before an action, so that the entire speech episode may be Tacitus' way of pointing out Calgacus' position; but this need hardly be conclusive. After all, Caesar, in Gaul (*Gallic War*, VII, 77), described a warrior who was certainly not the Gallic commander making a suspiciously similar speech before the start of the battle of Alesia (again we do not learn his fate). So was Calgacus officially in command (if such a term can be said to apply here)? Or, was he just one of many petty 'clan' or group leaders present: perhaps just a name that happened to come to the Romans' attention as someone important? Perhaps, he was simply a man whose renown and character made him someone the other chieftains, and possibly their men, would listen to, and whose ideas would carry above average weight. Perhaps he was also, since Tacitus is so coy, a man who eluded Roman capture. To go one step further, was he, in fact, essentially a fictional character: a *dramatis personae* created only because of the usual Roman literary convention of including pre-battle speeches? One recent book comes close to attempting a biography of the man (on no evidence), tracing his influence on the Caledonian campaigns over several years (Fraser 2005): but even his name, which means simply 'swordsman', is suspicious and he may well be an imaginary protagonist in a barely less overblown battle. What all this can be reduced to is that we have at Mons Graupius a British army formed *ad hoc* solely for the event and only then, according to Tacitus, towards the end of the campaigning season. This was merely a gathering at a particular, presumably well-known, landmark, which may have had no overall commander and whose survivors, after the battle, simply melted away, making no attempt (according to Tacitus) to regroup to fight again, despite facing a Roman army at the end of both the season and its supply lines. None of this looks like an army drawn from an organised, structured society. Nor does it sound like the effective fighting force of a warlike people for, if we are not to dismiss Tacitus' account as mere hyperbole, it was beaten by the Roman *auxilia* alone, without the legions becoming engaged.

Whatever the circumstances of Mons Graupius, there is evidence that Roman/ native relations in the occupied area may have been much more peaceable than we had expected. Studies of this issue are, admittedly, still in their infancy, but the evidence is still suggestive. There is, for example, the effect on native agriculture. A violent conquest, followed by a brutal occupation might have been expected to cause battle deaths and what are now called collateral casualties: especially as ancient warfare often brought starvation and disease in its wake. This should have been detectable as a decline in farming, but pollen data has shown that grazing pressure on the land increased (Woolliscroft 2002b, 66) under Roman rule, in other words agriculture actually intensified. This may have been a response to Roman supply needs, but it certainly does not suggest large-scale deaths, let alone anything approaching the genocidal picture given by the famous line that Tacitus (*Agricola* 30) puts into the mouth of Calgacus: that the Romans 'make a desert and call it peace'. Likewise a number of excavated Iron Age sites not only survived, but actively prospered through the occupation, acquiring Roman trade goods in the process. For example, the authors' excavations at the large roundhouse of East Coldoch yielded Roman pottery, along with bottle glass, which implies the import of Roman wine. A lot of the Roman material on native sites all over northern Europe relates to drinking, but the East Coldoch finds also suggest an openness to new foods, which are often a more conservative cultural area. The presence of grape pips might suggest imported raisins and there were also quantities of bread-wheat, which is a Roman staple, but rare on Iron Age sites. The site did not, however, produce any wheat pollen, so it is possible that the grain was not grown locally, and thus that even bulk agricultural goods were being traded, either with the Romans, or between the locals themselves.

A largely neglected, but potentially valuable resource for future study, is the unusually large number of native sites which lie in close proximity to Roman installations. To begin with, there are a surprising number of native structures actually inside Roman sites: both permanent installations and temporary camps. It is tempting to see these in terms of a stereotyped image of rapacious legionaries throwing native families out of their homes, to make way for the military sites,

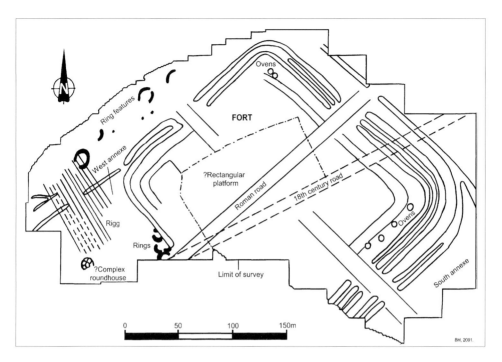

89 Cardean, the geophysical results

and on occasions this may well have been true. In practice, however, many of these features are only known from aerial or geophysical work and so we know nothing of the sequence involved. Nevertheless, there are certainly sites where the native features post-date the occupation, and where local people may have just reused the defences; whilst, on others, the Iron Age sites had been long abandoned when the Romans arrived. There are, though, still more native features close to, or even right outside Roman sites, and these may prove particularly revealing. We have already seen a group of at least 15 ring features outside the fortlet of Cargill (*70*), which has produced Roman finds to suggest that it was contemporary with the occupation. A similar group has been detected by the geophysical work to the north of Cardean (*89*), whilst antiquarian accounts record a souterrain in the same field. Bertha, Inverquharity and Drumquhassle had similar concentrations, as does the camp at Dun (*colour plate 31*), which we have suggested as a possible fortified landing facility. Other forts may prove to have had similar settlements, and the Roman Gask Project is currently mounting a series of large geophysical surveys to investigate. Moreover, if Armit (1999) is correct – that souterrains served to store native produce destined for the Roman army – it may be significant that we now have such features outside at least Cargill, Cardean and Inverquharity.

The significance of these settlements remains uncertain, for although a number of potential scenarios spring to mind, a lot more work will be needed before it will be possible to express a preference for any of them. For example, the sites all tend to occupy good defensive and settlement positions, often on firm, well-drained promontories, close to water sources, but clear of any flooding. It may well be, therefore, that the Romans simply picked them for the same reason the natives had, possibly displacing local inhabitants in the process. Secondly, it could be that the Roman's were deliberately positioning themselves on power centres, to either monitor or even support local leaders. On the face of it, this might seem improbable, as none of the native sites involved seem particularly impressive: but recent work by F. Hunter (2002) at the Iron Age site of Birnie (in Moray) has made it clear how ill-equipped we are at present to recognise contemporary power centres from the air. For,this apparently unremarkable site has produced substantial hoards of Roman coins and, again, it may be that the local Roman-period, Iron Age society was not much interested in demonstrating status through architecture. A final possibility is that the Roman sites welcomed the continuation of native settlement, or even deliberately attracted it, to act in the manner of fort *vici*. These are almost universal further south, but it has long been noted that very few of the forts of Scotland have anything resembling the normal, Romanised towns outside their walls, even though they seem to have been actively encouraged elsewhere. Indeed, to date, the only forts north of the Forth and Clyde to produce even tenuous traces of what might be a normal *vicus*, are Doune, and Strageath on the Gask, where we have already seen a network of roads, and a possible field system (*colour plate 14*). Elsewhere, however, it may be that we have been looking for the wrong thing, and that locals, or even non-locals, using local architectural techniques, were able to step in to perform the role of a *vicus* and profit from the army's presence.

It is also worth noting a tendency for Roman temporary camps to be sited close to native communities, some of which were quite large by local standards. For example, the camp at Eassie (NO 351466), near Cardean, is surrounded by at least three different native settlements (*86*). Likewise Lintrose camp, to the north of Perth (NO 220376), sits amongst a concentration of at least four souterrain settlements. In fact the camps of northern Scotland are a suspiciously impressive collection. Some, such as Raedykes (NO 841902), have substantial rock-cut ditches (*90*), which seem overly engineered for what are supposed to be mere overnight stopping places. They also tend to be superbly well sited and, if they really do represent no more than lines of march, one wonders whether Roman short-range reconnaissance was really that good, or whether they might in themselves be a pointer to active native collusion in Roman campaigns through the area. We should, after all, expect regional differences in attitudes to Rome amongst

90 Raedykes temporary camp, showing the rock-cut defensive ditch

the patchwork of tribal groupings: just as there are archaeological differences (Hunter 2001); if the local societies in the occupied area had previously felt under threat from tribes further north, they might have welcomed the Romans as potential protectors, and provided operational as well as logistical support.

Interestingly, there are tenuous clues that the invasion might have been preceded by diplomatic moves that would have been well suited to uncover such differences. Under the Flavian emperors we see signs of an empire-wide shift in foreign policy, accompanied by a burst of literary references to strange new lands, and to missions of exploration (e.g. Silius Italicus, *Punica*, 3.10). We hear of Romans going south towards Germa in the Sahara, and then beyond to Agisimba (probably on Lake Chad). Others explored towards the Baltic, to discover the source of the amber trade, and we see the development of the Egyptian, Red Sea harbours, to channel the incense and silk trades. An expedition to explore islands off the coast of Britain is mentioned, and there is an enigmatic reference in the Chinese annals to a communication from Rome (which the Chinese chose to regard as a surrender) reaching the Chinese emperor in what is now Vietnam. Within a few years of his accession, Vespasian took over the eastern kingdom of Cappadocia (now eastern Turkey), and an inscription to him was set up as far to the east as Azerbaijan. Late first-century Roman finds abound along the southern and eastern Baltic; the Black Sea; along the Silk and Incense Roads; in Nubia and in the Central Sahara (e.g. Leskow 1989, 29f). In fact, Rome was generally stretching her wings and exploring her surroundings, in search of trade opportunities and, to judge from later results, potential targets for conquest. In Britain, we have already seen Agricola dispatching an exploratory naval mission to circumnavigate the island for the first time: but there may have been significantly earlier activity on land. A number of Scottish, native sites have produced millefiori glass which is too early to be contemporary with the occupation. There are also a number of large, high-quality, Campanian bronze saucepans (e.g. the Stormont trulla in Perth Museum), which were also produced before the occupation (Hoffmann forthcoming, c). These seem to have been highly valued by the natives and were frequently mended: often before being finally deposited in the ground or, more frequently, in rivers or lochs. Given what we know of the methods and history of Roman exploration, these may be a sign that existing trade networks and/or dedicated diplomatic/espionage missions had been used for some time, to explore the area prior to conquest. These could have established contacts with local leaders, using Roman luxury goods, such as the expensive cooking vessels, as diplomatic gifts. The contacts and political information thus gathered might have been invaluable, and the missions could also have been used to reconnoitre the ground, identify potential garrison sites and to soften up the area for conquest, by detecting local enmities and exploiting them to recruit potential allies. This process of what might be called 'saucepan diplomacy' is well attested for other periods, and can be shown to have existed in the south of Britain, where the pre-conquest period of contact was longer.

There are also just a few indications that the Romans may have actively sought to avoid impinging on native ritual and funerary sites, which may be a deliberate mark of respect, or at least a desire to avoid unnecessary antagonism. One good example is the Gask tower of Raith, where a series of burials can be seen from the air immediately outside the Roman site. As we have seen, Raith has the best potential vantage point of any of the Gask observation towers, and yet the site was built about 40m to the east of the ideal position (now marked by an O.S. trig point (53, G)), conceivably to avoid these features. Other examples include the northern ditch of the largest of the Ardoch temporary camps, which passes through an area of marshy ground, apparently to avoid another barrow-field, whilst Inchtuthil left at least one large barrow untouched, immediately to its east. This may be a sign of tact (however self interested), but it is also consistent with Rome's general, often reverential approach to allies', and even opponents', gods and other sacred entities: which might include the dead. The Romans saw their relationship with gods in very businesslike terms and would often try to recruit or bribe them to join their own cause rather than, in the case of enemy gods, defeat them: and we may see something of this process at work here. Indeed, elsewhere in Britain, for example the fort of Great Chesters on Hadrian's Wall (Jones & Woolliscroft 2001, 109), there are signs that the Roman army may have adopted established native cemeteries to bury its own dead, presumably because they already had a suitable air of sanctity.

We may thus have a story of surprisingly friendly Roman/native relations, at least in the occupied area; and the fact that trade goods continued to reach sites such as East Coldoch into the fourth century, long after the Roman army had departed, may show that these good relations were maintained. Indeed, we might even see the area as some sort of protectorate, or buffer zone, after the end of formal occupation: perhaps with Rome offering some form of security guarantee in exchange for military and political intelligence. If so, this might feed back into a mystery which has fascinated Scottish archaeology for centuries: the hunt for the site of Mons Graupius. Phenomenal effort has gone into this search over the years and it is easy to see the attraction. Archaeology has been described as the handmaiden of history (although it is now unfashionable to say so), but in Mons Graupius it has a rare opportunity to look for what is supposed to be a great historical event; a real, some would say decisive, battle. The temptation is just too hard to resist. Many locations have been suggested, ranging from Fife, to Inchtuthil, to Aberdeenshire. In recent decades, attention has focused (e.g. Maxwell 1990b) on Bennachie Hill, and the nearby temporary camp of Durno, (NJ 697273), near Inverurie in Aberdeenshire. At present, however, there is no objective evidence in its favour and the most recent book on the subject has tried to place the battle back around Strathearn: on the Cairnie Braes, on the Gask Ridge (Fraser 2005). Assuming that a battle of some sort did actually take place, outside of Tacitus' imagination, the possibility that the occupied zone may have been largely welcoming (or indifferent) might be of some help in this search. Specifically, it might point to a northern location, where more fierce resistance could have been encountered. Whether this would turn the spotlight back on Bennachie is an entirely different matter: but it would certainly tend to argue against Strathearn.

The Fraser hypothesis is anyway difficult to take seriously, on purely tactical grounds. The Cairnie Braes are a natural amphitheatre of steep, south-facing slopes (NO 0218), which enjoy a commanding view over Strathearn. They lie to the south of Midgate and Westmuir, and to the north of the temporary camps at Dunning (NO 024150) and Forteviot (NO 039175): with the Earn itself at their base. As Fraser points out, they represent tactically very strong ground against an attack from the Strath. In fact, in ancient times, they would probably have been even stronger than they now look, because much of the valley bottom here is artificially drained and, like Strathmore, would have contained a great deal of wetland in its natural state. Even today, extensive areas are subject to regular flooding: so the river would have been fringed by marshes, to present an even more formidable natural defence. Fraser's supposition, is that the Caledonians exploited this strength by occupying the Braes, thus forcing the Roman army to attack them from a most disadvantageous position. He suggests that Agricola would have advanced up Strathearn on the eve of the battle, seen the Caledonian army on the Braes, and made camp at what he calls the first-century, claviculate camp at Dunning. In the morning, he would then have made a frontal assault; wading through the swamps; fording the river and storming up the steep hills: all in the teeth of Caledonian opposition and all without needing to commit the legions.

There are serious problems with this picture, however. Aside from the fact that Dunning is titulate, not claviculate, and that all of the finds recovered from it are second century in date, the Braes are nothing like as invulnerable as they first appear. They may be strong from the direction of Strathearn, but from virtually any other, they would be a military death trap: terrifyingly easy to outflank. In particular, there is higher ground to their rear, as they lie south of the summit of the Gask Ridge. In other words, they are overlooked from the direction of the Roman road and watch system which, on the likely new chronology, might already have existed at the time. Worse still, depending on the efficiency of the Caledonian pickets, it would be perfectly possible for an attacking force to get within well under 1km of the site without being seen. Fraser seems to assume that if the Caledonians had occupied the Braes, they would have taken Agricola by surprise, and so forced him into a frontal attack; but even an inexperienced general should not have been easily tricked into such a dangerous move. By this late stage in his term of office, Agricola should have known the ground well enough to understand the alternatives full well: and if he did not see the opportunity, he had seasoned officers with him who would. To be sure, he was in a position to overrule them, but under these conditions it would have taken a mad man to have done so.

Roman armies on the march always sent out reconnaissance units to scout out the ground and detect enemy activity in their path. The Cairnie Braes can be seen from many miles up Strathearn (from at least Auchterarder) and, as a large camped army tends to generate a great deal of campfire smoke, Agricola's scouts would have been able to detect the Caledonians without being noticed themselves; and long before the main Roman column came into view. This one fact handed all of the cards to Agricola. Even if he had originally planned to take the Strath route, he now had the option to switch north to the Gask undetected. Depending on how far his main body had reached, there are a number of routes which could have taken him to the Strageath river crossing, without coming in sight of the Braes: and, from there, he could advance along the Gask Ridge to take the enemy from the rear. Thus caught, the Caledonians could have been pushed down the steep slopes and caught in a killing ground on the fringe of the marshes, where they might well have been all but annihilated. Standing on the ground, however, the danger is so apparent that, in practice, it seems unlikely whether even the most disorganised rabble of a Caledonian force would ever have placed themselves in such a suicidal position.

8

ROME'S FIRST FRONTIER?

In the mid-second century AD, the Greek orator Aelius Aristides (*On Rome,* 80-4) wrote a speech in praise of Rome, as seen from his perspective as an admiring provincial. In it, he says that the Romans considered it beneath their dignity to put a wall around their city (it would not be fortified for another century). Instead, they surrounded the entire empire with a ring of fortified frontiers. He considered these so impressive that he made an early call for tourism, by suggesting that people should go to see them: although he also warned that the empire was so large that it took a long time to reach them. Interestingly, there may actually have been some degree of frontier tourism in the ancient world, because a number of Roman vessels have been found which seem to be souvenirs from Hadrian's Wall. The basic truth, however, was that the empire had, indeed, become ringed by defences at the time Aristides was writing. We have already discussed the Gask as being one of these systems, and possibly Rome's first fortified land frontier (frontiers based on rivers such as the Rhine and Danube certainly began earlier). Indeed it is often simply referred to as 'the Gask frontier', with barely a second thought: but it is, perhaps, worth re-examining this identification to make sure that it is really appropriate.

Roman frontiers, like the proverbial giraffe, are surprisingly hard to define, although we still hopefully know one when we see it. In fact, it is often easier to say what these frontiers were not, than it is to prescribe what they actually were. For a start, although we are used to systems like Hadrian's Wall, which had significant running barriers, by no means all of the frontiers had such features, especially in their earliest days. For example, large parts of the Eastern and North African frontiers never acquired a barrier. Instead, they looked very like the Gask:

an open chain of towers and forts strung out along a road. Likewise, the German and Dacian frontiers began life in this configuration and only later acquired barriers. Moreover, even when a running barrier was present, it was usually far less impressive than Hadrian's Wall. It might be a timber palisade, a simple bank and ditch, a much lighter stone wall, or a turf rampart, like that of the Antonine Wall in Scotland. The net result, therefore, is that many Roman frontiers looked exactly like the Gask line and, to quote the old saying: something which looks like a duck and quacks like a duck, seems highly likely to be a duck.

Another thing that a Roman frontier can, but need not be, is the political border of the empire. For this reason, the very word 'frontier' is probably ill chosen, and some scholars prefer to adopt Latin terms, such as *limites*, to describe these systems, whilst still arguing over exactly what the Romans themselves meant by them. The very idea of international borders was probably rather more diffuse in the ancient world than it is today. We are used to sharp lines drawn on large-scale maps, so that it really is theoretically possible to stand with both feet in different countries. But Rome was always reluctant to admit that her power had limits at all, so the empire was probably wherever her writ could be made to run. Aristides makes the interesting claim that Rome sent settlers beyond the fortified lines, who were subsidised and provided with craftsmen and other necessities. To what extent this may be true is uncertain, but there are definitely areas where Roman territory may have extended well beyond the frontier. For example, both Hadrian's Wall and the Antonine Wall had extensive systems of outposts, and there are reasons for believing that these were not beleaguered positions imposed on outside peoples, but that their surroundings were still very much part of the empire (Woolliscroft 1988). Likewise, many of the military units on the Rhine and Danube maintained territories, for their own use, on the far side of the rivers (Kurzmann forthcoming) and, elsewhere, protectorates, buffer states and alliances extended Rome's influence far beyond the lines.

The frontiers performed a range of functions. Firstly, of course, they had to protect the empire from full-scale invasion, but it is easy here to misinterpret their design. It is tempting to look at a spectacular system such as Hadrian's Wall and see it, quite literally, as a scaled-up city wall, or as an early precursor to the Maginot Line (itself not on a political border), which was designed to be defended and fought from. In fact, most Roman frontiers would be utterly indefensible against large-scale attack, not least because their garrisons were spread out along the line, so that it would be easy for even a relatively small attacking force to achieve local superiority. Instead, invasion defence would be done in the field, and relied on the fact that the frontier forces could be concentrated to form a large, single army, which could itself be augmented by other units, when necessary. Invasion defence would, in fact, have been better served by continuing the pre-frontier practice of maintaining large battle groups at strategic points, where they could also have been used offensively. The more familiar dispersed approach, through which large swaths of frontier were guarded and watched in detail, reflects a Roman desire for what Luttwak (1976) has called 'preclusivity'. This means total control of all movement into and out from the line, and it served a number of purposes. Firstly, it allowed the frontiers to become collecting points for the import (and export) duties on which a significant part of the empire's tax revenues depended. It also, however, allowed the Roman government to maintain one of its proudest public relations achievements: the so-called *Pax Romana*, or 'Roman peace'. This was, in effect, a guarantee of total internal peace and security and represented at least the attempt to ensure that any citizen would be safe anywhere on Roman soil. This was important not only as a propaganda plus, to popularise imperial rule by giving it an active benefit, but also for logistical and economic reasons. For if agriculture and industrial production could be carried out in security right up to the garrisoned lines, there would be less need for expensive long-haul transportation of goods to supply the troops, and tax revenues would also benefit. What this meant, however, was that the frontiers had to be virtually airtight. They had to protect the empire from the smallest of raiding and sheep-stealing parties, and the fortified lines were functionally better suited to this policing role. They would also have propaganda value for, as Aristides says, many of these systems would have looked extremely impressive, which must have added to their deterrent value, as well as reassuring (but still cowing) the frontier provincials. One final role might even relate to internal politics because, frankly, the frontiers also served to keep the army busy, and well away from the political centre: for there are few things more dangerous to any government than an army with nothing to do (Mann 1974, 532).

Man-made running barriers were not always necessary or even helpful. For example, rivers and seas can act as barriers (although they can also be highways), whilst controlling movement in deserts, mountains and swamps can often be done by holding individual points such as oases, passes and lines of dry ground. Roman frontiers do, however, have two final, but universal characteristics which might help in their identification. Firstly, they tend to have a recognisable inside and outside, albeit the exact dividing line might be somewhat nebulous. Secondly, they show a much denser pattern of military bases than an internal, but still militarily occupied area. The first-century Roman deployment to the north of the Forth and Clyde seems to meet both criteria. A glance at a map of Flavian Scotland (*6*), shows that it had far more closely packed garrisons than the area to the south of the isthmus, and the manpower disparity was even greater, because of the presence in the north of a legion. Likewise there is also a definite outside. The Highlands remained untouched, but in a way that is not the crucial issue because, in other parts of the empire, Rome did hold mountain areas without placing military installations within them. Instead, they occupied more easily supplied, key points on their fringes, as did King Edward I of England, in Wales. The Hanoverian forces also used a similar approach in Scotland, although it is worth noting that their dispositions depended on occupying certain strategic points on the western seaboard, such as Fort William, which the Romans ignored. More importantly, however, Rome left significant population centres unoccupied, of which the most conspicuous is Moray. We might thus be forgiven for assuming a first-century frontier, but a final test would be to try to model how such a system might actually have worked.

The likelihood of a longer chronology for the first-century occupation, and especially for the life-span of the Gask, allows (indeed forces) us to reassess the likely workings of the Roman defences. As already outlined, it used to be thought that the Gask and the Highland fringe line were not in operation together. It might even be thought that it would have been superfluous for them to have coexisted. As a consequence, various suggestions have been offered in which the two deployments would perform separate roles at slightly different times. For example, two possible functions have been proposed for the Highland line forts, which are not mutually exclusive. One is implied by the name 'glen blocker forts' that is often assigned to them, i.e. that they formed a defensive screen to prevent marauding hoards of hill people rampaging down the glens to attack Roman occupied territory (e.g. Ogilvie and Richmond 1967, 76). Alternatively, they might have been intended as springboards, for assaults into the Highlands, that ultimately never materialised (e.g. Mann 1968, 308). Certainly the forts do lie on or near glen mouths and this must be an important clue to their function. Moreover, the presence of the Inchtuthil legionary fortress in Strathtay might fit both scenarios. For invasion corridors can always work both ways and, as this is the largest route into and out of the Highland massif, it would suit both Roman and native aggression. There are problems, however, and the first concerns the putative invading hoards of hill people: because archaeology has not been able to find them.

The Highland areas are ideal for site preservation because, with the exception of a few fertile glen bottoms, much of the land has never been ploughed. Yet, although many air photographic and surface searches have been made in the mountains, they find little except for numerous much later, Highland clearance ruins. There are a few Iron Age sites, but not many, and certainly not enough to provide the basis for much of a hoard. Likewise, the forts are not well equipped to receive the best advanced warning of attacks down their glens. Under normal conditions, one assumes that the Romans would have maintained

91 Fendoch fort, from Stroness Hill, with the Sma' Glen behind

intelligence cover ahead of their lines to give advance warning of any major attack (Woolliscroft, 1988, 23-7). But, in emergency conditions, intelligence breakdowns could easily have placed the forts in serious jeopardy. Yet, even if one accepts the supposed Fendoch tower as Roman, it could give no more than a few minutes warning of a surprise attack down the Sma' Glen (*91*), and the positions of some of the other glen forts, where no such towers are even hinted at, would have been even worse. Some, such as Bochastle, can see only a few hundred metres into their glens and so, even at full cohort strength, their garrisons could easily have become hostages to fortune. On the other hand, the springboard theory has its own problems. Firstly, without people, there was little to invade in the Highlands. The land itself would have been of little value and, for large areas, there was nothing beyond it but sea. At the same time, only Inchtuthil had sufficient manpower to mount an invasion, albeit the legion could have been switched to an alternative jumping-off point if needed. The new chronology would, however, make it probable that all three of the northern defence elements did exist together, so that it becomes chronologically possible that each would only have formed a component of a much wider and more complex frontier: and it is not difficult to imagine advantages in their doing so.

The Gask line itself is fairly obviously designed to control Strathearn and Strathallan. These two valleys are strategically vital, for together they have always formed the principle, indeed virtually the only, viable invasion route into (or out of) northern Scotland. Such geographic determinism is currently much out of fashion but, in military matters, it remains inescapable: for armies, of whatever time period, can only operate where they can move and be supplied (Southern 1996). Even today, these are still by far the most important routes to the north, and it is no coincidence that the Roman road, and the campaign route marked by the temporary camps, are closely followed by the A9 dual-carriageway and the modern railway. The Gask towers would, no doubt, have monitored movements across the line, and passed on warnings of trouble to the main garrison forts, by signal. There have, in fact, been suggestions in the past that the towers were designed purely to act as a signalling system, to transmit messages up and down the line. In reality, there are far more towers than would have been needed for such a role, and they were almost certainly built to provide observation cover. Nevertheless, there is again little point in having observers unless they can report what they see, and the system seems to have been carefully designed so that almost all of the minor installations could see and thus signal directly to a fort (92) using the visual techniques of the day. The remainder could signal via just one intervening relay site (Woolliscroft 1993) and this design was to be copied on most, if not all subsequent Roman frontiers (Woolliscroft 2001a). Cross-system movements are likely to have been relatively insignificant, however, for there are very few natural routes across the line. Instead the Gask primarily watched the straths themselves, and this is particularly clear on the Gask Ridge, where many of the towers lie south of the ridge-top, in positions chosen to provide the best possible view over Strathearn. On occasions, this has even been done at the expense of their having little or no view to the north which, at first sight, seems curious; for it means that it would have been relatively easy to get close to the system from the north without being detected. This would have been much less of an issue, however, if the Gask and the Highland line were mutually supporting. Besides, some of the Gask installations (e.g. Raith and Midgate) do have superb long-range views to the north, which could have provided long enough warning of an attack (even by horsemen) for effective counter measures to be taken. Nevertheless, a presence in force ahead of the line would still have been extremely valuable, and the Gask could represent a back stop frontier to which the glen blockers acted, at least to some extent, as outposts. On the other hand, the support could act both ways. Firstly, the main Gask garrisons were well placed to act as a reserve to the Highland forts, albeit their potential would have been increased by better roads. Likewise, Pitts and St Joseph (1985, 278f) have argued that the Gask could have acted as a fortified supply line, which would have been a vital logistical life-line to the more forward bases.

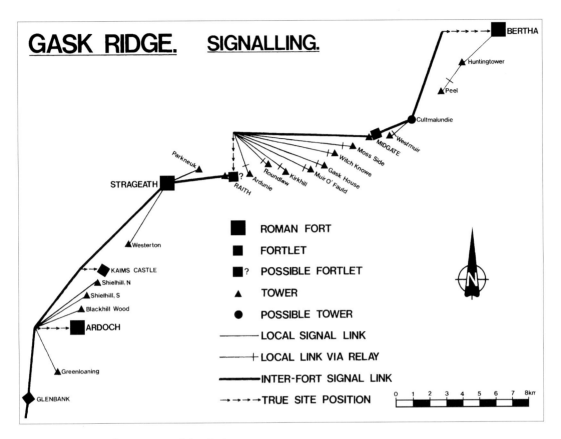

92 The signalling system of the Gask

Perhaps the most important clue to the frontier's operational rationale, however, concerns the nature of the Highland glens. A particular weakness of the springboard model for the role of the Highland line forts is the simple fact that most of the glens do not really lead anywhere. They do, however, most certainly interconnect: indeed so much so that it is possible to go up virtually any of the glen mouths between the Clyde and the Tay and emerge from any of the others (*93*). They also connect with two routes which do penetrate the far north, and in particular Moray, where in Roman times, as today, there was rich agricultural land which did support a significant population. To the north of the Tay there are two potential invasion routes into and out of northern Scotland. The main route follows Strathmore, where again we find a close relationship between the Roman temporary camps and the main modern road: the A90 dual-carriageway. Most post-Roman campaigns have also followed this route. For example, Balliol surrendered to Edward I, in July 1296, actually inside the Roman fort of Stracathro.

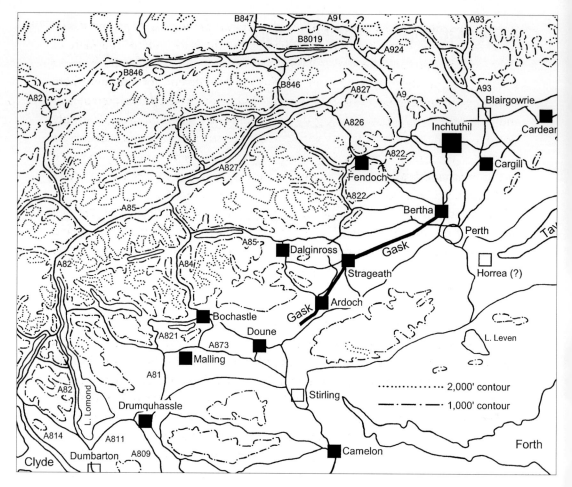

93 Topographic map of the Highland fringe

A less popular route, however, followed Strathtay through modern Pitlochry, Glen Garry and Strathspey, and then forked to head for both Elgin and Inverness. Such an interconnected route network would obviously undermine the Gask, because it would have made it frighteningly easy to out-flank, if it did ever stand alone. For example, one could slip down the Glen Garry route as far as Blair Athol, then turn west towards Loch Tummel or Loch Tay, and come out virtually anywhere between Crieff and the Clyde. The forts are thus blocking the glens, but not necessarily against forces which originated in those glens. Indeed, for this very reason, it would not be surprising to find a further Highland line fort somewhere between Loch Lomond and the Clyde, possibly at Dumbarton, which was the head of navigation until the removal (by explosives) of the Dumbuck shoal in the late eighteenth century. Alternatively, without the Strathmore forts and Inchtuthil, one could have moved down Strathmore, turned up Strathtay and entered this maze of glens to again out-flank the Gask. All three elements are thus vital for the frontier's security. The situation in Strathmore itself is rather different, for although there are still glens running north from it into the Highlands, these do not interconnect and do not generally provide long-distance routes to populated areas. The only exception is Glen Ardle, which affords a pass between Blairgowrie and Pitlochry, in Strathtay, and, again, it would come as no surprise if we were eventually to find a fort in or around Blairgowrie as a result. For the most part, however, the forts here could afford to be sited in mid-valley, blocking the main route.

This model makes it more obvious than ever why Inchtuthil was the key position of the entire frontier. For it is well placed to cover both Strathtay and Strathmore, whilst still screening the route to Strathearn and occupying a strong physical location. This explains why it received the legion, which was by far the most important single unit on the system, and thus single-handedly accounted for, perhaps, a third of the entire garrison. Even with the fortress in place, however, there was considerable value in the Strathmore forts operating in concert with the Gask: not least for early warning along what was still probably the most important potential invasion route. The strath was also worth holding in its own right, because it contained rich agricultural land which would have been a useful source of supplies. Nevertheless, the landscape would have looked very different in ancient times from how it does today, and this has greatly influenced its occupation pattern. The strath is now one of the richest arable areas in northern Scotland but, as we have seen, large areas are artificially drained and would have been wetland or water meadow until the eighteenth century (86). There were, however, dry routes down its north and south sides, with occasional cross routes between them, and the Strathmore forts are well placed to guard these. For example, Cardean blocks both the southern main route and a river crossing that gives access to a north–south passage to the northern route at Alyth. In short, the three elements of the northern defences are perfectly contrived to complement each other, and the efficiency of the design implies a good understanding of ground stretching well outside the occupied area, which in turn suggests detailed reconnaissance of the Highlands, at least as far north as the Great Glen.

Finally, Doune, Malling and Drumquhassle might also have had another role. Large tracts of the Forth valley were impassable marshland until they were drained in the eighteenth century and, as we have seen, there were a limited number of ways through or around them. Malling and Drumquhassle are well placed to monitor the swamp's western end, and this dual role might explain why these forts are set back rather further from their glens than the other members of the highland line. To the east, Doune controlled the ancient dry route known as the Fords of Frew, as did Doune Castle in the medieval period. To complete the pattern, it again seems likely that another fort would have been needed, in or around Stirling, to watch the eastern end of the mosses, and guard the lowest convenient bridging point on the Forth. A Stirling fort would also break what would otherwise be a rather long, 22.5km (14 mile), gap between Doune and Camelon, and so may seem likely on those grounds alone: for it is 10km (6 miles) from the former and 13km (8 miles) from the latter. Moreover, it is now all but certain that Doune was not brought back into use in the Antonine period, but the Gask forts, from Ardoch to Bertha certainly were. This would have resulted in an even longer 29km (18 mile) gap between Camelon and Ardoch, which seems too great to have gone without an intervening station: and again a fort at Stirling would have been the most likely position. Interestingly, the Roman deployment, both here and in Strathmore, shows a mastery of the use of marshland for defence. It might thus be worth noting that one of the candidates for the true invader of Scotland, Petillius Cerialis, arrived in Britain fresh from his victories amongst the fens of the Rhine delta, and so should have been Rome's most experienced expert in conducting warfare in wetland conditions.

The conclusion this chapter has reached is that the Gask line may not be a complete frontier by itself, despite being so often described as such. Instead, it is a key and, for its time, highly innovative element in a vastly larger frontier system, which stretched from the Clyde to northern Strathmore. This may be somewhat at variance with our traditional image, but such a modular approach was quite common amongst the many other Roman frontiers to which this prototype gave birth. For example, even that most iconic of systems, Hadrian's Wall, is not a frontier in itself. It is just one (albeit huge) part of a far wider network of outposts, coastal defences and hinterland forts, whose operational tendrils probably stretch back at least as far as the legionary fortresses of Chester and York. Likewise, the Antonine Wall had coastal defences (albeit less extensive) and a system of outposts, whose full extent we may still not fully understand. Other frontiers, elsewhere in the empire, show similar patterns and it is perhaps time that we encouraged the concept of 'frontier elements' in Roman frontier studies, to allow for this style of design. Knowing the modern world's fondness for jargon, these could perhaps be christened 'frontels' (if only half seriously), just as digital 'picture elements' have become 'pixels'. If so, then Hadrian's Wall would become one frontel, as would the Gask line, the Highland line, the Forth moss forts, and Strathmore. It would, of course, be possible for single sites to belong to more than one frontel: for example Malling, which belongs with the Highland line and the Forth mosses, whilst several frontels would combine to form a complete frontier: in this case, Rome's first.

APPENDIX:

THE BUILDING OF THE GASK SYSTEM

One final area where recent work has increased our knowledge, is the building and construction sequence of the Gask. This is more difficult to unravel than it might sound, because of the system's relatively open nature. On other Roman frontiers, we can often determine the sequence in which particular components were built, through their stratigraphic relationship with linear elements, such as a running barrier of some sort. The Gask denies us this luxury, however, for no such feature existed. Instead the only constant element is the road, and even this is not as helpful as it might be. For a start, the only stratigraphic link yet found between it and an installation is the still ambiguous presence of a quarry-pit in the entrance of Shielhill North tower. Likewise, there is no guarantee that the beautifully engineered line as we have it is not Antonine. That said, the fact that all of the minor installations have their entrances oriented towards the line would suggest that that the two were built (or at least planned) together, or even that the road (at least in some guise) predates the frontier. There are, though, a number of other clues that might be relevant to the system's construction. We have seen that the southernmost four towers have double ditches and a regular spacing system of ⅗ of a Roman mile, whilst other sectors have single ditches and, for the most part, more random spacings (*TABLE 1*). One possible explanation for this is that the southern sector was not fully contemporary with the rest of the line: but on other Roman frontiers, such as Hadrian's Wall, differences in design often represent not different building periods, but simply the work of different construction teams and the same may well be true on the Gask. If so,

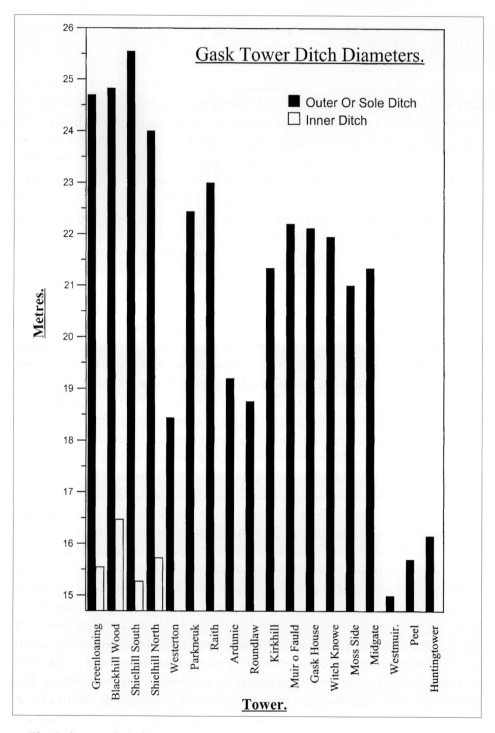

94 The Gask tower ditch diameters

can we find evidence for any other such building sectors? There are, for example, differences in the shape, size and ground areas of the towers but, on analysis, these seem to be fairly randomly distributed.

The tower ditches tell a rather different story, however, and have characteristics which may point to there being several building sectors. At one point, indeed, the system appeared to fall quite neatly into four, and we had come to believe that this might point to the line being built in a single season by detachments from each of the four legions in Britain at the time: which are the usual builder units (Woolliscroft 2002, 22). The geophysical results from Raith mean that this can no longer be sustained, however, and it now seems possible that there are actually six different sectors on the line. Firstly, again, we have the southern group of four which, with their double ditches, are not surprisingly the largest sites in overall diameter: at 24-26m (94). Secondly, there is Parkneuk and Raith, at the western end of the Gask Ridge proper which, although single ditched are, at c.23m, only 1-2m smaller in diameter than the southern group's outer ditches. There is also a group of six towers from Kirkhill to Midgate, towards the eastern end of the Ridge, with only fractionally smaller diameters of c.22m. Next comes Westerton and another group from Ardunie to Roundlaw, which are significantly smaller at 18-19m and, finally, an eastern group, from Westmuir to Huntingtower, whose diameters, at only 15-16m, are smaller than some of the southern group's inner ditches.

The ditch volumes, where known, also follow these divisions (95). Those of the southern group are abnormally slight: sometimes laughably so. They are often less than 0.5m deep and they are sometimes barely more than a metre wide. Indeed, Blackhill Wood was found to have an oven (39) set into one of its ditches (Glendinning and Dunwell 2000, 277f), and although this may relate to a somewhat later temporary camp, it does at least make the point that these features can have had little, if any, defensive value. The eastern Ridge towers, on the other hand, have substantial ditches of up to 1.8m deep and 4m wide, and it is interesting in this context that the controversial Midgate tower fits well with the rest of the group. Meanwhile, Parkneuk's ditch is just a little smaller, whilst Westerton, Ardunie, Roundlaw and the Eastern group have intermediate-sized ditches of around 2m wide and just under 1m deep. Furthermore, just as the southern sites have double ditches, most of the other groups have additional distinguishing features. For example, Westerton and Roundlaw, unlike the eastern Ridge group (but like the double-ditched sites), have their rectangular towers set with their long axes facing their entrances. They also have ditches of the asymmetrical *fossa punica* type, rather than the standard, V-shaped profiles known everywhere else on the line. Furthermore, Westerton, at least, had a pair of projecting slots running out from the tower, towards the entrance, which might be the foundation for a flight

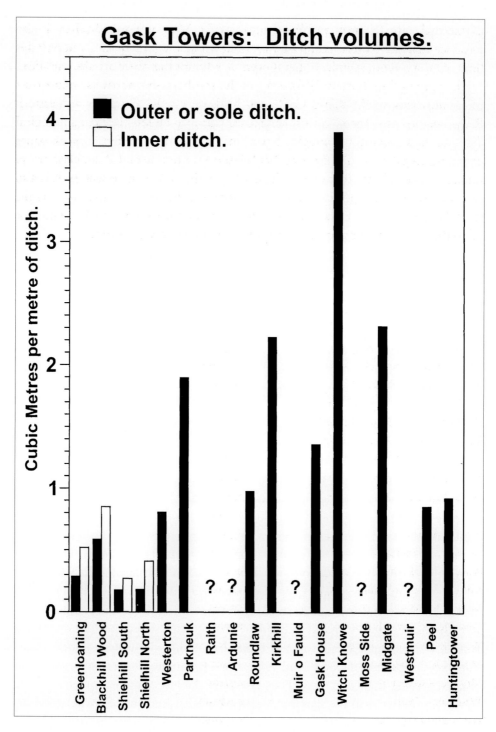

95 The Gask tower ditch volumes

of external steps (Hanson and Friell 1995, 502ff). More importantly, there is also evidence that the Eastern group may again be set at a regular spacing interval: this time of ⅔ of a Roman mile. It might even be relevant that there are also variations in the design of the fortlets: Glenbank, on the southern sector, has its entrance set in its short axis, whilst Kaims Castle and Midgate, on the Westerton and eastern Ridge sectors, have theirs in their long axes. This may be less clear cut and logical than we had previously thought, but it might still show different work gangs operating together; whilst the fact that Westerton, Ardunie and Roundlaw are so similar, might indicate that one of those gangs built two separate sectors. It is also noteworthy that the possible tower at Woodhead, between Bertha and Cargill, strongly resembles the Gask's double-ditched, southern towers, which means that (if confirmed) it might also have been built by the same work group.

TABLE I
THE GASK: INSTALLATION SPACINGS

Glenbank – Greenloaning	c.2,300m
Greenloaning – Ardoch	c.2,750m
Ardoch – Blackhill Wood	900m
Blackhill Wood – Shielhill South	875m
Shielhill South – Shielhill North	950m
Shielhill North – Kaims Castle	875m
Kaims Castle – Westerton	2,300m
Westerton – Strageath	c.4,200m
Strageath – Parkneuk	1,750m
Parkneuk – Raith	1,520m
Raith – Ardunie	1,510m
Ardunie – Roundlaw	1,110m
Roundlaw – Kirkhill	960m
Kirkhill – Muir o' Fauld	1,440m
Muir o' Fauld – Gask House	870m
Gask House – Witch Knowe	800m
Witch Knowe – Moss Side	1,120m
Moss Side – Midgate	1,400m
Midgate – Westmuir	c.915m
Westmuir – Peel	c.3,975m
Peel – Huntingtower	c.1,940m
Huntingtower – Bertha	c.3,175m

BIBLIOGRAPHY

ANCIENT WRITERS

Aelius Aristides, *On Rome*, Wissenschaftliche Buchgesellschaft edition, 1977, Trans: Klein, R.

Caesar, *De Bello Gallico*, Loeb Edition, 1917, Trans: Edwards, H.J.

Cassius Dio, *Roman History*, Loeb Edition, 1914-27, Trans: Cary, E.

Josephus, *The Jewish War*, Penguin Edition, 1981, Trans: Smallwood, E.M.

Pliny the Elder, *Naturalis Historia*, Loeb Edition, Trans: Rackham, H.

Pliny the Younger, *Letters*, Loeb Edition, 1969, Trans: Radice, B.

Pliny the Younger, *Panegyricus*, Loeb Edition, 1969, Trans: Radice, B.

Plutarch, *The Decline of oracles*, Loeb Edition, 1936, Trans: Babbitt, F.C.

Ptolemy, *Geography*, in Rivet & Smith 1981, 131ff

Sallust, *Bellum Catilinae*, Penguin Edition, 1963, Trans: Handford, S.A.

Silius Italicus, *Punica*, Loeb Edition, 1934, Trans: Duff, J.D.

Statius, *Silvae*, v,ii, *Laudes Crispini Vetti Bolani Filii*. Loeb Edition, 1955, Trans: Mozley, J.H.

Tacitus, *De Vita et moribus Iulii Agricolae*, Loeb Edition, 1914, Trans: Peterson, W.

Tacitus, *The Histories*, Penguin Classics Edition, 1964, Trans: Wellesly, K.

Tertullian, *Apologeticum*, Loeb Edition, 1931, Trans: Glover, T.R.

MODERN WRITERS

Abercromby, J. (1902) 'Account of the excavation of the Roman station at Inchtuthil, Perthshire, undertaken by the Society of Antiquaries of Scotland in 1901', *Proc Soc Antiq Scot*, 36, 182-242

Abercromby, J. (1904) 'Excavations made on the estate of Meikleour, Perthshire in May 1903', *Proc Soc Antiq Scot*, 38, 82-96

Adamson, H. (1774) *The Muses Threnodie*, Perth

Adamson, H.C. (1979) 'The Roman fort at Bertha', in Breeze D.J. (ed.) *Roman Scotland some recent excavations*, Edinburgh, 33ff

Adamson, H.C. and Gallagher, D. B. (1986) 'The Roman fort at Bertha: the 1973 excavation', Proc Soc Antiq Scot, 116, 195ff

Aikman, J. (1827) *The history of Scotland* (translation of G. Buchanan, *c.*1582), Glasgow

Alföldi, M.R. (1999) *Bild und Bildersprache der römischen Kaiser*, Mainz

Anderson, W.A. (1956) 'The Roman fort at Bochastle', *Trans Glasgow Arch Soc* (New ser 14), 35–63

Armit, I. (1999) 'The abandonment of souterrains: evolution, catastrophe or dislocation?', *Proc Soc Antiq Scot*, 129, 577–96

Baatz, D. (1997) 'Keeping watch over the *Limes*', *Arch Ael* (5), 25, 1–20

Bailey, G.B. (2000) 'Excavations on the Roman temporary camps at the Three Bridges, Camelon, Falkirk', *Proc Soc Antiq Scot*, 130, 469–90

Baird, R.D. (2005) 'The Roman road at Woodlea, Greenloaning, Perthshire: excavations in 1997/8', *Tayside & Fife Archaeological Journal*, 11, 1–8

Baradez, J. (1949) *Fossatum Africae*, Paris

Barclay, G.J. & Maxwell, G. S. (1991) 'Excavation of a Neolithic long mortuary enclosure within the Roman legionary fortress at Inchtuthil, Perthshire', *Proc Soc Antiq Scot*, 121, 27–44

Barclay, G.J. & Maxwell, G.S. (1998) *The Cleaven Dyke and Littleour: monuments in the Neolithic of Tayside*, Society of Antiquaries of Scotland, Monograph no 13, Edinburgh

Barclay, R. (1777) 'On Agricola's engagement with the Caledonians, under their leader Galgacus', *Archaeologia Scotica*, 1, 565–70

Bateson, D. & Hall, M. forthcoming, 'Inchyra, Perthshire', in *Coin hoards from Roman Britain* XI, London

Bennett, J. (1997) *Trajan, optimus princeps*, London

Bérard, F., Le Bohec, F.Y. & Reddé, M. (1995) 'Les Tuiles éstampilles', in Reddé, M. & Goguey, R. (ed.) *Le camp légionnaire de Mirebeau*, Römisch-Germanisches Zentralmuseum Monographien 36, 191–267, Mainz

Birley, A.R. (1976) 'The date of Mons Graupius', *Liverpool Class Monthly*, 1.2, 179–90

Birley, E. (1951) 'The Brigantian problem and the first Roman contact with Scotland', *TDGNHAS*, 29, 46–65

Birley, E. (1976) *Roman Britain and the Roman army*, Kendal

Bishop, M.C. (2002) *Roman Inveresk past, present and future*, Duns

Bishop, M.C. (2005) 'A new Flavian military site at Roecliffe, North Yorkshire', *Britannia*, 36, 135–224

Boyd, W.E. (1984) 'Environmental change and Iron Age land management in the area of the Antonine Wall, central Scotland: a summary', *GAJ*, 11, 75–81

Breeze, D.J. (1980) 'Agricola the builder', *SAF*, 12, 14-24

Breeze, D.J. (1982) *The northern frontiers of Roman Britain*, London

Breeze, D.J. (1983) 'The Roman forts at Ardoch', in O'Connor, A. and Clarke, D.V. *From the Stone Age to the Forty Five*, Edinburgh, 224ff

Breeze, D.J. (1988) 'Why did the Romans fail to conquer Scotland?', *Proc Soc Antiq Scot*, 118, 3-22

Breeze, D.J. (1990) 'Agricola in the Highlands', *Proc Soc Antiq Scot*, 120, 55-60

Breeze, D.J. (2000) 'The Romans in Perthshire', in Perthshire Society of Natural Science, Archaeological and Historical Section (ed.) *Dirt, dust and development, 50 years of Perthshire archaeology*, Perth

Breeze, D.J. Close-Brooks, J. & Ritchie, J.N.G. (1976) 'Soldiers' burials at Camelon, Stirlingshire, 1922 and 1975', *Britannia*, 7, 73-95

Breeze, D.J. & Dobson, B. (1976) 'A view of Roman Scotland', *GAJ*, 4, 124-43

Bushe-Fox, J.P. (1913) 'The use of Samian pottery in dating the early Roman occupation of the north of Britain', *Archaeologia*, 64, 296-317

Butler, S. (1989) 'Pollen analysis from the west rampart' in Frere, S.S. & Wilkes, J.J. *Strageath, excavations within the Roman fort 1973-86*. Britannia Monograph Series no 9, London, 272-74

Buxton, K. & Howard-Davies, C. (2000) *Bremetenacum, excavations at Roman Ribchester, 1980, 1989-1990*, Lancaster imprints series, 9, Lancaster

Callander, J.G. (1919) 'Notes on the Roman remains at Grassy Walls and Bertha, near Perth', *Proc Soc Antiq Scot*, 53, 137-52

Caruana, I.D. (1997) 'Maryport and the Flavian conquest of north Britain', in Wilson, R.J.A. (ed.) *Roman Maryport and its setting*, Nottingham, 40-51

Caruana, I.D. forthcoming *The Roman forts at Carlisle: excavations at Annetwell Street, 1973-84*

Christison, D.J. (1901) 'Excavations undertaken by the Society of Antiquaries of Scotland of earthworks adjoining the "Roman road" between Ardoch and Dupplin Perthshire', *Proc Soc Antiq Scot*, 35, 16-43

Christison, D.J. and Cunningham, J.H. (1898) 'Account of the excavation of the Roman station at Ardoch, Perthshire undertaken by the Society of Antiquaries of Scotland in 1896-97', *Proc Soc Antiq Scot*, 32, 399ff

Christison, D., Buchanan, M. and Anderson, J. (1901) 'Account of the excavation of the Roman station of Camelon, near Falkirk undertaken by the Society in 1900', *Proc Soc Antiq Scot*, 35, 329-418

Coleman, R. & Hunter, F. (2002) 'The excavation of a souterrain at Shanzie farm, Alyth, Perthshire', *Tayside & Fife Archaeological Journal*, 8, 77-102

Crawford, O.G.S. (1939) 'Air reconnaissance of Roman Scotland', *Antiquity*, XIII, no 51, 280-92.

Crawford, O.G.S. (1949) *Topography of Roman Scotland north of the Antonine Wall*, Cambridge

Cunliffe, B. (1971) *Fishbourne, a Roman palace and its garden*, London

Curle, J. (1932) 'An inventory of objects of Roman and provincial Roman origin found on sites in Scotland not definitely associated with Roman constructions', *Proc Soc Antiq Scot*, 66, 277-397

Dixon, N. (2004) *The crannogs of Scotland*, Stroud

Dore, J.N. & Wilkes, J.J. (1999) 'Excavations directed by J.D. Leach and J.J. Wilkes on the site of a Roman fortress at Carpow, Perthshire, 1964-79', *Proc Soc Antiq Scot*, 129, 481-576

Drack, W. & Fellmann, R. (1988) *Die Römer in der Schweiz*, Stuttgart

Dumayne, L. (1998) 'Human impact on the environment during the Iron Age and Romano-British times: palynological evidence from three sites near the Antonine Wall, Great Britain', *Journal of Archaeological Science*, 25, 203-14

Dundas, J. (1866) 'Notes on the excavation of an ancient building at Tapock in the Torwood, parish of Dunipace, county of Stirling', *Proc Soc Antiq Scot*, 6, 259-65

Dunwell, A.J. and Keppie, L.J.F. (1995) 'The Roman temporary camp at Dunning, Perthshire: evidence from two recent excavations', *Britannia*, 26, 51-62

Eck, W. (2002) 'Traian der Weg zum Kaisertum', in Nünnerich-Asmus, A. *Traian. ein Kaiser der superlative am beginn einer Umbruchzeit?*, Mainz

Erdrich, M. Giannotta, K.M. & Hanson, W.S. (2000) 'Traprain Law: native and Roman on the northern frontier', *Proc Soc Antiq Scot*, 130, 441-56

Fraser, J.E. (2005) *The Roman conquest of Scotland, the battle of Mons Graupius, AD 84*, Stroud

Frere, S.S. (1980) 'The Flavian frontier in Scotland', *SAF*, 12, 89-97

Frere, S.S. (1984) 'Roman Britain in 1983', *Britannia*, xv, 265-332

Frere, S.S. & St Joseph, J.K. (1983) *Roman Britain from the air*, Cambridge

Frere, S.S. & Wilkes, J.J. (1989) *Strageath, excavations within the Roman fort 1973-86*, Britannia Monograph Series no 9, London

Gillam, J.P. (1975) 'Possible changes in plan in the course of the construction of the Antonine Wall', *SAF*, 7, 51-6

Glendinning, B. and Dunwell, A. (2000) 'Excavations of the Gask frontier tower and temporary camp at Blackhill Wood, Ardoch, Perth & Kinross', *Britannia*, 31, 255-90

Gordon, A. (1726) *Itinerarium Septentrionale*, London

Grainger, J.D. (2003) *Nerva and the Roman succession crisis of AD 96-99*, London

Gregory, R.A. (2001) 'Excavations by the late G.D.B. Jones and C.M. Daniels along the Moray Firth littoral', *Proc Soc Antiq Scot*, 131, 177-222

Groenman van Waateringe, W. (1980) 'Urbanisation and the north-west frontier of the Roman Empire', in Hanson, W.S. and Keppie L.J.F. (ed.) *Roman Frontier Studies 1979*, Oxford (Brit Arch Rep Int Ser, 71, vol 3), 1037-44

Groves, C. (1990) *Tree-ring analysis and dating of timbers from Annetwell Street, Carlisle, Cumbria, 1981-84*, A.M. Lab. Report 49/90, London

Hanson, W.S. (1978) 'The Roman military timber supply', *Britannia*, 9, 293-306

Hanson, W.S. (1978) 'Roman campaigns north of the Forth-Clyde isthmus: the evidence of the temporary camps', *Proc Soc Antiq Scot*, 109, 140-50

Hanson, W.S. (1980) 'The first Roman occupation of Scotland', in Hanson, W.S. and Keppie, L.J.F. (eds) *Roman Frontier Studies 1979: papers presented to the twelfth International Congress of Roman Frontier Studies*, Oxford

Hanson, W.S. (1987) *Agricola and the conquest of the North*, London

Hanson, W.S., Daniels, C.M., Dore, J.N. & Gillam, J.P. (1979) 'The Agricolan supply base at Red House, Corbridge', *Arch Ael (5)*, 7, 1-98

Hanson, W.S. & Friell, J.P.G. (1995), 'Westerton: a Roman watchtower on the Gask frontier', *Proc Soc Antiq Scot*, 125, 499-520

Hartley, B.R. (1972) 'The Roman occupations of Scotland: the evidence of Samian Ware', *Britannia*, 3, 1-55

Haverfield, F. (1922) 'The conquest of Britain' in Furneaux, H. & Anderson, J.G.C. (eds), *Cornelii Taciti de vita Agricolae*, (2nd ed), Oxford, XLIII – LXXIII

Hind, J.G.F. (1983) 'Caledonia and its occupation under the Flavians', *Proc Soc Antiq Scot*, 113, 373-78

Hingley, R.C. (1992) 'Society in Scotland from 700BC to AD200', *Proc Soc Antiq Scot*, 122, 7-53

Hobley, A.S. (1989) 'The numismatic evidence for the post-Agricolan abandonment of the Roman frontier in northern Scotland', *Britannia*, 20, 69-74

Hoffmann, B. (2004) 'Tacitus, Agricola and the role of literature in the archaeology of the first century AD in Sauer, E.W. (ed.) *Archaeology and Ancient History: Breaking down the Boundaries*, 151-65

Hoffmann, B. (forthcoming a) *The Roman and native glass from Newstead*, Edinburgh: NMS

Hoffmann, B. (forthcoming b) *Excavations at Cardean 1967-75, SAIR*, Edinburgh

Hoffmann, B. (forthcoming c) 'Cipius Polybius and the supply of bronze vessels in 1st-century Scotland' *Tayside & Fife Archaeological Journal*

Hoffmann, B. (forthcoming d) *Tacitus: the 'Agricola'*

Holmes, N. (2003) *Excavation of Roman sites at Cramond, Edinburgh*, Edinburgh

Horsley, J. (1732) *Britannia Romana*, London

Hunter, F. (2001) 'Roman and native in Scotland: new approaches' *J. Rom Arch*, 14, 289-309

Hunter, F. (2002) 'Birnie, buying peace on the Northern Frontier', *Current Archaeology*, 181, 12-16

Ingemark, D. (1998) 'Roman glass' in Main, L. 'Excavation of a timber roundhouse and broch at the Fairy Knowe, Buchlyvie, Stirlingshire, 1975-8', *Proc Soc Antiq Scot*, 128, 335-37

Jarrett, M.G. (1994) 'Non-legionary troops in Roman Britain', *Britannia*, 25, 35–78

Johnson, A. (1983) *Roman forts*, London

Jones, G.D.B. & Mattingly D. (1990) *An atlas of Roman Britain*, London

Jones, G.D.B. & Woolliscroft, D.J. (2001) *Hadrian's Wall from the air*, Stroud

Kamm, A. (2004) *The last frontier: the Roman invasions of Scotland*, Stroud

Keppie, L.J.F. (1983) 'Roman inscriptions from Scotland: some additions and corrections to RIB I', *Proc Soc Antiq Scot*, 113, 391ff

Keppie, L.J.F. (1986) *Scotland's Roman remains*, Edinburgh

Keppie L.J.F. (1996) 'Roman Britain in 1994, Scotland', *Britannia*, 26, 332–42

Keppie L.J.F. (2000) 'Roman Britain in 1999, Scotland', *Britannia*, 31, 379–84

Keppie L.J.F. (2004) *The legacy of Rome: Scotland's Roman remains*, (3rd ed), Edinburgh

Körtüm, K. (1998) 'Zur Datierung der römischen Militäranlagen im obergermanisch-rätischen Limes gebiet, Chronologische Untersuchungen anhand der Münzfunde', *Saalburg Jahrbuch*, 49, 5–65

Kurzmann, R. (2005) *Roman military brick stamps – a comparison of methodology*, unpublished Ph.D. thesis, University College Dublin

Kurzmann, R. forthcoming 'Prata, territorium & Co-Roman military territories and their terminology', *Hadrianic Society Bulletin*, 2006

Leskow, A.M. (1989) *Gold und Kunsthandwerk vom antiken Kuban. Neue Archaeologische Entdeckungen aus der Sowjetunion*, Stuttgart

Lockett, N.J. (2002) 'A geophysical survey in the annexes of the Roman fort of Strageath', in Woolliscroft, D.J. *The Roman frontier on the Gask Ridge, Perth & Kinross*, BAR (British Series), 335, 77–81

Luttwak, E.N. (1976) *The grand strategy of the Roman Empire*, Baltimore

Macdonald, G. (1918) 'Roman coins found in Scotland', *Proc Soc Antiq Scot*, 52, 203–76

Macdonald, G. (1919) 'The Agricolan occupation of north Britain', *JRS*, 9, 112–38

Macdonald, G. (1924) 'Roman coins found in Scotland II', *Proc Soc Antiq Scot*, 58, 325–29

Macdonald, G. (1937) 'Britannia statim omissa', *JRS*, 27, 93–8

Macinnes, L. (1984) 'Brochs and the Roman occupation of lowland Scotland', *Proc Soc Antiq Scot*, 114, 235–49

Maitland, W. (1757) *History and antiquates of Scotland*, London

Mann, J.C. (1968) review of Ogilvie, R.M. and Richmond, I.A. *Corelii Taciti: De Vita Agricolae*, in *Arch Ael* (4), 56, 306–08

Mann, J.C. (1974) 'The Frontiers of the Principate', *ANRW*, II, principat I, Berlin, 508–33

Mason, D.J.P. (2001) *Roman Chester, city of the eagles*, Stroud

Masser, P., Allason-Jones, L., Bateson, D., Evans, J. & Willis, S. (2002) 'Recent work at Drumquhassle Roman fort: Stirlingshire', *Scot Arch J*, 24.2, 147-68

Mattern, S.P. (1999) *Rome and the enemy, imperial strategy in the principate*, Berkeley

Maxfield, V.A. (1979) 'Camelon "South Camp": excavations 1975-79', in Breeze, D.J. (ed.) *Roman Scotland some recent excavations*, Edinburgh

Maxfield, V.A. (1981) 'The Flavian fort at Camelon', *SAF*, 12, 69-78

Maxfield, V.A. (1984) 'Camelon Roman forts 1899-1981', *Proc Soc Antiq Scot*, 114, 592f

Maxwell, G.S. (1981) 'Agricola's campaigns: the evidence of the temporary camps', *SAF*, 12, 25-54

Maxwell, G.S. (1983) 'Recent aerial discoveries in Roman Scotland: Drumquhassle, Elginhaugh and Woodhead', *Britannia*, 14, 167-82

Maxwell, G.S. (1984) 'New frontiers: the Roman fort at Doune and its possible significance', *Britannia*, 15, 217ff

Maxwell, G.S. (1989) *The Romans in Scotland*, Edinburgh

Maxwell, G.S. (1990a) 'Flavian frontiers in Caledonia', in Vetters, H. and Kandler, M. (ed.) *Akten des 14. Internationalen Limeskongresses 1986 in Carnuntum*, Vienna, 353ff

Maxwell, G.S. (1990b) *A battle lost, Romans and Caledonians at Mons Graupius*, Edinburgh

Maxwell, G.S. & Wilson, D.R. (1987) 'Air reconnaissance in Roman Britain 1977-1984', *Britannia*, 18, 1-48

McCord, N. and Tait, J. (1978) 'Excavations in the northern annexe of the Roman fort at Camelon, near Falkirk, 1961-3', *Proc Soc Antiq Scot*, 109, 151-65

Mellor, R. (1993) *Tacitus*, London

Millett, M. (1990) *The Romanization of Britain*, Cambridge

Nimmo W. (1777) *The history of Stirlingshire*, Glasgow

Ogilvie, R.M. and Richmond, I.A. (1967) *Cornelii Taciti de Vita Agricolae*, Oxford

Pennant, T. (1774) *A tour in Scotland: 1772*

Perth Museum & Art Gallery (1994) *Perth glass*, Perth

Pitts, L.F. and St Joseph, J.K. (1985) *Inchtuthil, the Roman legionary fortress*, Britannia Monograph Series no 6, London

Price, J. (1985) 'The Roman glass'. in: Pitts, L.F. and St Joseph, J.K. *Inchtuthil. the Roman legionary fortress*, Britannia Monograph Series no 6. London, 303-12

Price, J. (1989) 'The Roman glass' in Frere, S.S. and Wilkes, J.J. *Strageath, excavations within the Roman fort 1973-1986*, Britannia Monograph Series no 9, London. 192-203

Price, J. (1999) 'Bottle fragment', in Dore, J.N. and Wilkes, J.J. 'Excavations directed by J.D. Leach and J.J. Wilkes on the site of a Roman fortress at Carpow, Perthshire, 1964-79. *Proc Soc Antiq Scot*, 129, 481-575

Proudfoot, V.W. (1978) 'Camelon native site', *Proc Soc Antiq Scot*, 109, 112-28

Rabold, B. (1988) 'Neue Untersuchungen zum römischen Gebäude in Heidenheim', Weimert, H. (ed.) *Zivile und militärische Strukturen im Nordwestern der römischen Provinz Raetien*, Heidenheim

Ramsay, S. (20020 'Pollen analysis from Peel Roman tower', in Woolliscroft, D.J. *The Roman frontier on the Gask Ridge, Perth & Kinross*, BAR (British Series), 335, 66-7

Ramsay, S. & Dickson, J.H. (1997) 'Vegetational history of central Scotland' *Botanical Journal of Scotland*, 49(2), 141-50

RCAHMS (1990) *North-east Perth an archaeological landscape*, London

RCAHMS (1994) *South-east Perth an archaeological landscape*, London

RCAHMS (1997) *Catalogue of aerial photographs 1993*, Edinburgh

Richmond, I.A. (1940) 'Excavations on the estate of Meikleour, Perthshire 1939', *Proc Soc Antiq Scot*, 74, 37ff

Richmond, I.A. and McIntyre, J. (1936) 'The Roman fort at Fendoch in Glen Almond', *Proc Soc Antiq Scot*, 70, 400ff

Richmond, I.A. and McIntyre, J. (1939) 'The Agricolan fort at Fendoch', *Proc Soc Antiq Scot*, 73, 110ff

v. Ritterling, E. (1924) 'Legio' in Pauly's Realencyclopädie der classischen Altertumswissenschaft 12, 1, 1186-837

Rivet, A.L.F. (1964) 'Gask signal stations', *Arch J*, 121, 196-98

Rivet, A.L.F. & Smith, C. (1981) *The place names of Roman Britain*, London

Robertson, A.S. (1950) 'Roman coins found in Scotland', *Proc Soc Antiq Scot*, 84, 137-69

Robertson, A.S. (1964) 'Miscellanea Romano-Caledonica', *Proc Soc Antiq Scot*, 97, 180-201

Robertson, A.S. (1970a) 'Roman finds from non-Roman sites in Scotland', *Britannia* 1, 198-227

Robertson, A.S. (1970b) 'The Roman camp(s) on Hillside Farm, Dunblane, Perthshire' *GAJ*, 1, 35-36

Robertson, A.S. (1974) 'Roman "signal stations" on the Gask Ridge', *Trans Perthshire Society of Natural Science*, (Special Issue), 14-29

Robertson, A.S. (1977) 'Excavations at Cardean and Stracathro, Angus' in Haupt, D. & Günter Horn, H. *Studien zu der Militärgrenzen Roms II*, proceedings of the 10th International Congress of Roman Frontier Studies, Cologne

Robertson, A.S. (1978) 'The circulation of Roman coins in north Britain: the evidence of hoards and site-finds from Scotland' 186-216 in Carson, R.A.G. and Kraay, C.M. *Scripta Nummaria Romana*, (London)

Robertson, A.S. (1979) 'The Roman fort at Cardean', in Breeze, D.J. (ed.) *Roman Scotland Some Recent Excavations*, Edinburgh, 42ff

Robertson, A.S. (1983) 'Roman coins found in Scotland, 1971-82', *Proc Soc Antiq Scot*, 113, 405-48

Rogers, I.M. (1993) 'Dalginross and Dun: excavations at two Roman camps', *Proc Soc Antiq Scot*, 123, 277-90

Roy, W. (1793) *Military antiquities of the Romans in Britain*

St Joseph, J.K. (1951) 'Air reconnaissance in North Britain', *JRS*, 41, 52-65

St Joseph, J.K. (1955) 'Air reconnaissance in Britain, 1951-5', *JRS*, 45, 82-91

St Joseph J.K. (1958) 'Air reconnaissance in Britain, 1955-7', *JRS*, 58, 86-101

St Joseph J.K. (1965) 'Air reconnaissance in Britain, 1961-64', *JRS*, 55, 74ff

St Joseph, J.K. (1969) 'Air reconnaissance in Britain, 1965-68', *JRS*, 59, 104ff

St Joseph, J.K. (1970) 'The camps at Ardoch, Stracathro and Ythan Wells: recent excavations', *Britannia*, 1, 163ff

St Joseph, J.K. (1973) 'Air reconnaissance in Britain, 1969-1972', *JRS*, 63, 214-46

St Joseph, J.K. (1976) 'Air reconnaissance of Roman Scotland 1939-75', *GAJ*, 4, 1ff

St Joseph, J.K. (1977) 'Air reconnaissance in Britain, 1973-76', *JRS*, 67, 125ff

St Joseph, J.K. (1978) 'The camp at Durno, Aberdeenshire and the site of Mons Graupius', *Britannia*, 9, 271ff

Salway, P. (1982) *Roman Britain*, Oxford

Sarwey, O., v. Fabricius, E. & Hettner, F. (date depends on volume) *Der Obergermanisch- Raetische Limes des Römerreiches* (Usually: ORL), in BAG. 2005 facsimile edition, Remshalden

Shirley, E. (2001) *Building a Roman legionary fortress*, Stroud

Shotter D.C.A. (1996) *The Roman frontier in Britain*, Preston

Shotter, D.C.A. (2000a) 'Petillius Cerialis in northern Britain'. *Northern History*, 36:2, 189-98

Shotter, D.C.A. (2000b) 'The Roman conquest of the North-West', *CW (2)*, 100, 33-54

Sibbald, R. (1707), *Historical Inquiries*, Edinburgh

Simpson, F.G., Richmond, I.A., Hodgson, K.S. & St Joseph, J.K. (1936) 'Report of the Cumberland excavation committee for 1935: the Stanegate', *CW (2)*, 36, 182-91

Southern, P. (1996) 'Men and mountains, or geographical determinism and the conquest of Scotland', *Proc Soc Antiq Scot*, 126, 371-86

Steer, K.A. (1958) 'The early Iron Age homestead at West Plean', *Proc Soc Antiq Scot*, 89, 227-49

Steer, K.A. (1964) 'Ardoch fort', *Arch J*, 121, 196ff

Stuart, R. (1852) *Caledonia Romana*, Edinburgh

Swan, V.G. (1999) 'The twentieth legion and the history of the Antonine Wall reconsidered', *Proc Soc Antiq Scot*, 129, 399-480

Syme, R. (1958) *Tacitus*, Oxford

Welfare, H. and Swan, V. (1995) *Roman camps in England, the field archaeology*, London

Whittington, G. & Edwards, K.J. (19930 'Ubi solitudinem faciunt pacem appellant: the Romans in Scotland, a palaeoenvironmental contribution', *Britannia*, 24, 13-25

Wilmott, A. (2001) *Birdoswald Roman fort*, Stroud

Wilson, D.R. (2004) 'The North Leigh Roman villa: its plan reviewed', *Britannia*, 35, 77-114

Woolliscroft, D.J. (1988) 'The outpost system of Hadrian's Wall', *CW (2)*, 88, 23-8

Woolliscroft, D.J. (1993) 'Signalling and the design of the Gask Ridge system', *Proc Soc Antiq Scot*, 123, 291-314

Woolliscroft, D.J. (1999) 'The Roman Gask Project' in Gudea, N. (ed.) Roman Frontier Studies 1997, *Proceedings of the XVIIth International Congress of Roman Frontier Studies*, Zalau, 293-301

Woolliscroft, D.J. (2000a) 'More thoughts on why the Romans failed to conquer Scotland' *Scot Archaeol J*, Vol 22.2, 111-22

Woolliscroft, D.J. (2000b) 'The Roman Gask series tower at West Mains of Huntingtower, Perth & Kinross', *Proc Soc Antiq Scot*, 130, 491-508

Woolliscroft, D.J. (2001a) *Roman Military signalling*, Stroud

Woolliscroft, D.J. (2001b) 'The Roman Gask Project: interim report 1995-2000', in Higham. N. J. (ed.) *Archaeology of the Roman Empire, A Tribute to the Life and Works of Professor Barri Jones*, BAR (International Series) 940, 85-94

Woolliscroft, D.J. (2002a) 'The Roman Gask frontier', *History Scotland*, 2.3, May/June

Woolliscroft, D.J. (2002b) *The Roman frontier on the Gask Ridge, Perth & Kinross*, BAR (British Series), 335

Woolliscroft, D.J. (2002c) 'The Roman Gask Project 1997-99', in Freeman, P., Bennett, J., Fiema, Z.T. and Hoffmann, B. (eds) *Proceedings of the XVIIIth International Congress of Roman Frontier Studies*, BAR (International Series) 1084, vol 2, 867-72

Woolliscroft, D.J. (2005) 'A possible Roman Road cutting at Innerpeffray library, Perthshire', *Tayside & Fife Archaeological Journal*, 11, 9-18

Woolliscroft, D.J. & Davies, M.H. (2002) 'Parkneuk Wood Roman road, Perthshire: excavations in 1967 and 1997', in Woolliscroft, D.J. *The Roman Frontier on the Gask Ridge, Perth & Kinross*, BAR (British Series), 335

Woolliscroft, D.J. & Hoffmann, B. (1997) 'The Roman Gask system tower at Greenloaning, Perth & Kinross', *Proc Soc Antiq Scot*, 127, 563-76

Woolliscroft, D.J. & Hoffmann, B. (1998) 'The Roman Gask series tower at Shielhill South, Perth & Kinross. Excavations in 1973 and 1996', *Proc Soc Antiq Scot*, 128, 441-60

Woolliscroft, D.J. & Hoffmann, B. (2001) 'Excavations at Cuiltburn on the Roman Gask system', *Proc Soc Antiq Scot*, 131, 149-66

Woolliscroft, D.J. & Hoffmann, B. (2003) 'Iron Age and Roman period native sites at East Coldoch, Stirling: an interim report for work up to 2002', Web publication, http://www.romangask.org.uk/Pages/Papers/Coldoch2.html

Woolliscroft, D.J. & Hoffmann, B. (2005) *The Romans in Perthshire*, Perth

Woolliscroft, D.J. Hughes, A.J. & Lockett, N.J. (2002) 'Six suspected small Roman temporary camps' in Woolliscroft, D.J. *The Roman Frontier on the Gask Ridge, Perth & Kinross*, BAR (British Series), 335, 29-39

Woolliscroft, D.J. and Swain, S.A.M. (1991) 'The Roman "signal" tower at Johnson's Plain, Cumbria', *CW (2)*, 91, 19-30

Woolliscroft, D.J. & Woolliscroft, J. (1993) 'Britannia Ltd: the profits of a loss making Roman province', *Liverpool Classical Monthly*, April

INDEX